Introduction

Leisure is widely recognised as an increasingly significant component of life in modern Western society and has for some time been given serious attention by sociologists and a variety of social commentators and planners, yet it is an area which until recently has been greatly neglected by historians. In the latters' conventional hierarchy of human activities, leisure has most often been a mere appendix, an unexplored and scarcely acknowledged minor tributary to the mainstream of history. The subject has been left to the amateur student of manners, the antiquarian or the folklorist, whose enthusiasms and industry have rarely been matched by any regard for historical perspective or social context. Within the last few years, however, the increasing range and confidence of the modern social historian (a pullulating breed) have brought several aspects of the field under scholarly examination. In the new canon of studies, leisure time and its activities are acknowledged as a significant element of social experience, whose history is of particular importance in the broader exercise of reconstructing the kind of life lived by the ordinary people of the past. To this end, the main focus of recent attention has been on popular rather than élitist recreations, though the best of the new work has been concerned to understand them not only in the context of their own culture but in relation to the structure of society as a whole and the wider patterns of social change. From such endeavours in modern British studies some kind of intelligible and coherent map of the field is emerging.

It is obvious from early reconnaissance that the nineteenth century saw great changes in popular leisure patterns in Britain as part of a fundamental transformation in the culture of an industrial working class. According to Briggs and Hobsbawm, the 1830s and 1840s were the 'dark age' of working-class culture (a phrase which echoes the diagnosis of the Hammonds – honourable exceptions to the rule of previous scholarly neglect). In these decades an older, pre-industrial culture broke up, leaving amid its wreckage many of the people's traditional recreations. Another culture formed, better adapted to the milieu of a modern urban industrial society, and by the last quarter of the century the British working class were settled into a new way of life which boasted a distinctive new range of popular recreations – music halls, association football, seaside holidays and the like – recreations which, as Hobsbawm points out, have become so familiar to us that they have in turn come to be regarded as 'traditional'. In the 1890s, it is suggested, a cluster of new techniques in communications and the complementary development of modern advertising and consumer capitalism signalled a further phase in the history of leisure, when a virtual leisure industry emerged to shape and service the mass culture of the twentieth century.[1]

This elementary schema is gradually being filled out. In particular, our knowledge of the world of traditional or pre-industrial leisure has been enhanced by Robert Malcolmson's account of English popular recreations in the eighteenth and early nineteenth centuries. Here we learn of a robust and ritualistic popular culture rooted in the tightly knit, inward-looking world of the country village, its calendar generously studded with festivals and holidays that derived their warranty and meaning from an intimate connexion with the seasonal rhythms of the agricultural year and the working life of the community. In common with other pre-industrial societies there was no clear-cut division between labour and leisure and the daily round was seasoned with a good deal of complementary sociability. The material apparatus of recreation was rudimentary and for the most part freely available from the common resources of the community. With little discrimination between generation or sex the people made their own amusement, though itinerant professional entertainers often contributed to the excitement of local fairs and wakes. Popular leisure was public and gregarious, and both its great and small occasions were heavily bound by the prescriptive ties of communal custom reinforced by a powerful oral tradition. The general good humour of the common people at play was punctuated at fairly regular intervals by the rituals of violence and excess: cruelty to animals and other kinds of brutality were commonplace as entertainment, and certain major holidays evoked the ancient licence of carnival when all social restraints on the human appetite were lifted and eating, drinking, fighting and love-making were celebrated in orgiastic fashion. On such occasions, too, the authority structure of village society could be temporarily inverted in the time-honoured ceremonies of saturnalia – the common man was king for the day and the world was turned upside down, as villagers thumbed their noses (and worse) at their betters. Far from taking offence, the governing classes tolerated and often patronised these and other popular festivities; as Malcolmson and others show, their goodwill was in part a reflection of their own membership of the village community, in part a recognition of the utility of such rites in dissipating popular frustrations and thus reinforcing the authority of the rural oligarchy. Though we have no similar account for London and the big towns where social life was obviously more diverse and volatile, it seems clear enough that popular recreations there displayed many of the same characteristics. Work and leisure intermingled in the life of the workshop where traditional craft practices laid down the ritual patterns of celebration and good fellowship. The symbiosis of town and country in this era meant that the seasonal flux of urban leisure carried a strong echo of the cyclical rhythms of the agricultural year. Certainly many of the town worker's recreations were bucolic in form and inspiration and displayed a similar zest for the brutal and the carnivalesque; this also was likely to be indulged by an urban ruling class which recognised the stabilising effect of intervals of licence.[2]

We are dealing with the institutions of a predominantly stable and conservative society, but as Malcolmson shows, the complex of powerful social changes that overtook English society in the eighteenth century undermined the material and cultural base of the traditional way of life and began the breakdown of the old pattern of popular recreations. The Enclosure movement, the growth of cities, the rise of evangelicalism and the rigorous disciplining of labour under the new industrial capitalism destroyed the old community of interest and generated a new temper among the ruling class; thus their paternalist tolerance now gave way to a sour impatience with plebeian culture as morally offensive, socially subversive, and a general impediment to progress. From the middle of the eighteenth century folk recreations came under direct attack from a new puritanism and Malcolmson describes the growing momentum of class hostility that hastened their demise amid the general dislocation of traditional culture. Though the area lies outside his chosen brief, he alludes to the even greater severity of the crisis in the big towns and cities. Thus we are back again in the dark or bleak age of the second quarter of the nineteenth century, on the brink of that reconstruction of popular leisure which takes place after 1850 and the closing of Malcolmson's enquiry.

Though some significant contributions are beginning to appear and a small army of researchers are beavering away off-stage, we have nothing like a comprehensive account of this next phase. What we do have, however, from historians as well as sociologists, is a sharper awareness of the proposition that leisure took on a fundamentally new form and meaning in this era. The demands of mechanised factory production and the accelerated growth of big cities led to a radical restructuring of the temporal and spatial patterns of economic and social life. 'During the industrial revolution', observes de Grazia, 'leisure disappeared under an avalanche of work.' When it re-emerged it had not only been reduced but relocated in the life-space, forming a separate and self-contained sector in an increasingly compartmentalised way of life. Work and leisure were no longer intertwined in the continuum of shared activities that characterised the daily and yearly round within the closed world of the small and homogeneous traditional community. In the populous and extensive industrial city, leisure was time clearly marked off from work, to be pursued elsewhere than in the workplace and its environs, and undertaken in company no longer in the nature of things comprised predominantly of workmates. Moreover, the activities of this leisure time were no longer regulated as a whole by the tight mores and collective obligations of traditional social life. Thus the characteristic recreations of the second half of the nineteenth century were radically different from their predecessors: not only were they in many cases the products of a new technology and new social groupings, but they now took place within the unique circumstances of modern leisure, a condition of individual free choice specific to industrial society and a qualitatively new dimension in the experience of the masses. When a man walked out of the factory gates in the big industrial city he was in a sense freer than in any previous age.[3]

In this respect then, modern leisure made its début in Victorian England, the first mature industrial society. Of course, it was not all so cut and dried: the creature of custom that was the homo ludens of traditional culture was not transformed overnight into the free agent of an atomistic modern world. Traditional modes and mentalities persisted, community norms in one way or another were maintained, and severe material constraints often made a mockery of leisure's putative freedoms. We are dealing in what might be called the sophisticated crudity of an ideal typology that needs elaborating, qualifying and, above all, humanising. Yet by the second half of the century leisure was to a significant degree an area of relative autonomy in the everyday life of all classes – 'a sort of neutral ground which we may fairly call our own', as one Victorian cleric observed neatly in the 1870s.[4]

It was, however, precisely this feature of leisure which made its growth a source of considerable tension as well as gratification, for this fluid and open territory threatened to outstrip the reach of existing systems of social control. The middle class, as the most substantial beneficiaries of the new bonus, were themselves uneasy about the potentially corrupting effect of leisure on the internal disciplines of their own class; all the more so then were they apprehensive about the effects of leisure and its freedoms on a working class with a traditional taste for wantonness and an uncertain allegiance to the authority of its betters. Viewed from above, leisure constituted a problem whose solution required the building of a new social conformity – a play discipline to complement the work discipline that was the principal means of social control in an industrial capitalist society. In contrast to the harsh offensive of the earlier period of industrialisation, however, this policy was now to be pursued through the reform of popular recreations rather than their repression; but this more liberal disposition did not ensure it an easy passage in a society with a recent history of severe class conflict, for working people evinced a determination to make their own leisure in ways which resisted assimilation to middle-class ideology. In trying to respectabilise popular leisure, reformers also met with hostility and competition from powerful vested interests in working-class life – most notably the licensed trade, for whom the traditional appurtenances of popular recreation, most notably strong drink, represented both a basic livelihood and a chance to exploit fat new commercial opportunities. Leisure was one of the major frontiers of social change in the nineteenth century, and like most frontiers it was disputed territory.

This book examines the contest and interaction between these social forces and the part they played in creating the new leisure world of Victorian England during the fifty years or so of cultural reconstruction from the 1830s to the 1880s. It describes the indigenous process of renewal in popular culture, and the ways in which the working class realised the freedoms of modern leisure amid the unique complex of opportunities and constraints that defined an urban industrial society; attention is given here to themes of continuity as well as change, and the climacteric of the 'dark age' is looked at for evidence of growth as well as destruction. In turn the book investigates the role of the middle-class activists who sought to shape working-class choice by providing an alternative world of reformed recreations which would immunise workers against the alleged degenerations of their own culture and counter the more corrupt appeals of an embryonic leisure industry; here I have considered the reform ideal in relation to the changing experience and significance of leisure in the lives of the middle class in general. After examining the cultural politics of three specific areas of development in popular recreation, the Working Men's Club movement, the new athleticism and the music hall, the book concludes with a consideration of the significance of leisure for the broader questions of class relationships and consciousness in Victorian society.

If at times I have talked of leisure in a loose and common-sense fashion as man's general pursuit of enjoyment or some such readily identifiable social phenomenon I have none the less had in mind throughout this book the sociologist's more specific usage of the term. Defining leisure in this company can be a complex and controversial exercise, but leaving aside the idealism of the neo-classicists and the more obvious ambiguities the arguments seem to reduce to two main propositions: modern leisure is a certain kind of time spent in a certain kind of way. The time is that which lies outside the demands of work, direct social obligations and the routine activities of personal and domestic maintenance; the use of this time, though socially determined, is characterised by a high degree of personal freedom and choice.[5] The Victorians talked less about leisure than recreation (in itself a significant preference) and this term also carries a specialised meaning for some of today's writers. I have explained at certain points in the text the particular sense in which Victorians could use the word, but in general I have simply taken recreation or its plural to denote those activities and interests that form the typical occupations of leisure time.

The campaign for improved recreation – rational recreation – was a piecemeal operation which was part of a broader front comprising the more clearly defined and institutionalised movements for temperance and educational reform. Abstinence and edification were common prescriptions of rational recreation, but I have paid more attention to reform schemes which were sensitive to the popular need for recreation in entertainment, play and relaxation. Source material for this kind of study is abundant but diffuse. The state of popular recreation was a perennial topic of public comment but its discussion was often incidental to that of other issues. Certain reform schemes generated their own literature and particularly sports and entertainments were often served by a specialist press, but there is no single major corpus of documents. I have had, therefore, to track chronicle and debate over a wide area, through an extensive sampling of press and periodicals, reports of government committees, sermons and pamphlet literature, works of social commentary, memoirs, novels and ephemera. To a considerable extent I have let the Victorians speak for themselves, attempting to catch the authentic voice from below as well as that of the official or dominant culture. This book is not meant to be a comprehensive leisure history of the period (such a work is a long way off), but I have tried to capture the essentials of the common experience of leisure in urban and metropolitan England in these years, while providing a modest running case study in local history in the references to Bolton, Lancashire as a typical new industrial town.[6] I should add, too, that I have left quantification to others – as an individual and a historian I am by temperament and talent a craft worker not a technician.

Introduction to the paperback edition: Leisure, culture and the historian – confessions of a vulgar culturalist

The reissue of a book argues for its continuing soundness and utility, and in consequence I have made only very minor revisions in the main text. The notes and bibliography, however, have been substantially updated in acknowledgement of the considerable development in the history of leisure and popular culture, and this introduction offers a review of recent scholarship in the field.

Though the volume of work addressed directly to the history of leisure has been less than that in other new fields in social history, it has been sufficient to provoke significant critical ambush. At the same time, the reading of leisure as a constituent element in the broader category of culture has implicated it in the theoretical and political issues of a contentious neo-Marxist historiography and the complementary pre-occupations of the new and radical field of cultural studies. In all there is a good deal for the historian of leisure to chew on.

From its beginnings as an academic specialism, the history of leisure has been regarded as a mixed blessing. The earliest strictures came in the mid-1970s in Gareth Stedman Jones's cogent if overstated critique of a collection of conference papers on working-class leisure.[1] Himself then engaged in making an effective connection between history and social theory, he found the emergent field defective under both counts. As history, its knowledge was still poorly grounded and uneven (the neglect of gender was here early registered); as theory, it was conceptually confused. His targets included the simplistic application of modernisation theory with its scheme of successive stages of development which led historians into the characterisation of previous ages as unproblematically 'traditional', but more pointedly he warned against the sloppy use of the social control model as an explanation of class domination, suggesting, like the lady at the second-hand stall, that we not only need to know if something fits, but also need to know where it came from. The social control model's roots in functionalism, argued Jones, made it suspect, for it assumed an ideal or natural state of equilibrium whose periodic breakdowns were almost mechanically correctible, a model at odds with the facts of enduring social conflict inherent in a class society. The materialist logic of the critique then however turns in upon itself: class societies are conflict-ridden but the prime locus of conflict and its social determinations is the work place, not leisure which is devoid of the persistent antagonisms built into the factory and its relations of production. There was a danger in overpoliticising leisure as an arena of struggle, or crediting its increasing market function as a more powerful agent of capitalist domination than work. While Jones allowed that time away from work was a potentially valuable area of research, he warned against the study of 'leisure' – the inverted commas ring like leper's bells – as a separate and self-contained field.

The problem with social control is less its own ideological presumptions than its reductionist application, which casts the controllers and the controlled in roles coterminous with stereotyped class interests, the dominant one seeking in purposive fashion to engineer the conformity of the subordinate other, who either accepts or rejects it. This ignores the complexity of motive and division of interest within ruling groups and the variable and ambiguous response their prescriptions meet with. Though this book talks the language of social control and thus might be found guilty by association, it is more concerned with the ways in which control was contested by a relatively autonomous working class with its counter strategies of resistance and selective adaptation; indeed its evidence on this count has been adduced to support a further indictment of the social control model.[2] What I do plead guilty to is using the terminology without taking full account of the theory (merely a glance at the entry in the social sciences encyclopaedia as I shamefacedly recall); the offence is one of ornamental sociology – 'a well-intentioned gesture in the direction of a non-existent rigour', as Jones puts it. Er, well, yes. Other scholars have shown that social control can be a far from bankrupt concept,[3] but the theoretical articulation of this book's arguments about leisure and class would, I think, be better rendered in the formulations of Gramsci's hegemony, though the one reference to that ventured in the conclusions is also little more than gestural. More rigour needed all round.

Hegemony (if initiates can bear with recapitulation) is the process whereby dominant forces in society reproduce their dominance through the orchestration of an ideological harmony or consent among subordinate groups, a process pursued in what Gramsci identifies as the realm of civil society, that area of social life in which we lay claim to the freedoms of the private citizen and family – typically that of leisure. The operation of hegemony is located primarily in specific ideologies reproduced in specific institutions and practices (rational recreation is an example, though some might conceive of it rather as discourse), but the totalising grip of hegemony lies in its potentiality for defining the 'common sense', the 'natural' reflexes of a society and its consciousness as embedded in the whole repertoire of conduct and expression that pattern everyday life and its informal power relationships.[4]

There is a danger that hegemony may be used to explain too much, as an hermetic order that effects complete ideological closure. But a central point in hegemonic theory is that its controls are never complete; at best it achieves only what Gramsci termed a temporary or 'moving equilibrium'. Alignments within the ruling or leading class shift and compete as do its points of access to its subordinates, whose response may be similarly disjointed, variously resistant, modificatory or accommodative (here one might example the qualified embrace of respectability discussed below). The emphasis is thus on the flux and complexity of cultural formation and offers an effective mediation of the cruder oppositions of the structuralist/culturalist dualism where the underclass is either wholly enmeshed in the structures of bourgeois ideology or breaks free in the assertion of its own authentic people's culture. There may be the further objection that hegemony provides no account of the movement or circulation of culture upwards, but this seems remedied by newer readings of Gramsci that move closer to the less doctrinaire model of appropriation in conceptualising popular culture as an area of exchange or negotiation between the classes, though the benign and diplomatic associations of such terms should not obscure the tensions that inhere in any hegemonic order – relationships are not always so civil in civil society.[5] Where it is worked through rather than misrepresented, hegemony is more than just social control with Marxist knobs on, for it renders class interaction as an historically specific process which operates not through the formalised apparatus of social engineering, but through the concrete experience of culture as a dynamic ensemble of practices and relationships.

It is by siting it in the larger context of culture that Stedman Jones disinfects 'leisure' in his influential article on the re-making of the London working class at the point of transition to a putative mass society in the 1870s and 1880s.[6] Leisure here is a crucial indicator (though not agent) of social change; its characteristic activities are related to the culture of working people as a particular way of life whose primary determinants are fundamentally material – the casualisation of the East End economy, the decline of artisanal production and the exigencies of daily life at the bottom. The response to the insecurities of such a life was 'a culture of consolation' absorbed in the pursuit of the small pleasures so readily supplied by commercialised leisure, notably the music hall: leisure is now little more than a series of relishes for the feast that never comes. The emergence of such a culture severely weakens independent working-class political activity (the main point of the argument). There is a deep pessimism in this account. There is no overt theorisation, but it does seem that while the social control of middle-class reformers may have failed, the people are gripped by deeper structures (Althusser's baleful ISA?) which extend into leisure; conflict is restricted to incidental skirmishes over music hall regulation and the working class are almost inert customers of escapist tosh. But in scholarly terms leisure has been rehabilitated as an organic component in an historically specific culture.

More commonly, however, social historians, while recognising the constraints within which popular leisure/culture is bounded have seen it as a more active vehicle of class expression and agency. A collection of essays, edited by Eileen and Stephen Yeo, whose provenance was the conference that occasioned Jones's critique of leisure history, constitutes a comradely corrective and an affirmative redefinition of the field and its significance, not least in its title, *Popular Culture and Class Conflict 1590–1914: Explorations in the History of Labour and Leisure* (1981). The Yeos' spiky editorial commentary is plainly influenced by the reformulation of the classic Marxist relationship of base and superstructure in acknowledgement of the latter's self-determining potential. The history of 'leisure' (within culture) is, they argue, 'as much about the history of production – social production – as is, for example, the history of boots, coal or beans'. Inherently then, *pace* Jones, leisure involves struggles over social relations which make it a highly politicised area. To the constraints that cramp and cage working-class life, the Yeos and their collaborators add the power of the state, no longer a happily alien phenomenon, but alive and tentacular here in England in the structures of class control and the market (though perhaps they too readily represent still independent interests as part of its alignments).[7] At the same time they offer an alternative history of cultural development which picks out the creative capacities of popular culture, revealed fitfully as 'clusters of potential' in the moments of struggle, and reconstructed here to encourage their realisation in the present, for this is a political manifesto as well as a history book. The essays are strong on context and offer a suggestive typology of associational forms in popular culture, though there is a tendency (observable elsewhere) to render the commercial forms of leisure as analogous to those of industrial manufacture, without regard for their cultural singularities – the production of music and entertainment, for example, may be similar to, but is also in many ways different from the production of boots, coal or beans.

In his admirable *Leisure in the Industrial Revolution, c. 1780–1880* (1980), Hugh Cunningham also locates leisure in culture, conceived as a productive and material practice that is 'active and influencing'.[8] Leisure was thus an important nexus of various interlocking and conflicting forces, but here too it becomes a positive instrument through which people make their own history. In a parallel treatment of the middle-class campaigns for rational recreation Cunningham finds further evidence of effective popular resistance, though he concludes that the outcome of a century of battles over the problem of leisure was a victory for the dominant culture who reduce leisure to 'the safely residual', primarily through the hegemony of the market. In an extended postscript he relates the theoretical assumptions of the book to his own intellectual odyssey through E. P. Thompson to Gramsci; if the points of reference are Marxist, the stance is engaged but non-doctrinaire, a prominent credo of the new social history. Cunningham also mounts his own critique of leisure history. In the first place, he maintains, it has failed to connect meaningfully with larger contextual issues and, second, it has been preoccupied with the transformation of leisure and thus failed to appreciate its significant continuities. As a corrective to the latter deficiency, he argues against the idea of a vacuum or climacteric in popular recreations in the first half of his period and reinforces his claims for the autonomous strengths of popular culture by demonstrating the persistence of traditional forms and the vigorous growth of new forms in the circus and popular theatre.[9] He also found more continuities between town and country than the abrupt developmental model of modernisation allowed. Another critic, Chris Waters, stresses the unevenness of change and commercial penetration, emphasising rather the diversity of leisure experience in a variety of social contexts and 'taste publics', concluding that the fluidity of mid-nineteenth century leisure may have made it an important area for the construction of new group identities within the working class – a mini golden age?[10]

Historians have certainly become more sensitive to the persistence of traditional forms alongside or in interaction with the more rational modes of an industrial urban society. A recent collection of essays on popular culture in the nineteenth century, edited by Robert Storch, provides examples across a range of forms and contexts, from Guy Fawkes night in small southern towns to the mixed economy of Lancashire wakes and the moral economy of big city music hall audiences. There is a welcome attention here to the symbolic content of popular recreations, reflecting the influence of social anthropology and reconstructions of early modern *mentalités*, and an account of Birmingham's wakes and fairs suggests how their various functions might be comprehended within the larger conceptual frame of the carnivalesque.[11] The utility of this increasingly influential historical model might be pressed further in time and place than the still relatively compact communal practices considered here (most of which, for all their latter day folk vigour, do not seem to have survived beyond the 1880s). Modern popular culture does have a significant symbolic and ritual content, but its modes have become fragmented, displaced, piecemeal and optional, and we need to be alert to the persistence of carnival and much else in more dispersed if no less intense forms. One place to look may be in the neglected field of language and what Bakhtin in his classic study of carnival noted as its 'regenerative ambivalence'.[12] Attention to literacy, education and the popular press tends to obscure the fact that popular culture in the nineteenth century was still very much an oral culture in its everyday transactions and key areas of its leisure.

The history of popular culture has also been an important area in the emergent field of cultural studies, less a discipline than a convergence of interests across disciplines concerned primarily with the analysis (and political reclamation) of a broadly conceptualised contemporary popular culture. History is valued as a necessary contextual corrective to the ahistorical perspectives of other component disciplines such as literature and sociology, and for its reconstruction of the concrete experience of lived cultures as inspired by Thompson. At the same time Thompson and his followers have been rebuked for overestimating the function of culture as an independent oppositional force in popular life and neglecting the determinant grip of the unconscious structures of ideology, as disclosed by theoretical rather than empirical investigation. Hence the intellectual melodrama of the culturalist/(Marxist) structuralist prize fight and the attempt to make a necessary reconciliation between the concrete and the theoretical, the heroic and the narcotic readings of culture and ideology in the more flexible formulations of Gramsci. A further reproach for the social historian is that the necessary recovery and contextualisation of cultural practices has been insufficiently informed by any study of their internal codes and mechanisms. Historians are urged to reconsider culture as a configuration of texts or sign systems on the model of language, whose latent, complex, and often contradictory meanings have to be laid bare by the interpretative techniques of what may be variously labelled semiotics, deconstruction or discourse analysis.[13] Work on the more spectacular subcultures has shown how cultural forms can be reworked by subject groups, making consumption a process of active engagement and the rearticulation of meaning in 'the struggle for the sign'.[14] Cultural studies can be too strenuously theoretical and preoccupied with its own inner demons, but it can also be open and stimulating; if leisure in history is to be fully reconceived as a cultural construct then there must be more attention to what leisure means as well as how it works.

Meanwhile a non-marxisant, more empirically bounded history of leisure/popular culture continues in fruitful production from social historians for whom leisure and culture are largely unproblematical operational categories.[15] Another recent collection of essays, bunched mainly in the nineteenth century, extends the range of comparative evidence through local and regional case studies, and pursues the theme of continuity and change, discovering, for example, a moral panic among opponents of the cinema in the inter-war years that echoes the anxieties and prescriptions of Victorian rational recreationists.[16] There are now also major studies of some of the prime sites and activities of nineteenth-century leisure. John Walton's social history of the English seaside resort takes a hard-nosed look at the specifics of popular demand, and the politics of urban development and local government (the latter a less ideological usage than the state). In the experience as well as the provision of seaside holidays he reports a complex diversity, but in a class-based analysis of styles he argues for the emergence of 'a common recreational culture . . . for the pleasure-loving of all classes' by the 1890s.[17] In a study of another major element in the late-century reshaping of popular culture, Tony Mason provides an extensive breakdown of the social composition of players and supporters of soccer, giving substance and refinement to its characterisation as the 'people's game'. Yet he finds soccer's relationship to what he wryly labels 'the philosopher's stone of working-class consciousness' far from straightforward: if it brought a new kind of solidarity to its working-class supporters it was one fragmented by an intense localism, and though such partisanship was at odds with middle-class prescriptions of sportsmanship the game generally served to reduce class tension.[18] Another dominant institution, the music hall, has also become the subject of considerable research interest, both for its singularities as a modern entertainment industry and its complex mediation of ideologies of class, gender and race.[19]

Yet if such work fails generally to meet, or chooses to ignore, the growing appetite for theorisation, its reach for interpretive generalisations continues, albeit amid the qualifications that closer study often imposes. Thus Cunningham – 'most comfortable when my feet are firmly planted on empirical ground' – mobilises sufficient hard evidence to question the assumptions of a new abundance in working-class leisure between 1871 and 1914 as represented in mass culture theory (more of it and worse), or golden age nostalgia (lots of it and lovely).[20] But for all his reservations, he allows some real growth in opportunity and a possibly greater valuation of leisure, finding in its practices a new fixity of expectations and behaviour as a changing cultural formation took on 'the force of custom'. That the leisure – and work – of this period became both newly routinised but far from deadened is the conclusion of Ross McKibbin's revisionist study of work and hobbies from 1880 to 1950.[21] He suggests that the increasing absorption of workingmen in their hobbies was a consequence of the latters' considerable intrinsic satisfaction rather than a reflex compensation for alienation at work, a condition he goes some way to disprove. Changes at work nonetheless increased the appeal of leisure activities that provided privacy, solitude, and a high degree of individual competition, and help explain the presence of such values in terms other than those of borrowed middle-class ideologies. For McKibbin the re-shaping of late-nineteenth century working-class culture is the consequence neither of hegemony nor of convergence – the common culture thesis – but of an independent response at an individual (male) as much as a class level; nor is this a culturalist victory wrested from the dominant class, but a demonstration of the British ideology of live and let live, of separate and largely self-sufficient class worlds. The study of one aspect of working-class leisure becomes by extension part of a larger reinterpretation of class and culture in which British society in the period is represented as at once both 'highly cohesive yet poorly integrated'; leisure is cast as a formidable competitor to party politics, not as the escapism of the petty consumer but as a densely compelling world of alternative loyalties, private as well as associational.[22]

The remaking of popular leisure/culture from the 1870s and 1880s is still an underworked and challenging field. No longer can it be claimed as Thompson did for the early century that this was the most distinguished popular culture England has known. We are not obviously dealing with the heroic; it is not banners and barricades, but bicycles and banjos. Though media re-creations of this world often now emphasise its singular 'period' flavour, arguably it is its comparative ordinariness and familiarity that limit our further understanding.[23] Not that we are short of interpretations of this culture, as we have seen. It has been variously represented as massified and manipulated under a new corporate consumer-oriented capitalism; as less than totally manipulated but at the same time more complicit with the hegemonic 'national-popular' culture of an imperialist state; as newly 'traditional' and custom bound; as predominantly consolatory; as vigorously populist and self-determining; as typically associational *and* individualist; as independently class-based; as class convergent. What might be allowed within all of these interpretations is that, for all the undoubted limitations within which it was realised, leisure in this period does seem to take on a new saliency in the emotional economy; to reverse Patrick Joyce's striking verdict on work in the previous period, it is possible now to argue that it is leisure that gets under the skin of life. If class yet remained a powerful determinant of leisure choice, collectively prescribed forms were yielding to or co-existed with a more generalised and indefinite condition of freedom given over to the more or less conscious construction of individual or family-based life-styles and identities.[24] We are dealing with a pluralist culture – more structured than voluntarist – but still pluralist in the sense of the multiplication of its roles, sites, forms and expectations, both actualised and lived out only or partially in the head.[25]

Popular leisure in the late century may have restabilised as a newly customary round of pleasures pursued amid various communities of place and interest, but it can also be represented as a more plastic pattern of experience, subjective as well as social, moving across a more dispersed, discontinuous, and typically more urbanised field of action, with shifting situational thresholds of inclusion and exclusion, identity and status. In a new world of mass individualism leisure became not only more homogenised but more atomised, and its characteristic mode became that of performance or what Simmel termed 'exploit'. The theorising is there in the classic studies of contemporary European urban life and in various strands of recent, mostly North American sociology on interactionism and the modernisation of consciousness (critical heavy breathing), which might be usefully tempered with the structuralist emphasis on the construction of the subject;[26] the historical evidence is there, in the imaginative literature, in the canon but also in popular or mass texts.[27] Clearly great caution is needed in employing such formulations, but a qualified concept of pluralisation may be as important in understanding an emergent modern leisure *mentalité* as concentration on the set pieces of collective class expression and encounter.

The recasting of the subject/individual, together with the identification of significant second-order collective categories – fractions, strata, taste-publics, subcultures – and the new emphasis on the competing primacies of gender, generation and race seem at times to dissolve or displace the operations of social class, in culture as in much else. If the material and normative determinations of class remain inescapable for historians, they have become more sensitive to the shifts and ambiguities in their cultural formation, and among the passages in this book with which I now feel least comfortable are those which claim to identify such and such a phenomenon as being 'authentically' of a particular class (the sin of 'essentialism'). Yet the reconstruction of the historic class cultures, however nuanced, remains on the agenda. Here the obvious deficiency is the still marked lack of attention to the middle class, compared to that directed to the workers.[28] There is a great deal of substantive work to be done here, but in speculative terms the concept of leisure as performance in a pluralist world seems particularly plausible – H. G. Wells in *Tono-Bungay* discovered middle-class couples practising their social skills in weekends away at posh hotels. At the same time it seems necessary to continue to conceptualise leisure as a 'problem' in middle-class lives beyond the limits of the investigation first opened up in this book, for leisure remained a crucial province for the defence or aggrandisement of class identity and status: the operation of hegemony imposed limits and controls on the dominant class, and it continued to be engaged in its own restrained yet still intense ideological 'struggle for the sign', most notably in negotiating the extended cultural code of gentility.[29]

Equally important is the need for studies of the leisure culture of the lower middle class. Recent research suggests that they qualify least as a coherent class entity,[30] and indeed in the late nineteenth century they might be as well understood as a geological fault line running through the system, variously collapsing, bulging and eliding the classcape. It is they who most plainly live out the contradictions of the mass individualism of consumer capitalism, projecting a kind of collusive antithesis to the dominant ideology that seems characteristic of much of modern popular culture.[31] It is here too among the most stifling of conformities that self-realisation can seem most complete: Talleyrand located the only true *douceur de vivre* in the France of the *ancien régime*; J. B. Priestley reclaimed it for life in a lower-middle class villa in pre-1914 Bradford.

Another acknowledged shortcoming in the new history of leisure is the concentration on its more public, associational, visible and accessible forms to the exclusion of the private, personal and informal.[32] This in turn has reinforced the neglect of women and the question of gender in leisure. Always on the agenda, but nowhere apparently in hand, this task of recovery seems doubly difficult; women's leisure remained mostly private, and its interweave with other activities further obscures its practice and function. One way of demarginalising women might be to exploit what we have more efficiently. Certain prominent leisure sites such as the pub and music hall can be interpreted as intermediate institutions that bridged the public and private divide. Such settings, of course, gave employment as much as leisure to women, as barmaids, waitresses, entertainers and prostitutes, but they were important sites for the construction of gender and sexuality and social laboratories for the rehearsal of gender roles and relationships still underworked in scholarship.[33]

Leisure history over the past decade or so has made a real if still relatively modest contribution to the new social history of the period. Most notably it has demonstrated in a variety of ways the significance of leisure in the formation of class cultures and the mediation of their relationships, culturally and ideologically. The implication in some critiques that leisure has become the new opiate of the intellectual seems overdrawn but yet the field could do with some recharging. Of course, in the language of the trade, there are still a great many gaps to be filled, but the necessary work of recovery needs to venture beyond the worthy but somewhat leaden categories of provision, use and control; for all the insistent appeal from experience in history writing, our rendering of experience in leisure, its quality, dynamics and meaning is still elementary. We do seem in need of more imaginative, theoretically informed work – suitably rigorous, preferably lucid and properly integrated with historical practice. Recent work in the field has helped rid leisure of its leper's bells by locating it in the wider contexts of society or culture, but it has not generated much in the way of major reinterpretation across this larger canvas. As Richard Johnson has remarked, it has been one of the additional kinds of history that has grown up alongside the old without transforming it. That challenge still stands.[34]

*

Though the research for this book was undertaken in England much of it was written in Canada and is marked by its distance from as much as its engagement with the society under analysis. If this dualist provenance (as much cultural as intellectual) accounts for whatever originality the book may lay claim to, it has made it at points more of a personal history than an academic exercise and has given the argument an *ad hominem* derivation that it now seems appropriate to acknowledge.

With no disrespect to my Canadian mentors I have to report that I entered the academic profession by the side door, as a jaunty but immature fugitive from Oxford. The perplexed product of a respectable working-class family, the welfare state and a grammar school education, I had spent little time on history at university being more preoccupied with negotiating its alien yet seductive social world. Overcoming if not entirely eradicating the deferential reflexes of the grammar school 'grey man', I paradoxically represented myself both as more proletarian than I had full claim to be and as what I took to be an increasingly plausible impersonation of the typical Oxbridge bourgeois gentilhomme. I eased the anxieties of pursuing identity in two opposite directions at once by playing a great deal of social piano and drinking a greater deal of beer – *bibo ergo sum* – and left Oxford with a third-class degree (my one unimpeachably genteel achievement), unfitted for any other occupation than that of a state-subsidised poseur.

With the subsidy abruptly withdrawn, I spent a sub-picaresque interlude as advertising salesman, would-be professional jazz pianist, 'mudder-up' in a boiler factory and trainee teacher, before exporting myself to Canada, the land of the second chance. In search of academic redemption as a graduate student at the University of British Columbia, I was not only made to work but made to think (novel experiences both), while my new location as external (compare Raymond Williams's internal) migrant gave me the detachment to see my own previous history as the product of a specific social and historical determination, and led me to question (if not entirely relinquish) the priority of style over substance as an adequate strategy for life.

At UBC I was also encouraged to move into what was then unconventional territory. Even so, the cautious liberalism of my Oxford inheritance meant that I began my study of Victorian leisure in the respectable tradition of studies of the reformer and reform institutions in 'the age of improvement'. And though I returned to Britain to research at a time when social history generally was taking off and work on leisure getting underway, the albatross of my genteel undergraduate performance and the stigma of my new 'colonial' status made me a solitary student, largely unaware of the political and theoretical fermentations about me – I was more likely to have mistaken the *New Left Review* for a cabaret act than the broadsheet of a reinvigorated intellectual radicalism. As with all scholars I borrowed from the work of others and was enthralled by some (inevitably, of course, E. P. Thompson), but in a sense I had to invent my own history, and as my interest shifted to the responses of those who had been the objects rather than promoters of improvement, I projected on to them my own experience as a latter-day improvee and minor combatant in a class system that I was revisiting in the present as well as the past.

Thus it was that on return to Canada I wrote up my Victorian working people as role-conscious actors skilled in social artifice and dissimulation, playing the system and winning back small but relishable gains in a class war gone underground.[35] I feel confident enough, as I have argued above, in the interpretation of leisure (life) as performance in the more fluid, pluralist world of the late century, but I confess to feeling some unease at the Goffmanising of what may have been the more stolid workingmen and women of the mid-Victorian period. Yet it is significant that the book's representation of respectability as a role situationally adopted for instrumental advantage rather than induced as ideological reflex – style over substance – has been the point most favourably and frequently singled out by other historians. Is this testimony to its historical validity or a displaced act of collective self-recognition by other survivors of the great English game of class among the lumpen professoriat?

Winnipeg, 1986   P.C.B.

1

Popular recreation in the
early Victorian town

The early historians of England as an urban industrial society have left us with an overall picture of popular recreation which is cramped and joyless – the Hammonds, for example, concluded that 'the new towns were built for a race that was allowed no leisure . . . recreation was waste' – yet, while it must be recognised that the town worker suffered from lack of time and space for recreation, and that the amusements of the poor were still under frequent attack from the superior classes, what is just as remarkable is the vitality and adaptability displayed by popular recreation under these siege conditions.[1]

I

In seeking first to demonstrate the vitality of popular recreation in this period, one must allow that the evidence for this does in part help to confirm the Hammonds' picture of gross deprivation. Foreigners had frequently been alarmed at the exuberance of the Englishman at play – a Frenchman who witnessed a football game in Derby in 1829 was moved to remark that, if Englishmen called this playing, it would be impossible to say what they would call fighting – but it becomes clear enough that such occasions were often now formless and convulsive compensations for the strains of a coercive industrial society, rather than the ritualised exercises of a traditional popular hedonism. The new industrial wage-earner was still in a minority in the workforce, but the unprecedented regularity and intensity that characterised his working hours were gradually being demanded of all sections of the labouring population and, in general, the pattern of tension and release in working life had become tauter. Contemplating Manchester in 1844 another Frenchman, Léon Faucher, was much disturbed at the immoderation in all things which characterised the new industrial Englishman. He thought that overworking was a malady which Lancashire had inflicted on the whole country;

it was balanced only by another extreme, the incontinence of the Englishman's recreation. 'They cannot partake of anything in moderation; they must partake of it to repletion.' Francis Place, recalling the grinding demands placed on his early working life, remembered how he would tear himself away from his work and rush out to some park or open space in the city for a brief respite before 'returning to his vomit'. Given such experience, he professed himself well able to understand the reactions of the 'uninformed man', and the latter's urgent need 'to procure the excitement which MUST be procured'. Looking back at the improvement in manners from the vantage point of 1867, two students of working-class life recalled the pattern of the 1830s as one of 'noisy, drunken riot . . . alternated with sullen, silent work'.[2]

Noise and drink were common accompaniments of popular recreation – in some minds no doubt their dual presence thereby constituted a riot – but they did not always or necessarily indicate a simple reflex action of despair to the grinding tedium of work. Mention of them should, however, remind us that working-class leisure was for the most part public and gregarious, and that its principal everyday setting was that of the public house. As an old workingman pointed out in recalling conditions in industrial Yorkshire in the 1830s:[3]

> There were only two places to go in spending spare time away from one's own house – church, chapel or alehouse; the former were seldom open, while the latter was seldom closed. The first was not attractive, the second was made attractive.

Among the attractions of the pub were a great variety of recreations which brought enrichment as well as escape to the life of the town worker.

Reports in Bolton's local press reveal how diverse and extensive were the activities held in the pub or its gardens: bowling, quoiting, glee clubs and free and easies, amateur and professional dramatics, fruit and vegetable shows, flower shows, sweepstake clubs and the meetings of trades' and friendly societies.[4] The latter occasions combined business with pleasure, and serve as an example of how the pull of the public house as the institutional hub of working-class recreation was reinforced by the wide range of social and economic services which it offered. The pub served as a labour exchange, a pay station and a port of call for the tramping artisan. Initiation into particular trades and other customs of the workplace still often demanded the treating of workmates, which tied men further to the credit of the local pub. For the single man in lodgings the pub was the closest thing to a home – here he would take his meals and read the newspapers. And always there was beer – 'the friendly mug of beer' – which, as Charles Booth later remarked, 'was the primordial cell of British social life'. Thus in an age of social dislocation the pub remained a centre of warmth, light and sociability for the urban poor, a haven from the filth and meanness of inadequate and congested housing, a magnet for the disoriented newcomer and the disgruntled regular alike. 'There is plenty of gas and company to keep us alive', explained the customers who were quizzed by an enquiring cleric; 'there is always society in the pubs, and the men there are so very agreeable.'[5]

The most prominent among the many clubs and associations which met on pub premises were the friendly societies. Their activities were well reported in Bolton where membership grew during the 1830s and 1840s despite frequent hard times, and in 1850 there were over 200 lodges of the various societies in the town. Sociability and entertainment were among the prime functions of these fraternities of working people and the *Grand Lodge Circular* of the Bolton Oddfellows records the recitations and songs with which members regaled one another throughout the year, but the annual feasts were the great occasions. As many as thirty or forty might be held on a single night, with the lodge banners decorated with evergreens flying from the pub windows. Foot races and dancing were held in the street, but it was the inner man (and woman) who came first, for it was food and drink in abundance which marked the successful anniversary.[6] The staples of roast beef and strong ale were not merely customary – they were part of the birthright of the freeborn Englishman; 'a mechanic at a feast', noted a contemporary, 'thinks himself scurvily used if he is supplied with less than a gallon of strong ale.'[7]

But as the previous inventory of activities demonstrates, pub life was not all cakes and ale, and there was enough 'rationality' in popular recreation inside and outside the pub, to secure the acknowledgement of middle-class contemporaries alert to such qualities. In Nottingham, reported James Hudson, in his survey of adult education written in 1851, 'there are several Working Men's libraries HELD IN PUBLIC HOUSES' (the emphasis seems more intended to counter the incredulity of the reader than to underline the exceptional). 'At two of these houses', Hudson continued, 'political discussions are also held under judicious regulations.' A churchman in Bolton recorded how two workingmen explained their absence from a Sunday lecture at chapel – they were attending a discussion at their local pub on the existence of God. From Manchester, Faucher reported that Handel and Haydn were 'as household words' in the manufacturing districts of Lancashire; there was no difficulty in raising choirs among the factory operatives.[8] The popularity of clubs and choirs confirms the continuing communal nature of working-class recreation, but one must note here too the already familiar exception of the working-class solitary: Job Legh, the weaver botanist, in Mrs Gaskell's *Mary Barton*; Joseph Gutteridge, a weaver from real life who studied natural history in the fields around Coventry; Charles Manby Smith, a journeyman printer from London, who painted water-colours and studied the pianoforte.[9] In these and certain other interests individual workingmen found a private freedom of expression in their leisure time. Thus literate and intellectual interests coexisted with the more boisterous traditional recreations among a working class whose culture had been as much stimulated as disrupted by economic upheaval and social conflict. Whatever the partisan emphasis, Samuel Bamford's pride in listing the accomplishments of his Lancashire work-mates in 1844 seems well justified:[10]

> they are the greatest readers; can show the greatest number of good writers; the greatest number of sensible and considerate public speakers. They can show a greater number of botanists; a greater number of horticulturists, a greater number who are acquainted with the abstruse sciences; the greatest number of poets, and a greater number of good musicians, whether choral or instrumental.

II

Together with this resilient and diverse vitality, popular recreation displayed the further strength of adaptibility, as revealed in the response to those constraints noted by the Hammonds: the curtailment of time and space, and the hostility of the superior classes.

Conditions of regular employment in the manufacturing towns appeared to allow only the merest scrapings of free time. In the previous century normal working hours had been long enough – ten hours was the traditional day's labour – and in many trades the week had culminated in a feverish climax of activity to catch market deadlines, but the rhythm of work had been largely self-imposed and often leisurely, weekends had been elastic and holidays numerous. The stricter work discipline of capitalist production had severely curtailed such liberalities.[11] In 1840 the prominent factory inspector, Leonard Horner, found that the twelve-hour working day that was now normal in textile mills left the worker 'utterly unfit for anything like mental improvement . . . and not very fit for much social enjoyment with his family'. John Fielden, the reforming manufacturer, was greatly struck by the testimony of a youngster in one of the mills that there was 'never any time to play'; another millowner admitted that the time left for recreation and improvement after the average working day was scarcely two hours.[12] Sunday was the only day commonly free from work, but for the working wife it was the one day available for the washing and other accumulated domestic tasks; for the rest of the family the propensity to stay in bed on a Sunday was no doubt less a matter of choice than a necessary recruitment of strength.[13] By 1834 there were only eight statutory half-holidays in England, and the traditional calendar of religious feast days and the celebrations of seasonal tasks or particular trades had been considerably pruned, both by the employers and the Church.[14]

But the working classes stretched the meagre allowance of free time. Sunday's leisure, for example, could still be extended through the largesse of 'St Monday', who continued to claim many devotees. Disraeli recorded the popularity of the extended weekend in describing the industrial town of Wodgate in *Sybil, or the Two Nations*, his novel on the 'Condition of England' in the 1840s:[15]

> The social system is not an unvarying course of infinite toil. The plan is to work hard, but not always. The men seldom exceed four days of labour in the week. On Sunday the master workmen begin to drink; for the apprentices there is dog-fighting without stint. On Monday and Tuesday the whole population is drunk. Here is relaxation, excitement.

It was in the 1840s too that the factory commissioners reported frequent occasions when extra holidays were conceded. 'It was', they remarked, 'not due to liberality on the part of the masters, but to custom.' In one area of Lancashire it was averred that the workers enjoyed a fortnight's break at Christmas, a full week at Whitsun, 'three or four days at Ringley Wakes, about the same at Ratcliffe Races, and at odd times besides'. Often it was sport as much as drink that was irresistible. Thus the exploits of Ben Hart, Bolton's pedestrian champion of these years, drew crowds which left the local mills half-empty. From the Warwickshire pits a witness reported:[16]

> When there is such a matter of universal interest as a prize fight most go to see it, and it is a day's play. Upon the average there may be five or six such occasions in the course of a summer.

Elections also occasioned impromptu holidays – when an MP complained of a certain bill in 1828 which proposed to limit the duration of elections, that 'it abridged the constitutional enjoyments of the people', he was not referring to their rights of suffrage; similarly, *The Times* noted that the great reform demonstration in Birmingham in 1833 had 'the appearance of a great fair . . . the excuse for making holyday'.[17] Also relevant here, of course, is the measure of what might be called involuntary leisure in working-class life, when the work schedule was interrupted by structural breakdowns in production, seasonal drops in particular trades or periods of general business depression. Though they rued the economic consequences, men habituated to such fluctuations must have developed some capacity for improvising casual diversions in these breaks. In any case, enough has been said to nod in agreement with one experienced contemporary who concluded that the workingman 'possesses more facilities for getting holidays than is generally supposed'.[18]

The practice of such time-honoured delinquencies as St Monday obviously varied according to the economic setting. In Disraeli's Wodgate (modelled on the lockmaking town of Willenhall in Staffordshire) small workshops rather than factories provided the typical work situation, and there masters and men shared a common indulgence. Domestic outworkers were less confined than factory hands – in Bury in the 1830s the handloom weavers would drop their work whenever the hounds passed by and join in the chase.[19] Men in relatively minor trades, on the other hand, might lack the numbers necessary to outface their employers – we learn from the *Bolton Chronicle* for 9 August 1834 that five apprentice combmakers 'who seemed to consider that they had a prescriptive right to a holiday on the Horse Fair Day' were successfully prosecuted for absenteeism. Among factory workers, for whom industrial discipline was tightest, the claims of St Monday and other unscheduled and illicit breaks were far from extinguished, but here labour's principal response to the new rigorism was that of organised protest rather than the sporadic reaffirmation of traditional rights. The northern textile workers' struggle for the Ten Hours Bill (passed into law in 1847) was in a sense conservative, for it sought a return to the traditional measure of a normal day's work, but its logic was modern and forward-looking. The movement implicitly acknowledged the separation of work and leisure into exclusive domains while trying to negotiate a more humane balance between the two; in principle labour was now prepared to accept the austere regimen of factory production in return for the guaranteed regularity of a fair level of leisure time. The simultaneous demand for a Saturday half-holiday reflected the same philosophy and was supported by a substantial minority of employers who appreciated that such a concession on their part might not only win better attendance and punctuality in working hours, but might also effectively stabilise the workers' leisure within the fixed limits of a mutually defined weekend. The 'short Saturday' written into the 1847 act was still eight hours long, but a further measure in 1850 obliged textile mills to cease work at 2 p.m. on Saturday and in Manchester the new hours soon became standard for most other trades. Elsewhere these gains were still to be won, but in the north-west the modern English weekend was clearly taking shape.[20]

Restrictions on space were severe in the industrial town, and were more difficult to overcome. Open space vanished before the march of bricks and mortar: in Coventry, the mayor complained of the enclosure of the town's open park which had deprived the young men of 'much active exercise' and driven them into the public house; in Bolton, the gardeners' club, which had been formed to encourage workingmen's allotments, had become the preserve of gentlemen's gardeners from the suburbs as the patches of old cottage gardens disappeared from the town itself.[21] One common resort, the pub garden, was vulnerable to the pressure on building space, rising ground rents and neighbours' complaints of the crowd nuisance. In London, the somewhat more ambitious pleasure gardens, often descendants of eighteenth-century institutions, had long since lost their fashionable clientèle, and were similarly prone to complaints from the respectables.[22] It is commonly suggested that even in the 1850s and 1860s few towns or cities were so large that the countryside was more than a few minutes' walk away. It should be pointed out, however, that, on the evidence of Bolton, it seems that such an apparently simple excursion could be extremely hazardous where it meant negotiating the often hostile streets beyond one's immediate neighbourhood. In any case, access to the countryside was further limited by the denial of footpath rights by the landowners.[23]

The most obvious escape from confinement was the mass breakout such as Dickens described in the Londoners' 'spring rush' to Greenwich Fair. Bolton held major fairs in its market square at New Year and Whitsuntide, but equally popular were the wakes, a succession of fairs celebrated in late summer in the villages and townships surrounding the borough. At Whitsun the country cousins came to town and their awe at beholding the big city gave the break its local title of 'Gaping Sunday'; in August and September the flow was reversed and the town workers burst out into the villages.[24] Race meetings were other great occasions in the popular calendar. The progress of the London crowds from the metropolis to Epsom Downs on Derby Day was advertised by the huge swirling cloud of dust which hung over their route. On race days Mancunians debouched to Kersal Moor, the 'mons sacer' of the cotton towns as Engels called it. Belle Vue pleasure gardens (the scene of early brass band contests) also provided an important outlet for Manchester.[25] Trains and steamboats increased the range of the excursionist: a depressed Gravesend was revivified by boatloads of London pleasure-seekers; hitherto remote country race meetings, such as Goodwood, were inundated with townspeople; the wakes at the Cheshire villages of Hale and Tranmere were transformed into major proletarian festivals by the regular descent of the Liverpool working class from across the Mersey. From Bolton Henry Ashworth reported on the excursion travels of his workpeople: 'They will go to Ireland, or London, or Scotland, wherever the coach or the steamboat will carry them, and spend their time rationally.'[26]

Such occasions, however, provided only temporary relief, and the problem of open space for everyday recreation and exercise remained chronic. As footpaths, public gardens and common land were swallowed up or subjected to a more exclusive interpretation of property rights, the street alone was left as the new commons of the industrial poor. Street life in the Victorian town and city was much enlivened by the diversion and entertainment of its many professional habitués: Punch and Judy men, buskers, ballad hawkers (the 'flying stationers'), street preachers, stump orators and patent medicine salesmen. The street also provided an informal meeting place for gossiping neighbours, and a seasonal promenade for the young and flirtatious. In some cases traditional recreations were adjusted to suit its particular dimensions – thus the processional Whit walks in northern England can be seen as linear expressions of the round dances of the village green. But traffic and pollution limited its amenity, and the street was at best a constricted and unsalutary playground.[27]

It was not just a problem of open space but of adequate indoor facilities as well; moreover, as a corollary, there was the problem of the increasing pressure of sheer numbers. A London tradesman appearing before a parliamentary inquiry into drunkenness in 1834 made the point that all the pubs seemed much fuller than ever he could recall. When asked where the new customers came from he replied simply enough: 'I think they came from the current in the streets.'[28] Thus the pub was the natural resting place for this increase in human traffic.

The pub changed to accommodate the increasing volume of callers. Many old pubs were little more than the parlours or kitchens of private houses, presided over by an ex-butler or the like (when the Sedleys' business collapsed in *Vanity Fair* the butler, 'with the infatuation of his profession', set up a pub); new pubs built in the 1830s – the so-called gin palaces – were entirely different in scale, in lay-out, in style and in management. They solved the problem of space by doing away with seats; this also discouraged dawdling, which in turn meant a more rapid turnover in customers. Any feeling of congestion among the new generation of 'perpendicular drinkers' was relieved by an upward spaciousness provided by higher ceilings and the illusion of roominess contrived by the generous use of mirrors and plate glass. The huge gas lamps (a feature which impressed itself so greatly on contemporaries) hung outside as well as inside, and extended the territory of the pub into the street at all hours of the night. A bar counter separated the customers from the liquor and its dispensers, indicative of a more businesslike approach by the proprietors, some of whom were alleged to spend more time in the counting house than waiting on their customers. That function was increasingly taken over by barmaids, who constituted as much of an attraction as the elaborate fittings, and in some cases were just as garish. The domesticity of the old pub had given way to the commercialised glamour of new people's palaces, gaudy compensations for the meanness of everyday life. They were, as Dickens noted, 'invariably numerous and splendid in precise proportion to the dirt and poverty of the surrounding neighbourhood'. But in that they were vast as well as spectacular they offered some solution to the problem of the spatial as well as the social limitations of town life.[29]

Drinking, the simple company of the pub – these could be a recreation in themselves; but the working population demanded entertainment too. This was provided by the 'free and easy', an informal and predominantly amateur sing-song of longstanding popularity in the history of the pub, which was developed into a more formalised and frequent kind of tavern concert. Here again, new space was created by the more economical use of existing space: inn yards, billiard rooms, skittle alleys, even the publican's own sleeping quarters, were converted into 'singing saloons', the prototype music halls.[30] At a London licensing session in 1834, a sympathetic magistrate passed the following comment on the new phenomenon:[31]

He rejoiced in seeing so many applications for music licenses, as they proved the growing desire on the part of the public for intellectual and rational amusements. At the same time, he regretted the number of applications, as they proved that a power had too long been exercised to abridge popular recreations.

Such a remark brings us to a consideration of those who discerned little or no intellectual or rational content in the amusements of the people; their hostility constituted the other major constraint upon popular recreation.

III

The concern to police the amusements of the poor had a long history in English life but, as has been noted, it took on a new severity from the middle of the eighteenth century, and this preoccupation had scarcely lessened by the early Victorian period. Among its principal agents were the factory employers. In their drive for greater economy and efficiency they extended working hours, outlawed the traditional workshop pranks and diversions of the old craft culture – particularly those involving drink – and curtailed the number of local holidays. Some of the more single-minded of them used their considerable local influence to extend their surveillance beyond the factory and maintain a formidable discipline over their employees outside working hours.[32] More pervasive was the increasing influence of evangelicalism which by the 1830s had found support among clergy of all denominations and taken firm root in the middle classes. Its teachings stressed the need to strengthen personal and social standards of morality and evinced a deep suspicion of all worldly pleasures. In the Nonconformist churches its sentiments reinforced a long-standing hostility to traditional recreations, and the Methodists in particular were credited with some remarkable reforms of popular behaviour.[33] The Established Church, on the other hand, though it too had censured popular recreations in its time, had also traditionally been their patron – the northern wakes, for example, were originally parish feasts, and the old holiday calendar was as much ecclesiastical as agrarian in inspiration. But during the eighteenth century the Anglican clergy had increasingly distanced themselves from plebeian culture and withdrawn their patronage from its traditional festivities. Under the influence of evangelicalism estrangement was converted into an active hostility. In the 1820s this was accentuated by leading churchmen anxious to exorcise the surviving image of the traditional sporting parson with his love of field sports and country dancing. (Sidney Smith parodied the new commandments against clerical worldliness thus: 'Hunt not, fish not, shoot not, dance not, fiddle not, flute not.')[34] So church and chapel, as the old Yorkshireman had remarked, provided little for the workingman's recreation and indeed condemned such that he had. This greater censoriousness was noted in a snatch of popular verse from Peacock:

> The poor man's delight
> Is a sore in the sight
> And a stench in the nose of piety.

By the 1830s there were several active reform movements – predominantly evangelical in inspiration and middle class in membership – whose campaigns against certain abuses in public life threatened the form and content of much popular recreation. Principal targets were animal cruelty, sabbath-breaking and intemperance. The Royal Society for the Prevention of Cruelty to Animals included in its brief the suppression of all blood sports, and its inspectors were zealous in reporting infringements of the act of 1835 which had made the sports illegal. The society played a prominent role in suppressing the traditional bull-running at Stamford in Lincolnshire in the late 1830s, though many smaller-scale blood sports continued to flourish clandestinely.[35] The sabbatarians, operating principally through the Lord's Day Observance Society, offered a greater threat to popular recreation, for they sought to close all institutions (including the pub) which required the employment of labour on a Sunday, or otherwise distracted the populace from attending church. Sunday, as noted previously, was sanctified to the working classes in other ways – it was generally the one day a week which was regularly free for recreation and domestic tasks. The cause was not popular in Parliament and its proposals were often greeted with ridicule or disdain, not least because its spokesman in the Commons, Sir Andrew Agnew, had a peevish and almost inaudible voice; in the street his bills were known as Agony Bills which, according to vulgar wit, forbade even the working of Epsom salts on a Sunday. But the sabbatarians were well enough organised as a lobby and their flourish of petitions ('greater than on any subject other than those against West Indian slavery') earned them some deference from succeeding administrations – they won select committees in 1831, 1847 and 1851, successfully postponed the opening of the British Museum on a Sunday for over fifteen years, and secured the passage of some important restrictive legislation in the mid-1850s.[36] The Temperance movement comprised many local and several national organisations, but there was a common trend in the mid-1830s away from general appeals for moderation in drink-taking to an insistence upon complete abstention or teetotalism. The movement was split as to how this could best be achieved, but its hostility to drink and its purveyors cut at the roots of much popular recreation. Its early champions in Parliament were received as derisively as Agnew, but out of doors the local organisations proved formidable in petitioning the magistracy for the restriction of drink licences.[37] Temperance reformers often formed a common front with sabbatarians in opposing the Sunday opening of the pub.

It is clear that local authorities often played a major part in abridging popular recreations, either on their own initiative, or as servants (reluctant or otherwise) of the reform interests. In Bolton, for example, the magistracy proved amenable to a campaign by local clergy against the leading singing saloon in the town, the Star Museum and Concert Hall. In 1843 the proprietor, William Sharples, was frustrated in his bid for a theatre licence for his expensively remodelled premises by petitioners to the bench led by Bolton's vicar, who complained of the degeneracy of the concert room. The following year the same lobby secured a magistrate's order prohibiting Sunday performances at the Star. But the local mill-hands voted with their feet and the Star's popularity continued to grow. When the Star burnt down in 1852 church and chapel took the lead in forming an anti-singing saloon association pledged to prevent its resurrection, and successfully petitioned at the annual brewster sessions for the suspension of Sharples's licence. But the magistrates' action is not necessarily evidence of a single-minded concern for public morality, for a revealing commentary in the *Era*, the national trade paper of the licensed victuallers, claimed that the bench discriminated against Sharples for political and commercial reasons: as Liberals, the magistrates were anxious to retain the chapel vote in a forthcoming municipal election; as landlords of other public houses in town, they were securing their own tenants against the powerful competition of the Star.[38] Elsewhere, as we have seen in the remarks of the London JP quoted above, magistrates were actively sympathetic towards popular recreation – several who appeared before the select committee on licensing in the early 1850s clearly recognised the adequate social controls built into the singing saloons and were prepared to defend them. On other occasions magistrates were respectful of popular traditions; some invoked the Stuart *Book of Sports* in defence of Sunday sport and evinced great distaste for actions brought on the evidence of common informers, a frequent device of the sabbatarians.[39] Thus there was obviously great local and individual variation in the attitudes of the magistracy, though on balance they were probably more repressive than benevolent.

Other local bodies were frequently hostile to traditional amusements. In London, the Common Council in the City (largely under the prompting of its Methodist contingent, so we are told) strangled the historic

Bartholomew Fair by degrees. During the 1840s it raised the rents for stall-holders, limited the duration of the fair and succeeded in forcing it to use another, less convenient site. Thus 'old Bartlemy' was dead by 1854, following the fate of several other London fairs (some dispatched by private bills).[40] Robert Slaney, an MP greatly concerned with the contraction of popular recreation, accused local authorities of allowing nuisances at fairs to go unchecked in order to build up a case for their complete suppression.[41] Municipal incorporation in the mid-1830s gave office to a generation of councillors preoccupied with retrenchment, often at the expense of traditional festivities – certainly the fat geese roasted to celebrate success at Michaelmas elections disappeared in most boroughs. Other administrative rationalisations could trim away time-honoured local recreations – W. E. Adams recalled how the introduction of the new Poor Law in Cheltenham in the 1840s put an end to the agreeable annual ritual of 'beating the bounds', for it discontinued the subsidy which, under the old law, had paid for the wagonloads of drink. Incorporation could produce an officious local bureaucracy – in Bolton, the new inspector of nuisances was indefatigable in his campaign to exterminate pigeon-flying, already a popular working-class sport.[42]

The officers who had the greatest impact upon popular recreations were the officers of the new police. They were organised in both town and countryside during these decades, following the model of Peel's reform of the metropolitan police in 1829. Constables were soon a prominent feature of the fairground and race track: intercepting the Swell Mob, flushing out the pickpockets and other small fry, and harassing the itinerant showpeople whom they regarded as a cover for the criminal nuisance. The police enforced the law against blood sports. In Spitalfields in London, for example, they put an end to the bull-running on Easter Monday, an occasion which the old specials had been powerless to control. The bobbies were also effective in curtailing other wild sports, such as the Shrove Tuesday football game in Derby, which engulfed the streets with its mob of players, but which yielded to official limitations in 1846.[43]

There was considerable opposition to the introduction of the new police from all levels of society, and there is some indication that they were initially cautious in interfering with popular pleasures; eventually, however, it was only by conspicuous zeal in such matters that they could justify their existence to the more cantankerous and influential among the ratepayers. 'Where are the new police?' became a common cry in letters to the Bolton press in the 1840s – why did the officers of this offensive new institution (maintained at great local expense) do nothing about the young men playing pitch and toss in Great Moor Street, about the boys playing 'piggy' (a Lancashire game of tip-cat) behind Walmsley's Warehouse, about the crowds of louts who gathered to cheer on pedestrian races and obstructed rights of way?[44] The list of cases before the local courts show that the police did indeed come to bear down heavily upon these 'nuisances'; the players and spectators of street games were prosecuted for obstruction, trespass, breaches of the peace, vagrancy and desecration of the sabbath. Thus the police invaded the daily occasions for recreation as well as the popular festivals of the fair and race meeting. In clearing the streets, they not only threatened to deprive the working class of its last resort of public assembly, but also cut off many of its diversions by moving on the street performers.[45]

The hostility of the reform associations and local authorities was only the most forceful expression of a general middle-class impatience with the intractable crudities and excess of so much of popular recreation. The respectable citizens of Bolton who demanded police action against street games were not just concerned to criticise the efficiency of a distasteful new service, but were generally affronted by what they saw and heard of. In an age of progress and rationality it was frankly incomprehensible that people should amuse themselves by eating scalding porridge with their fingers or stripping the wicks from a pound of candles with their teeth, all for the sake of a wager and the applause of an audience of like-minded boobies. These folk pleasures were popular contests at the yearly Halshaw Wakes held near Bolton, but similar feats took place all the year round – eight pounds of treacle consumed in twenty minutes by a butcher's assistant (the commonest of participants) provides a ready example.[46] Such displays were generally attended by a great deal of drinking and gambling. The gentry and the respectable middle classes recoiled from such uncouth congenialities and, like the clergy, no longer appeared as patrons of the local fairs and feasts.

One persistent defence of the aberrations witnessed at the annual festivals – that they provided a safety valve for the discontents and frustrations of a hard-driven working people – found no support among the middle classes, particularly since this traditional licence encouraged recrudescences of saturnalia which they found offensive to their sense of station and social order.[47] In Lancashire at Eastertime the ancient practice of begging for eggs or 'pace-egging' provided sanction for gangs of youths to dress in outlandish garb and march in procession from pub to pub, blowing trumpets and banging on the tables till free drink was brought. Respectable passers-by were badgered into contributing drink money, and Henry Richard recorded an occasion when 'a rabble sort' stormed the Commercial Room of his hotel in search of tribute. At Ashton in Cheshire, revellers demanded beer money for the Black Knight, who was paraded in effigy at the annual fair – missiles hurled at the Knight had a way of breaking windows or spattering the better-dressed bystanders.[48] In many of these cases the full flourish of the traditional ritual had been pared away, but this attrition seems to have given the celebrations a sharper retaliatory edge – a popular retort to the studied neglect, compounded by official harassment, which character-ised the attitudes of the superior classes to the workingman's amuse-ments.

Before turning to consider the general response of the lower orders, it should be noted that there were some great popular festivals which significantly resisted curtailment, though castigated as morally degener-ate. Race meetings head this category. Racing had long been a target for the reformers of manners – an early sign of Wilberforce's conversion had been his pointed refusal of the stewardship of York races in 1790 – but the aristocracy and its county allies were successful in protecting the sport from its enemies. A committee of the House of Lords considered that the traditional arguments for the defence still held good in the 1840s:

> The Committee think it desirable that this amusement should be upheld, because it is in accordance with a long-established national taste, because it serves to bring together for a common object, vast bodies of people in different parts of the country, and to promote inter-course between different classes of society.

The committee went on to recall how Manchester races had been allowed to take place immediately after the Peterloo massacre; despite official misgivings, the meeting had not provided a new rallying ground for the disaffected, but had afforded a three-day armistice. The sport could also be defended as necessary for maintaining the good quality of English blood-stock. There were problems of public order on the Turf, but the Jockey Club, the aristocratic governing body, went some way to putting its own house in order during the 1840s and 1850s.[49] So the race meeting remained a stronghold of aristocratic patronage and life-style, trading on the patriotic claims and status associations of equestrianism; its broad and harmonious social mix received its apotheosis in Frith's classic picture, *Derby Day*, painted in 1858.

Racing increased in popularity with the working class in this period, and certain big city meetings became almost exclusively proletarian occasions. This was true at Manchester, Newcastle and at Doncaster, where by 1850 it was a matter of comment that 'the family carriage has been superseded by the bus'. The spread of excursion traffic and the continuing lure of a day in the open account for some of the growth, but an additional attraction was quite obviously the betting market. There was an immense increase of on-course betting for individually small sums, and the editor of *Bell's Life in London*, the leading sporting paper, concluded: 'The great majority of betters are persons from the manufacturing towns.' As a betting medium, racing was also popular away from the track: off-course betting shops were numerous (some as lavishly appointed as the gin palace), carrier pigeons relayed the results from the meetings and avid punters hung over bridges to catch the name of the big race winner from the fireman as the express train flashed through.[50] Gambling was a familiar vice among English workmen and it was well within living memory that such enthusiasms had been encouraged by a state-run national lottery; by the mid-century, however, the common man as gamester appeared as a threat to property in government eyes, for it was feared that gambling debts would lead the workman to theft, and the shopman to plunder his master's till. The remedy was the 1853 act for suppressing betting shops, which also outlawed the promotion of betting lists in the pubs. The legislation was meant to eliminate excessive betting from the towns, though the gentleman's right to wager was protected by significant loopholes in the new law (Lord Palmerston was supposedly responsible for cutting out some of the bill's more drastic proposals in the committee stage). The act was never a very watertight measure and, in any case, betting was still permitted at the race meeting itself. To prohibit betting on the course would have invited political disaster, but this relative tolerance suggests that, as a safety valve, the race meeting was regarded by the authorities as a manageable explosion which could be left to crackle away in a kind of quarantine on the edges of towns or beyond. Local opinion could be reconciled to any disturbances by the extra business brought by the influx of gentry and excursionists.[51]

The prize ring deserves some attention at this point, since it displayed a social formula similar to that of the Turf. It had a long history of aristocratic patronage, but all classes and callings were found among its followers, giving the sport its dominant feeling of social equality. In the mythology of the Ring, the fist was England's national weapon and the skilful and courageous wielding of it in public kept alive the spirit of Waterloo. Prize matches were generally fought in the countryside, and the style of the sport was heavily rustic; 'on the whole', observed Dickens, 'the associations entwined with the pugilistic art are much in the manner of Izaak Walton.' As with the Turf, there was much gambling, considerable piecemeal commercialisation, and a pronounced criminal fringe. The Ring was also very popular with the working class. The champion fighters were great popular heroes who often provided a focus for fierce local loyalties, and news of the big matches brought excitement to the slums. As the costermongers told Mayhew, fighting was considered a necessary part of any boy's education, and the rather portly muscularity and rubicund complexion of the pugilist embodied popular ideals of physical health. A successful career in the Ring for a working-class professional could mean substantial enrichment and the company of nobility – at least it generally meant enough money to open a pub.[52]

But the prize fight was a bloody and unruly affair, and it came under heavy attack from humanitarians and reforming magistrates. Publicans who promoted fights were prosecuted for breaches of the peace, or were unable to renew their liquor licence at the next brewster sessions; on the not infrequent occasions when a pugilist was slugged to death, his adversary was charged with homicide. The coming of the new police increased the odds against the sport's survival, but a few hardy promoters continued to trade upon such intelligence as that 'the Constables and Justices slept more soundly in Cambridgeshire than in Essex', and the Ring survived in a somewhat attenuated but largely unreformed state.[53] In 1860 the great international match between Sayers and Heenan provided the final climax for pugilism and revealed the subterfuges to which its supporters had had to resort. A special train left London before dawn, bound for a secret rendezvous beyond the reach of mounted police patrols; the contenders had gone before, in disguise. The press generally treated the event as a brutal anachronism, but assertions of the traditional warranty for the sport were still heard: in the Commons, Palmerston (who was accused of conniving at the outwitting of the authorities) made plain his personal approval of the Ring as a manly exercise in self-defence.[54] The lordly patronage of prize-fighting had by then greatly declined, but on such occasions, and in their continuing presence on the Turf, the aristocracy showed themselves the custodians of certain of the great myths of the English at play – the egalitarian bonhomie of the sporting fraternity, and the necessary role of the fist fight in building a sturdy national character. As an apologia for two heavily criticised institutions these sentiments provided some protection for popular participation.

IV

Generally, however, the working classes could count on little protection for their amusements from their betters; how, then, did they react to the

campaigns against popular recreation? Reformers often met with harassment: parish officers attempting to enforce Sunday closing were seren-
aded with 'rough music' and the clanging of dustmen's bells; racegoers
and fairground crowds man-handled religious fanatics who harangued
them on their sinfulness.[55] There were also occasions of fiercer and more
sustained resistance. The new police were ambushed and stoned and a
two-day mêlée ensued when they attempted to disperse the gambling
tables at Lancaster races in 1840. Attempts to suppress bull-baiting in
West Bromwich provoked extensive rioting, and such was the defiance
of the crowds at the annual bull-running at Stamford in Lincolnshire
that the dragoons had finally to be called in to assist the police in its
suppression.[56] A similar though comparatively minor incident in Berkshire is a reminder that these occasions were not only sporting events but
expressions of community, and defended as such: in Wokingham, a local
alderman donated the bull, and the proceeds from the sale of the dead
animal (whose meat was allegedly improved by baiting) went to charity,
together with the hide, which made shoes for the poor.[57] In a small
country town such an occasion would dominate the calendar. In the
cluster of manufacturing towns and industrial villages in Lancashire
there were so many feasts and wakes that some succumbed to reform
pressures without arousing any recorded popular protest – in Bolton and
district, Horwich races, the Cross Keys Fair and Tonge Fold Fair
disappeared quietly within a few years of each other in the late 1840s, at
the apparently uncontested promptings of 'moralists' and 'influential
gentlemen'.[58] What excited determined resistance in the big towns were
measures which theatened the more commonplace occasions of recreation and sociability. In Bolton in 1853, the working-class secularist
society successfully organised mass protest meetings against sabbatarian
proposals to close the pubs on Sunday. Two years later there were
serious riots in London against similar measures; in this case not only
recreation but domestic habit was threatened, for Parliament was
proposing to stop all trading in the city on Sunday.[59] Such campaigns
were interpreted as an attack upon the whole fabric of working-class life.

The language of resistance shows that workingmen often saw these
confrontations as part of a broader social and political conflict. There is,
for instance, a story (its origins as yet still obscure) of how the Chartists
took up the case of the proprietor of a London saloon theatre who was
prosecuted for playing the drama, at a time when dramatic licences were
still restricted to the patent theatres. The Chartists picketed Westminster carrying placards with the following legends: 'Freedom for the
People's Amusements'; 'Workers Want Theatres'; 'One Law for the

Rich, Another for the Poor'.[60] A more reliable example is provided by the Bolton protesters against sabbatarianism, whose leaders were veterans of the radical politics of the 1840s; the latter repeated a long and well-rehearsed catalogue of grievances against the local clergy – how they had sabotaged the Peel Park scheme, obstructed Sunday excursions, vetoed the Mechanics' Institute, and neglected the welfare of the people in the hard times of previous years. In Newcastle-upon-Tyne in the same year a workman warned his mates against the shopkeepers and clergymen of a local anti-race committee in words which carry the authentic note of class hostility:[61]

> They promise nought to replace this workman's holiday. . . . They would legislate for our morals . . . in their desire to deny us recreation and amusement they only add another to the many proofs they have already given us of their utter ignorance of human nature. . . . They are very fond of indulging in invectives against the publican, but the most casual observer among them cannot fail to have perceived that this body furnishes the only instances of providing amusements which, judging from the patronage they have received, appear to be most in demand. . . . They only speak of workmen's intelligence on rare occasions and display concern for their welfare when they want to use us to promote a scheme of their own. . . . I would say to you then, my fellow working men, be up and stirring in this matter; you, more than either the publican or the brewer, are interested in it, as it is only the prelude to a series of attempts to prevent, if possible, all recreation and amusement – it is the thin edge of the wedge which they will use all their efforts to drive home.

Given these examples of defiance it is difficult to explain away the apparently uncontested truncations of popular festivals in terms of working-class indifference. In an open letter to the Prime Minister in 1856 attacking the cessation of Sunday band concerts in London parks under pressure from the bishops, the radical, G. J. Holyoake, was anxious to counter this impression. 'It is', he said, 'a farce to talk of, and a wrong to assume, the "indifference of the people" from their silence – even on questions vital to them.' It was, however, in Holyoake's experience, difficult to marshal popular opposition, and thus many abridgements of popular recreation seemed to pass without offence, until accumulated resentment finally exploded in riot, as in the case of the Sunday trading riots in London in the previous year.[62] Holyoake's contentions are sound, but it seems likely too that the workingman was better able to accept and overcome many of the undoubted losses of these years because of the emergence of a new urban popular culture whose recreations were more appropriate to the environment of the modern industrial town.

In moving on to consider the singing saloons as one of the more prominent and, in middle-class eyes, more disturbing manifestations of the new popular culture, we meet up with the most formidable vested interest in popular recreation – the publican. The primacy of the publican derived in large part from his dominating position in the food and drink trade, and the traditional social skills he displayed in his stewardship of the pub. He sang in the pub harmonic society and presided over the Derby sweepstakes; he provided the prizes for the clubs which met on his premises; he played host and stakeholder to the various sporting fraternities, and gave cover to 'listmen', the early bookmakers; he put up the leg of mutton or the new chemise for which contestants danced or ran at the local fair. He also sold the refreshments for the fair, like Jack Entwhistle of the Falcon and Four Factories at Cross Keys Fair in Bolton, 'better known as Happy Jack – there in all his glory, surrounded by beer barrels and beer buyers'.[63] This was the 'genial Boniface', the people's friendly major-domo. Moreover, his central position in popular recreation, as the workingman from Newcastle had indicated, was reinforced by the withdrawal of such erstwhile patrons as the clergy and other local worthies.

The publican had to defend his commanding position against the reformers, particularly the Temperance movement. His free beer fuelled many of the working-class demonstrations noted above, and publicans (or licensed victuallers as they increasingly preferred to be known) formed trade protection societies whose function included propaganda in which the publican stood for the very ideal in good living, as we may learn from a report of the Manchester licensed victuallers' annual dinner in 1850: 'Here were jolly faces, healthful countenances and athletic men, whose thews showed the strength that roast beef, plum pudding and John Barleycorn create.' The glowing image was contrasted with that of Temperance diners picking at their food – 'as pale, decayed and thin a set of human beings as ever scowled on humanity'. In his defence the publican also laid claim to a unique professional expertise. 'Public amusements', argued the *Era*, 'is a trade and a mystery and requires to be learned like any other trade . . . no amateur ever ventured into it without damaging its character, and injuring its professors.'[64]

This retort was made in criticism of a particular attempt by clergymen to provide amusements which would counter the attractions of the pub, but the publican was more threatened during this era by competition from within his own bailiwick. The Beershop Act of 1830 had thrown open the retail trade in beer, allowing any ratepayer to brew and sell beer on his premises; licences were available from the local excise officer, and the beershop proprietor did not, like the publican, have to present sureties of solvency and good character, or submit to the magistrates for the annual renewal of his licence. Beerships proliferated. The publican was also likely to find himself in competition with his own kind, for the conditions of entry into public house proprietorship had also become easier under the influence of the free licensing movement.[65] Publicans made shift to out-face their rivals – as one of them explained to a government committee in 1831, the search for extra attractions had led him and his fellows to resort to 'very great show and ornament'. Hence the elaborations of the gin palace and the regular entertainment of the singing saloon, which show the publican on the defensive as much as on the make. Given the burgeoning 'current in the streets', the situation was almost certainly never as bad as the trade made out – one witness who knew the business from the inside maintained that some London publicans had increased their profits so substantially in the 1830s that they were diversifying into steamboat excursions.[66] But many of them were worried about hanging on to their share of the drinking public; as rival leisure attractions multiplied in the following decades, publicans came to conform less to the popular image of a genial Boniface than to Dickens's picture of the proprietor of a Liverpool singing saloon: 'Mr Licensed Victualler . . . a sharp and watchful man, with tight lips and a complete edition of Cocker's arithmetic in each eye.'[67]

The commercial operation of the singing saloons reveals also that despite growth there were significant economic and social limitations to the leisure market of the period. Revenue came from the sale of food and drink, particularly the latter. Admission to the saloons was by purchase of a refreshment check, a bronze or copper disc bearing the name of the pub and the value of the refreshments for which it was exchangeable inside the hall (in some areas this practice relieved the publican of the need to hold a music licence, and also obviated an old law forbidding the taking of money for admission on Sundays, often a popular night at the saloons).[68] The publican tried to sell more drink than that provided on the refreshment check – he had to cover rising rents and increased overheads. The chairman, who conducted the entertainment, was therefore required to ensure frequent breaks for ordering drinks, setting a personal example by his own readiness to accept a glass from the audience. His duties were graphically described by a Lancashire magistrate:

there were diverting pleasant fellows who had what is called 'the run of their teeth'; that is, they were allowed to eat and drink, and they were employed by the publicans to sing songs and tell stories, and badger any country fellow who came till they made him drink.

The waiters, too, kept up the pressure, as another witness recorded: '[Visitors] are soon made to understand by the waiter coming to them that they must order drink or leave the place . . . they are compelled to order drink as the condition of remaining to witness the performance.'[69] These practices demonstrate that however numerous popular demand might have been, it was not very effective in terms of spending power – a full singing saloon did not automatically guarantee a full till. The refreshment ticket and the importunities of the saloon staff were necessary devices to prise revenue from the meagre competences of a working-class public with no established habit of direct payment for entertainment, particularly not for entertainment as familiar and largely self-generated as the free and easy. The singing saloons were called into being by the working classes, and the working classes asserted a remarkable degree of popular control over them. Not until the 1850s did certain of the more enterprising publican entrepreneurs devise a new and more remunerative market formula.

In the meantime the saloons flourished as a popular institution. The new tavern concerts were most numerous in London and the north. Between 1829 and 1849 applications for music and dancing licences to the Middlesex bench increased eightfold, and an increasing proportion of these were granted. By the 1840s London had a substantial body of professionals working the singing saloons; they had their own benevolent society and used the Hope Tavern off Drury Lane as a clearing house for engagements.[70] Here was evidence of a growing commercialisation and regularity. There were thriving music rooms in Manchester by 1834, there being six to one street in Ancoats alone. 'Many of them', reported one observer alert to the conspicuous consumption of the poor, 'have an organ, or a pianoforte, or a musical clock worth one hundred and fifty guineas.' From Preston in 1851, James Hudson reported: 'Singing-rooms are numerous, prosperous and constantly well-attended.' At first the music had only been provided in the winter months, but by the 1840s concerts were being held throughout the year, and the entertainment and appointments were on a grander scale. William Dodd has left us a good picture of a thriving singing saloon in his description of The Jolly Hatters in Stockport in 1842, where a large extension had just been opened. This annexe, the 'Thespian Gallery and Temple of the Muses', was 'beautifully painted and well furnished',

and could accommodate 400 to 500 customers for its nightly performances.[71]

A good example of the rise of the singing saloon to a dominating local
position in working-class recreation is provided by the Star in Bolton.
Opened in 1840 by Thomas Sharples, a prominent publican of the town,
the Star had gradually expanded under his son William's management to
incorporate a picture gallery, a museum and a menagerie. The museum
held historical relics such as the axe reputed to have been used at Derby's
execution, geological specimens, stuffed birds, a photographic studio
and a ship's mainmast complete with rigging. Lectures on these various
exhibits and topical subjects such as emigration were held in the Star, as
well as the music and dancing associated with saloon entertainment.
'The principle of the concert room', explained George Gray, the
manager, 'is to combine social enjoyment with wholesome instruction.'
Referring to disappointing experiments in popular education, he championed the saloons as 'the only engines for public instruction now existing in society'. Gray's formula was certainly attractive to the Bolton
working class. The Star could hold over 1,000 folk, and at weekends in
particular it was bursting at the seams with the influx of excursion
crowds from surrounding towns. A score of minor rivals operated in its
shadow, but in 1852 it accounted for the biggest share of the estimated
nightly attendance of 3,000 to 4,000 at Bolton's singing saloons. Though
family groups were reported among the audience, the Star was particularly attractive to the young of both sexes, who used it for their courting;
most of them were unattended by their parents. William Sharples's
account books provide several examples of the headaches of management, but they show too, amid the confusions of his own personal style
of accounting, that the Star yielded a handsome and regular profit.[72]

The entertainment set before the saloon audiences was diverse in its
materials, illustrating the wide resources of popular culture; the songs,
dances and tricks were derived from the travelling show and popular
theatre, the village green and the street, the drawing room and the
church, and the recently imported nigger-minstrel shows. The style was
boisterous, vulgar and irreverent – Dodd, in his 1842 description of The
Jolly Hatters at Stockport, noted a satirical song entitled 'The Parson
and his Pigs', a young woman 'in a stylish undress' and 'an indecent
mongrel kind of dance'. The saloon audience also had a taste for spectacle (tableaux of battle scenes and reproduction of great historic events)
but essential to all performances was the chorus singing, in which the
audience came into its own. The fierce enthusiasm of their participation
is described here by a member of the 'improving' press, who records

with some amazement the *lèse-majesté* visited upon some of his own favourite songs:

> By name, they are often the same as we see in music-sellers' windows and on our own drawing-room tables; but they are garbled and interpolated here in a manner to defy description. They are sung, or rather roared, with a vehemence that is stunning, and accompanied with spoken passages of the most outrageous character. At the end of every verse the audience takes up the chorus with a zest and vigour which speaks volumes – they sing, they roar, they yell, they scream, they get on their legs and waving dirty hands and ragged hats bellow again till their voices crack. When the song is ended, and the singer withdraws, they encore him with a peal that seems enough to bring the rotting roof on their heads.

Whatever the abandon, by the 1850s the procedure was well formalised in some of the halls: 'programme books thick as a magazine are laid upon the tables for our acceptance, and as the song is announced by the chairman, he refers you to the number in the volume, beneath which you may find the words.'[73]

The singing saloons in particular emphasise the continuing strengths of popular recreation – the vitality and capacity for adaptation. Their success represents a victory over the constrictions and impersonality of the new towns. They utilised and stretched existing resources to accommodate the increasing numbers from the street who were hungry for company and diversion. As with the gin palace (often one and the same set of premises with the saloon) the gas light and other advances in technology were pressed into service to allow for greatly enlarged assemblies, yet the gregarious intimacy of saloon entertainment retained an essentially human and personal pattern of contact within the new scale of things: the logistics were such that the audience could perambulate and intermingle at will; the performers – despite an incipient professionalism – were not yet irrecoverably distanced from their public; and the chorus singing was a compelling ritual that reaffirmed the common identity of its celebrants. It is significant too that despite the incessant clatter of bonhomie good order prevailed among the singing saloon crowds. In his tour of Lancashire in 1842, the journalist and historian Cooke Taylor recorded: 'I have gone into some of the concert-rooms attached to favoured public houses which they (the operatives of Manchester) frequent, and I have never been in a more orderly and better behaved company.' Some ten years later a spokesman for a Manchester association for the reform of public houses found no need to demand any alteration in the hours which the singing saloons kept because he allowed: 'The people regulate the hours – all the working people leave by 9:30.' The same witness also acknowledged that there was very little drunkenness among saloon audiences, and Sharples's accounts testify that ginger beer or 'pop' sold as well as the stronger stuff.[74] With emphasis on the north-west again, it seems plain that a substantial section of the working class was by now distributing its leisure time and energies to a more disciplined pattern, in closer correspondence than before with the parameters of a standardised industrial working week. If the nature of the experience was therefore modified, the satisfactions still appear real enough.

The Star in Bolton, with its wide range of attractions, shows how the saloon could meet the popular thirst for instruction as well as entertainment. From Bolton too, there is evidence of how the saloons could fight off the attacks of the reformers, for Sharples eventually defeated the designs of the local anti-singing saloon association and rebuilt the Star after the 1852 fire. On its reopening, the Bolton dialect paper recorded the cheers of popular satisfaction: 'We're so fain to see the Star oppen ogen, that we're just gettin' shut of a bit of eawr surplus emoshun . . . nearly every chops had a grin on it.' In a more reflective manner, another local correspondent drew the following conclusion from the controversy over the Star: 'The Singing Saloons, or Singing Halls, are the best guarantee for recreation, and approach nearer to the inclinations and customs of the working classes than any other institution of the present age.'[75]

These proletarian 'maisons de culture' advertised their success with a clamant assault upon the senses, for they were certainly more obtrusive than their more humble forerunners. With their powerful lighting, their enlarged capacity and the prevailing enthusiasm for chorus singing, they were a phenomenon of which few can have remained unaware. The saloons were blazing arcades of light. Customers crowded outside on the pavement waiting to get in, while the sounds of popular music-making were roared abroad – on Sunday nights such favourites as the Doxology and the Hallelujah Chorus dominated the repertoire. To Faucher's translator, a middle-class Mancunian, the inclusion of hymns was a sign of an improved taste among the working classes, but to other respectable citizens passing by on the other side the saloons afforded fleeting peep-shows of degeneracy, confirming the evidence of prison chaplains whose younger charges seemed ever ready to oblige with testimonies to the corrupting influences of such places.[76]

The saloons were particularly disturbing to the reformers.[77] They saw the brutality and crudeness of the older traditional amusements as the excrescences of a folk or rustic barbarism – noxious enough, but ultimately incapable of withstanding the moral advances of a modern society; they were now confronted with a thriving institution that was the direct product of a modern urban society, and which so fitted the tastes and conventions of a large section of the members of that society, that it theatened to engross all their leisure time. It was this marked capacity for autonomous renewal in popular recreation which demanded of reformers that their counter-attack be constructive rather than merely repressive.

2

Rational recreation: voices of improvement

In the 1830s and 1840s English society faced appalling problems of social order and public health which provoked a wide-ranging debate on the 'Condition of England'. One strand in the debate concerned popular recreations and the desirability of promoting their reform in such a way as to make a constructive contribution to the general drive for social amelioration or 'improvement'. In this scenario improved recreations were an important instrument for educating the working classes in the social values of middle-class orthodoxy. Rational recreation, as the new prescription was styled, commended itself to a variety of reform interests and attracted increasing public attention as the mid-century approached. By then the history of several schemes launched in its name had revealed the considerable problems of putting its rationale of social control into practice.[1]

I

Rational recreation proceeded from a basic humanitarian sympathy with the plight of the urban masses. Expressions of regret at the persecution and neglect of their amusements multiplied during the early Victorian era. 'The very essence of our laws', acknowledged Edward Bulwer Lytton, the novelist, 'has been against the social meetings of the humble, which have been called idleness, and against the amusements of the poor, which have been stigmatised as disorder.'[2] Such confessions became calls for action. In the Commons, Robert Slaney, a country gentleman with a utilitarian interest in the health of towns, argued that those who abolished the amusements of the poor were bound to find a substitute. There were, he maintained, 'great arrears to make up in this respect towards these neglected classes'. The concern to humanise life in the towns was reinforced by practical considerations of social stability. If relief was not forthcoming, warned Slaney, 'the working classes will fly to demagogues and dangerous causes'; it was, he claimed, 'alike wise and benevolent to provide, in regulated amusement for the many, safety valves for their eager energies'.[3] Chartism was the dangerous cause uppermost in middle-class minds. Edwin Chadwick was moved to argue for the provision of improved recreational amenities from the example of one occasion in Manchester, when potential demonstrators flocked to the zoo and museum (opened specially at the instigation of the police chief) rather than a Chartist meeting. A witness to the commission on the health of towns reminded its members that open spaces and sports were essential for diverting the lower orders from political disaffection. In particular, it was the unnerving spectacle of the Chartist agitation in 1842 which alerted a Manchester banker, Benjamin Heywood, to the alienation of the working class, and prompted him to reform the Manchester Lyceums; within these new recreational centres he hoped to create a 'community of enjoyment' which would engender 'reciprocal feelings' between employer and employee. Though the threat of Chartism receded, there still remained the problem of containing the 'dangerous classes', that indeterminate but volatile menace that lurked in the rookeries of the big cities.[4]

But rational recreation was not an old-fashioned exercise in placating the mob; Slaney talked of safety valves, but qualified the image by talking of the need for 'regulated amusement'. Existing popular recreations which served to dissipate tensions within society were generally dismissed. While middle-class reformers acknowledged examples of working-class improvement at play and derived considerable encouragement from them, they stood dismayed at the prodigality of much working-class leisure with its determined exploration of the limits of the human appetite to the point of repletion or collapse. Contemplating the Staffordshire miners in 1850, Hugh Tremenheere, a factory inspector of much experience, noted despondently: 'The half-savage manners of the last generation have been exchanged for a deep and almost universally pervading sensuality.'[5] Drunkenness was the most frequently indicated 'sensual' pleasure; feasting, brawling and (less directly stated) fornication were other regrettable indulgences. The reformers meant to cut back these excesses by providing alternative recreations which stimulated and restored the mind rather than merely debilitated the body, yet the new proposals also placed limits on the exercise of mental energies for there was the fear that these too could be misplaced if they were lured into the vigorous radical culture of popular social movements such as Chartism, where much that was undeniably recreational (and often enough well disciplined) was none the less socially subversive. Cooke Taylor, the journalist and historian met with previously in his tour of Lancashire in the early 1840s, concluded:[6]

There must be safety valves for the mind; that is, there must be means for its pleasurable, profitable, and healthful exertion. These means it is in our power to render safe and innocent: these means in too many instances have been rendered dangerous and guilty.

Those who gave the question serious attention in these years were coming to the realisation that its solution required more than an immediate rescue and repair operation; even if political tensions were reduced, there remained the continuing problem of ensuring a socially tractable working class in a fluid and anonymous urban society. Any realistic strategy of social control – or 'moral education' as contemporary usage had it – would have to devise techniques for legitimating its authority other than those of direct and coercive impressment. To most social reformers in the early Victorian period, formal education appeared as the single great lever with which the working classes could be moved into the light. Education, in the words of Dr Kay-Shuttleworth, its chief government policy-maker in the 1840s, was meant not only to teach occupational skills, but also 'the nature of his [the artisan's] domestic and social relations . . . his political position in society, and the moral and religious duties appropriate to it'.[7] But, as Cooke Taylor pointed out: 'The lectures of the schoolroom will be utterly ineffective when they are counteracted by the practical lessons of the playground.' 'It was', he asserted, 'the great but neglected truth, that moral education, in spite of all the labours of direct instructors, is really acquired in hours of recreation.' Some such dictum has no doubt appeared in the conventional wisdom of many previous eras, but in this age it carried a new significance, for reformers were being forced to recognise that the more effective control of popular leisure was an urgent and difficult undertaking demanding a particular sensitivity to the changing pattern of life in a modern world. The problems involved were thus considerable, but the task also had its exhilarations, for it offered the opportunity to contribute to what contemporaries conceived as a general remaking of society. Contemplating the state of popular recreation and the travails of modern life in 1838, William Howitt concluded that both had reached a turning point:[8]

There appears to have been a pause in that important portion of human life, amusement, so far as the common people are concerned; but it has been in appearance only. One of the greatest changes that ever took place in human society has been in this interval maturing: the change from the last stage of worn out feudalism to the commencement of the era of social regeneration.

II

How was rational recreation to assist in this regeneration? How was it to be implemented? Reformers were generally agreed upon the need to provide more recreational amenities in the manufacturing towns as a basic improvement. This was one of the 'immediate remedies' proposed by the select committee on drunkenness in 1834, which indicated the range and balance required of such provisions. The committee recommended:[9]

> The establishment by the joint aid of Government and the local authorities and residents on the spot, of public walks, and gardens, or open spaces for healthy and athletic exercises in the open air, in the immediate vicinity of every town, of an extent and character adapted to its population; and of district and parish libraries, museums and reading rooms, accessible at the lowest rate of charge; so as to admit of one or the other being visited in any weather, and at any time.

But governments and local authorities were generally dilatory in meeting such requests, despite the lobbying of men like Slaney who regularly promoted bills to secure public walks and playgrounds. In 1837 Joseph Hume, another Radical interested in the amusements of the poor, was successful in passing a motion in the Commons which instructed the enclosure commissioners to ensure that each enclosure left an open space 'sufficient for the purposes of exercise and recreation of the neighbouring population'. Two years later, after an inspection of the breviates of enclosure bills, an interested member reported back that 'the laudable object had been laxly looked after'. Members for the new towns in the reformed House recognised the problem but were sceptical of any municipal improvement which required an increase in the rates – 'There is', said Fielden to a select committee on public walks, 'an extraordinary jealousy in that respect.' In 1840 Parliament voted money to assist local authorities in providing parks, and in 1845 Peel made a personal example by a gift of £1,000 towards the establishment of Peel Park in Manchester; but the boroughs were slow in response – in Bolton the proposal for a Peel Park was first made in 1850 and was not brought to fruition till sixteen years later.[10] Official parsimony effectively restricted the improvement of mental as well as physical recreation. William Ewart, a Liberal backbencher, successfully introduced a bill in 1850 which enabled local authorities to provide public libraries out of the rates. It was, said one of his supporters, 'the cheapest police that could possibly be established'. The Libraries Act enabled town councils to levy a small rate which paid for housing and servicing the libraries, but not for buying books; the select committee on libraries had maintained that 'donation will abundantly supply the books'.[11] Once the authorities had grudgingly primed the pump, philanthropy was meant to complete the operation.

Thus recreational reform failed to command any real priority with the legislators. The Commons seemed happy enough to debate the issue of the amusements of the poor as a diversion – the image of Merrie England was freely invoked as members deplored the puritan zeal of certain magistrates who prosecuted sabbath-breaking cricket players, or applied the vagrancy laws to street singers – but members deprecated direct control as a means of improving the manners of the people. In its inquiry into the licensing of places of entertainment in the early 1850s, the Commons' select committee obviously preferred education as an agent of improvement to any extension of the magistrate's powers. Improvement outside the field of education, as one MP reminded the House, would come from 'the influence of an increased morality, diffused downward from the upper class'. This was the current orthodoxy: 'Opinions travel upwards, manners downwards.' No government action, whether through limiting the number of theatres, legislating for the better observance of the sabbath or imposing sumptuary laws, was any substitute for the operation of this mysterious and respected process.[12]

While reformers would not allow *laissez-faire* arguments to excuse the official neglect of amenities, they did accept the need for example-setting by the superior classes. Setting an example was, in any case, a salutary exercise for the superior classes, but it was hoped that their presence in recreation would engender a mutual moral vigilance in the community at large. Thus would be created the police of public opinion – 'mores sans legibus', rather than 'legibus sans mores', as the Lord Chancellor had put it in a debate on sabbath observance. In rational recreation the community restraints would be reinforced by imprinting the values of the superior example on the working-class mind, making them self-acting imperatives. 'SELF-ACTION FOR SELF-IMPROVEMENT', proclaimed the *Bolton Chronicle*, drawing a moral from the Factory Operatives Bazaar, 'was the only sure ground for hope of progress.'[13]

But if the working class needed an example to follow, exactly who among the rest of society was to provide it? The patronage of the nobility could be far from appropriate – commenting on the spectacle of the gentry going down to Newmarket on what had become a regular Easter Sunday procession, Bishop Blomfield of London declared that there was 'nothing more likely to unhinge the whole fabric of civil society than this evil example of the rich'.[14] Where the moral conduct of the aristocracy had greatly improved – and this was generally held to be the case – middle-class commentators suggested that it was the conspicuous rectitude of the middle classes which had shamed the aristocracy out of its old ways. If, therefore, the middle classes accepted the aphorism 'opinions travel upwards, manners downwards', they did so because they saw themselves as the central point of departure for the diffusion of improvement in both ideas and behaviour. If aristocracy meant rule by the best, then the English middle class was beginning to assert its claims to be better qualified – as Carlyle challenged: 'Not that we want no aristocracy, but that we want a new one.'

There was considerable apprehension among the middle class at the persistent attractions of aristocratic patronage among the workingmen of a nation proverbially enamoured of a lord. The fear was that aristocratic paternalism, even when purged of its traditional decadence, would obstruct the diffusion of middle-class values and stunt the growth of working-class self-help. Such misgivings quickened in times of political rivalry. In 1843, Lord John Manners, a supporter of protection and factory reform and a member of Disraeli's Young England group, accused the manufacturing interest of 'a utilitarian selfishness which has well nigh banished all unproductive amusements from the land', and demanded extra holidays for the people and a return of true recreation. The joys of the maypole and the sports of the village green were to be restored under the revived alliance of the nobility and the old High Church: 'Before the millions are taught to dance and sing, leisure must be obtained for them and obtained in a way which they shall be taught thankfully to acknowledge – the way of the Church Catholic in England.' The following year, with the campaign against the Corn Laws still undecided and Short Time agitation mounting, the Manchester Lyceum (the workingmen's club run by Heywood the banker) asked Manners to be its patron, but was privately warned off such a course by Cobden and the Anti-Corn Law League.[15]

Some working-class reformers were also wary of the insidious grip of the aristocracy and the persistence of habits of deference. Francis Place, for example, was dismayed by the initially strong influence of the aristocracy at Exeter Hall, the London rallying ground for evangelical reformers, for he feared it would seduce middle-class attenders from their duties to workingmen. In a prize essay written for a Leeds Mechanics' Institute in 1850, a workman applauded many of the proposals of Young England for joining the rich with the poor in common pursuit of sports and games, but suspected the group's motives: 'They would', he feared, 're-establish the bond of feudalism.'[16]

The one 'persona non grata' to all reformers was the publican. There were respectable workingmen who defended the 'social glass' and spoke well of the publican and the pub, but the experience of the Temperance Chartists had alienated men like William Lovett who had tried to provide rational recreation for their class. Lovett learnt at first hand of the ruthlessness of the drink interest when he was evicted from his People's Hall in Holborn by the machinations of the publican-entrepreneur Edward Weston, who took over the premises for conversion into a music hall. A Liverpool vicar who ran concerts for his working-class congregation put the reformers' case succinctly: 'The duties of publican and the duties of provider of public amusements for the people are quite incompatible.'[17] Reformers were at least agreed upon the principal figure in their demonology.

Whatever the rivalries over its direction, the general strategy of rational recreation was clear: new amenities would divert the workingman from the pub and provide the proper environment for his exposure to the superior example, whose values would ultimately be internalised. But how was the superior example to be projected to the working classes; was it to be by display or prescription? Slaney provided an example of the former in arguing for public walks:[18]

A man walking out with his family among his neighbours of different ranks, will naturally be desirous to be properly clothed, and that his wife should be also; but this desire duly directed and controlled, is found by experience to be of the most powerful effect in promoting Civilisation and exciting industry.

Family recreation in the company of social superiors would generate 'a pardonable vanity'. For those reformers untouched by whole-hog sabbatarianism, the 'Continental Sunday' offered an admirable model. French and Germans of all classes took their recreation together on their Sunday promenades; though drink was taken ('a glass of light beer') the moderation and decorum of these occasions seemed to prove to English witnesses how effectively the public parade of bourgeois respectability could impress the masses.[19] This was also the assumption behind the tea party or soirée, where the good manners of the middle-class guests were expected to rub off on the less genteel. Nature itself – where it plainly bore the mark of man's assiduous hand – might also set an impressive example: the *Bolton Chronicle*, 11 September 1852, commended the local horticultural society's annual show to the 'humbler classes', confident that, by their inspection of its awesome batteries of well-drilled fruit and vegetables, 'pleasurable emotions will be engendered and fostered, lessons of lasting importance will be learned, and high moral sentiment will be imbibed.' But, as the history of several schemes for recreational improvement shows, reformers felt the need to clarify the content of conformity more forcefully, and display and the conventions of polite social intercourse were generally reinforced and mostly overtaken by prescription.

III

Samuel Greg's report on the improvements he introduced on his industrial estate in Cheshire in the late 1830s provides a convenient point at which to begin an examination of rational recreation in practice, for it reveals something of the tension which developed between these two approaches as well as exemplifying a fairly common type of reform exercise in this field.[20] Greg was a substantial employer who provided a variety of recreations for his workpeople – music classes, gardens, a playground for games, and regular tea parties in the winter. He insisted that other schemes to improve the content of working-class leisure were often inappropriate – he dismissed the Mechanics' Institutes as offering 'mere intellectual pursuits', maintaining that:

> There are many whose minds are not sufficiently cultivated to avail themselves of these: they have little or no taste for them, and yet are quite capable of being made very worthy, sensible, respectable, and happy men. . . . By gently leading them, or rather perhaps by letting them find their own way, from one step to another, you may at length succeed in making them what you wish them to be.

Having professed his belief in the perfectibility of workingmen, he talked of 'letting them find their own way'; having seen something of the erratic and reluctant nature of their actual progress towards self-redemption, he felt the need to expedite the process by 'gently leading them'. The guiding hand of the reformer was frequently more impatient and intrusive than the latter phrase suggests, and Greg himself was more peremptory in practice than his comments allow; elsewhere in the report he remarked briskly that he had succeeded in 'breaking them [his operatives] into my system'.

Greg's schemes were not exceptional among manufacturers whose operations were confined to an industrial estate or factory village which constituted a closed community – 'a little Colony', as Greg put it. Robert Owen's New Lanark mills had included an annexe comprising a school, museum, music hall and ballroom. The Ashworth brothers provided similar facilities at their country mills at Turton, near Bolton. In the village of Flockton, near Huddersfield, the firm of Stanfeld and Briggs maintained a clubroom, choir, playground and gymnasium for their colliers, and there were several other examples of this kind of welfare capitalism.[21] The employers were applauded for their concern to humanise the factory system, and the *Spectator* commended Greg for providing his work people with a 'moral' or 'aesthetic' economy to balance the necessary exigencies of political economy.[22] Though some of them would have disdained the role and its associations, such men were readily cast as the new industrial lords of the manor; they were reaffirming the traditional social bonds of Merrie England, so the reports went, albeit a Merrie England bowdlerised by the twopenny pastoralism of the Victorian press. The ideal inspired Disraeli's picture of Trafford of Wodgate, the model employer in *Sybil*:

> In the midst of this village, surrounded by beautiful gardens, which gave an impulse to the horticulture of the community, was the house of Trafford himself, who comprehended his position too well to withdraw himself with vulgar exclusiveness from his real dependents, but recognised the baronial principle, reviving in a new form, and adapted to the softer manners and more ingenious circumstances of the times.

It should be noted, however, that the returns of this kind of paternalism could be disappointing. Greg was very hurt when his workpeople went on strike in 1847 over the introduction of a new process, especially since they made no attempts at negotiation with him before abruptly turning out. At Flockton in 1845 there was a thirteen-week strike which Tremenheere, the government inspector, regarded as 'an unhappy perverseness of conduct' on the part of employees who were so well provided for. Subsequent reports from Flockton recorded further disenchantment: 'The novelty having gone off, the amusements and rational occupations for leisure hours have fallen into some neglect.'[23]

It was a common contemporary assertion that such schemes were only practicable in industries and manufactories located in the countryside; as these centres of production declined or became absorbed by urban growth, the factory inspectors tried to encourage some attention to welfare and recreation on the part of employers in the towns, where the main thrust of industrial growth now lay. Welfare capitalism had made but slight progress in this sector, according to a government report of 1843:[24]

> Instances of personal attention on the part of employers to the welfare of their workpeople in general, and of the younger portion of them in particular can be regarded only as individual exceptions. It is a fearful thing to see how exempt the great body of employers hold themselves from moral obligations of every description towards those from whose industry their own fortunes spring. Even they who contribute at all to the education or moral improvement of their workmen do so in nineteen cases of twenty merely by money, and without personal pains or superintendence of their own. These vicarious benevolences are seldom availing.

As the decade progressed, however, the provision of recreational facilities did improve.[25] James Hudson provided one explanation. 'The manufacturer', he claimed, 'finds it PROFITABLE to form schools and factory libraries, to rear amateur bands of musicians among his workmen.' A further explanation must be that factory employers in the 1840s felt the need to counter growing criticism of their class, both in Parliament and out of doors. Hence the defensive tone to this declamation by Sir John Potter, manufacturer and mayor of Manchester, on the occasion of the inauguration of the public library in the town:

> Let it never be said hereafter that the masters, the employers, the richer classes of Manchester, have no interest in the improvement and advancement of those they employ. . . . Let it never be said that they are not willing to make sacrifices for the many. Let it not be said that they seek merely their own advantage: that they are content with making money for themselves.

Yet where employers offered recreational facilities on the site the workers' response was often disappointing – John Bright's brother reported that only a small percentage of his employees took advantage of the means he offered them for their improvement.[26]

The demand for public libraries exemplified the need for more open facilities than those attached to and indelibly associated with the workplace; some schemes set their experiments on more neutral ground and made bids for a broader clientèle. Heywood's Lyceums offer a good example. The Lyceums were formed in Manchester and Salford in the late 1830s as auxiliaries to Mechanics' Institutes. The institutes had generally failed to attract a substantial working-class membership; Heywood recognised that the formal lectures of the institutes were often too demanding for the exhausted factory worker, and offered a lighter regimen of social evenings, sports and excursions.[27] After the Chartist agitation in 1842 Heywood concentrated his full attention on the Lyceums as an instrument of community welfare and class reconciliation. He lowered the subscription and encouraged wives to attend; the Lyceums were to be a home from home, 'a match for the public house' and an agreeable meeting ground for masters and men. Despite the more relaxed and entertaining fare there was an underlying note of earnestness, as Heywood revealed: 'Beneath the tempting experience of amusements and exhibitions, valuable as they are, there must be an undercurrent of solid instruction to support your progress.' Thus Harriet Martineau's moral tales of political economy were read aloud while the workingmen took their coffee.

The Lyceums were a failure according to the criteria of their promoters. Reporting on the experiment in his history of adult education, Hudson concluded: 'Their moral influence has become inoperative against the singing rooms which have sprung up in the cotton metropolis.' Heywood found that his efforts to develop a common sociability among employers and employed were vitiated by social distance. The mechanics' parties were uneasy parades along the class frontier. The middle-class directors were self-conscious in their bonhomie, and the workingmen too obviously on their best behaviour to give these occasions any real conviviality. For the workingmen, trying to be festive in these circumstances must have been like attempting a clog dance on a tight rope. The propriety of such occasions disintegrated, as Heywood mournfully reported to his son in 1851:[28] 'The character of the thing is changed. I am glad you were there, however, for old sake's sake. It is somewhat humiliating that the sober speakers should be the stopgaps between the acts.' The danger that amusements might dilute or obliterate instruction was a constant hazard to improvers.

Yet amusements were undeniably important to the appeal of sectional interests no longer assured of a ready flow of working-class recruits. The churches may have turned their backs on traditional recreations, but in the Sunday schools of all denominations they were active in promoting counter-attractions. In Bolton in the 1820s, for example, the Sunday schools had instituted regular tea parties to keep their pupils from defecting on race meeting days. In the early 1840s they began to combine with the junior divisions of the town's Temperance association to dominate the popular holiday ritual of the Whit walks – street processions of witness complete with flags and decorations and marching bands (minus the spiced ale which had been served at Sunday school treats twenty years previously). *The Half-Holiday Hand-Book*, published in Manchester in 1846, was meant 'to assist conductors and superintendents of Sunday schools in selecting a locality for the periodical excursions of their pupils'. It was the Sunday school teachers in Bolton who took the lead in forming the anti-singing saloon association which campaigned against the Star; one teacher pointed out that the best counter to the concert room lay in expanding the schools' recreational programme.[29]

In the schools proper solid instruction predominated, though the policy-makers of education were aware of the didactic potential of recreation. Kay-Shuttleworth acknowledged the importance of the playground as 'a source of moral training', wherein children could be taught to maintain 'mutual good offices . . . and propriety of demeanour'. Playgrounds, however, remained scarce.[30] But in the 1840s the education secretary did promote one classroom subject with considerable recreational content. The Education Department gave warm encouragement to the new systems of class instruction in choral music – the Hullah and Tonic Sol-fa methods. Echoing Fletcher of Saltoun, Kay-Shuttleworth declared a people's songs 'an important means of forming an industrious, brave, loyal and religious working class'. 'They might', he ventured, 'inspire cheerful views of industry' and 'associate amusements . . . with duties'. A great many schools continued to pay no attention to musical instruction, but the new systems did make an extremely important contribution to popular music-making, particularly in the industrial cities of the north where they reinforced already strong musical traditions. The discipline of the adult choirs and the predominantly sacred content of their programmes continued to recommend themselves to those concerned with moral training in the mid-Victorian period.[31]

In the 1840s, however, the single most important agency of recreational improvement was the rising Temperance movement. Though most of its injunctions were prohibitive its founding fathers were not kill-joys. Joseph Livesey of Preston, for example, in testifying to the 'Drunken Committee' in 1834, had not objected to either music or dancing in beershops and pubs, provided there was some official regulation. Only later did Temperance become subsumed by the canon of restrictive respectability. Even then it maintained a constructive concern to defeat the pub by building up counter-attractions, in the tradition of James Silk Buckingham's 1834 proposals for parks and playgrounds, which had been meant 'to draw off by innocent and pleasurable recreation and instruction, all who can be weaned from habits of drinking'.[32]

The movement showed considerable energy and imagination in providing counter-attractions. Though hardly unique to the movement, the railway excursion became a common Temperance recreation in the 1840s – Thomas Cook, first Temperance reformer, later travel magnate, ran his first trip in 1841, to remove working-class children from the temptations of Leicester race week.[33] Temperance societies were as prominent as the Sunday schools in appropriating the popular Whit walks in the north, and just as keen in proselytising the young (the two institutions were, of course, frequently maintained under the same religious sponsorship). The enthusiasm of the Temperance youth fife and drum band in Bolton was such as to condemn it as a public nuisance in the eyes and ears of some residents. Temperance halls provided what was often the only facility for large popular assemblies before the great town halls were built: Bolton's Temperance Hall opened in 1840, its town hall in 1873. The movement developed its own friendly societies and produced a vast literature which was a recreation in itself. Though many Temperance meetings were dauntingly single-minded, the movement was, by the late 1840s, clearly providing an alternative world of recreation for the lower middle and working classes. Samuel Smiles made a note of its progress in 1846:

> Our temperance reformers have been slow to recognise the importance of these truths; but they are now beginning to act on them. They begin to feel that there is no other way to defeat drink but to outrival it with attractions of a higher kind – such as music, cheap railway excursions, cheap concerts, and cheap rural galas.

A few years later, William Howitt concluded: 'The Temperance Associations have approached nearer to the ideal of a popular festival than any other body yet. . . . They are finding out the art to be glad and social, merry and wise.'[34]

The appeal of Temperance recreations was, however, greatly restricted by the strong prejudice against the movement among the working classes. In a beer culture, workingmen regarded Temperance itself as a dangerously unhealthy practice (a point much emphasised in the counter-propaganda of the publican), and the missionary zeal of the reformers circumscribed enjoyment of the recreations. The call for forbearance was too often translated into unpopular campaigns to close the pubs, which brought down such recriminations from the working class as the Bolton and Hyde Park riots in the mid-1850s. On occasions, Temperance philanthropy was thrown back in the face of its promoters. In 1844, Thomas Trevaskis, the 'Temperance Father of the West', offered the people of Padstow in Cornwall a fat bullock to roast for seven years, to replace the usual revelry of the annual festival of the Padstow Hobby Horse – when he drove the first bullock into town, both he and his offering were driven out by a hail of stones. Temperance reformers were attacked by working-class critics for attributing solely to intemperance the evils which came from the general squalor and meanness of the urban environment – evils which could only be remedied by more comprehensive reforms than restrictions on the availability of drink. The feeling that the Temperance movement was a fundamental insult to the capabilities of his class stung Francis Place into a wholesale attack upon Buckingham's proposals, even though they recommended a general improvement of amenities.[35]

Working-class movements of the period spawned their own schemes of rational recreation, where Temperance was adopted as one of the necessary disciplines for realising a broader programme of political and social progress. As Chartism diversified in the 1840s, its local cells offered a wide range of activities which nourished recreation as well as the class cause. William Lovett in his autobiography recalled with distaste the crude amusements of his youth, and in their antipathy to drink and boorishness the ground rules that he laid down for his People's Halls echoed the prescriptions of other similar workers' institutions of the period: 'Let us blend, as far as our means will enable us, study with recreation, and share in any rational amusement (unassociated with the means of intoxication) calculated to soothe our anxieties and alleviate our toils.' Lovett was an early agitator for the Sunday opening of art galleries and museums, the epitome of 'study with recreation'. This was all part of his concern to promote a comprehensively rational life-style for his class. Thus he also emphasised the value of correct diet and proper exercise and encouraged greater attention to personal manners, rejecting in the process the rhetoric of Feargus O'Connor, for whom roughness of speech and bearing was a defiant badge of class. Wrote Lovett: 'Unshorn chins, unwashed faces, and dirty habits will in nowise prepare you for political and social equality with the decent portion of your brethren.'

Lovett displayed something of that puritan streak which appeared in other working-class leaders. Thomas Cooper, for example, another prominent Chartist, extended his strictures on loose entertainment to include all dancing and theatregoing. But, as Lovett's rebuttal of O'Connor indicates, respectability was not an end in itself, but a means to class advancement on a broad front (although the People's Halls were short-lived institutions, Lovett's tactics did pay off, for it was his representations on the part of the working class which did much to secure the favourable report on public libraries).[36] The Owenite movement with its Halls of Science also provided pockets of working-class activists with a meeting place and a regular programme of activities well leavened with recreation. Determinedly teetotal, and earnest and proselytising in tone, the Owenites nevertheless give the lie to any impression that the claims of reason must necessarily extinguish the joy and vigour of the play instinct; their love of music and, more particularly, their love of dancing contributed such an exuberance to their fiercely secular festivals that their clerical enemies were moved to accuse them of veritable orgies of rational recreation.[37] Other reform ventures appear to have achieved a similarly convivial mix of education and entertainment. Christopher Thomson was a lively character who started an Artisans' Improvement Society in Suffolk and revitalised the village feast. One day of the week's celebrations was devoted to 'intellectual training', to balance what he termed the 'beer and pudding business'.[38] But if improvement was not always the dour undertaking it often sounds (a point it is well for us to remember), it is clear enough that a heavy emphasis on discipline and propriety was a necessary policy for those workingmen who sought to make gains for their class within the system.

Only by demonstrating their commitment to the serious duties of recreation could the working class prove their fitness for the shortening of the working day, agitation for which drew increased attention to the question of popular recreation in the mid- and late 1840s. When the chief architect of the Ten Hours Bill, Lord Shaftesbury, was honoured by a public address in Bolton in 1850, he took the occasion to warn the working-class audience of the great responsibility they faced now that the bill had passed into law; he implored them to turn to good account the extra free time they had acquired – to ensure that they did not abuse their additional leisure by 'senseless and disgusting recreations'. He urged them to see the bill as a starting point in 'their great career of moral and social improvement'.[39]

In this, as in many other matters, the Bolton workingman, like his fellows elsewhere, did not want for good advice; but he still lacked adequate amenities. The town had been one of the earliest to take advantage of municipal incorporation and had received its charter in 1838, but this had done little to stimulate recreational improvement. One impediment had been the political and sectarian bitterness of the 1840s, which divided public life in Bolton as in many other towns. The Tories assailed the Liberals as 'political economists' whose retrenchments threatened popular amusements in general and the Cross Keys Fair in particular. The Liberals retorted by attacking the Tories for

celebrating their first election victory by calling a holiday and squander-
ing public funds on an inaugural procession to the parish church, an
innovation which gave added offence in its religious particularism.
Bolton's glee club was destroyed by quarrelling over the Corn Laws and
a project for public baths was delayed by party squabbling. The town's
public library, opened in 1852, was almost the only municipal improvement to recreation. There were enlightened employers like the
Ashworth brothers, but the *Chronicle* reported that 'the majority of
employers concern themselves only to see that their operatives do their
allotted work, and for nought beside.' The neglect was still extensive, as
the paper made clear in another lament in the mid-1850s: 'Where is
there a town which either in itself, its environment, or its public institutions, offers such scanty means of either physical or mental recreation
to the workingman?'[40]

IV

The wider evidence suggests that Bolton was far from being as exceptional as the local editor believed, for the overall gains in recreational
improvement in the 1830s and 1840s were slender. In the first place, the
number of schemes for rational recreation, whatever their provenance,
were relatively few in number. As we have seen, various factors help
explain this basic paucity: governmental lack of interest, reinforced by
the arguments of *laissez-faire*; the financial tightness of the new municipal authorities; the presence of other, infinitely more threatening problems, which tended to absorb both public and private reform energies.
Education was the great social panacea – recreation, where its importance was recognised, was still regarded mostly as an accessory, and the
philanthropy which was expected to assist in its improvement may have
been curtailed by the uneven performance of the economy.

Schemes that were introduced were often disappointing to promoters
and participants – why was this so? One common feature which undoubtedly affected working-class attendance was the insistence upon
certain prerequisites of conduct and appearance. At Flockton, admission
to the company clubroom and playgrounds was dependent upon 'a
respectable demeanour' and, among the children, evidence that they had
signed a Temperance pledge. At a Liverpool mill, an annual summer
fête was open to those employees 'whose general conduct entitles them to
a ticket, upon their being able to give satisfactory proof of being in the
habit of attending some place of instruction or of public worship on a
Sunday'. Samuel Greg considered that only about a half of his workforce

were eligible for more than one invitation per year to his parties; these were 'the superior ones – the aristocracy of the place'. Admission to a free exhibition in Bury's new Town Hall was denied to those wearing clogs. *The Times* provides another tell-tale example of this kind of discrimination in reporting on the passage of a private bill of Ewart's which threw open Regent's Park to the public in 1841. Here, claimed the paper, was an encouraging move in 'the redemption of the working class through recreation'; after all, it continued, why should the lower orders not enjoy 'the liberty of taking a walk in the more plebeian portions of the park, provided they have a decent coat on'. Provided they had decent coats on, provided they were regular attenders at Sunday school, provided they signed a Temperance pledge – all these conditions reduced the eligibility of workpeople. There were, moreover, some friends of improvement who found the working classes manifestly too unscrubbed to make a respectable public début. To Bishop Blomfield, speaking in the Lords, the way to social salvation lay through the bath-house: 'it must be obvious that before the needful recreation of the people can be attained, before museums and public places could be made available, habits of cleanliness must be diffused throughout the whole community.' Cleanliness came before godliness, but a broad hint of both was needed to gain entrance to the park or playground.[41]

More central to an explanation of working-class disenchantment is class hostility. Tremenheere discerned this in the collapse of a lending library scheme in the north-east, which he attributed to 'the spirit of jealous suspicion with which everything set on foot by the masters is regarded'. Sporadic benevolences could obviously not dispel overnight the working-class resentment of the assault on popular amusements which more frequently marked the interest of the middle class in such matters. Reconciliation may have been difficult where improvement was too crudely designed as an instrument of work discipline. *The Times* found this motive distressingly common:

> Popular gatherings and merrymakings seem, really, in this utilitarian generation, to be tolerated only as stimulants for provoking people to 'industry'. . . . It is entirely reprehensible to celebrate with misplaced festivities what is in reality the greatest disgrace of all – viz, the necessity of securing the good conduct of the poor by artificial and secondary contrivances.

It seems too that the employers' benevolences could carry a sting in the tail, if we take account of the experience of one workingman, who here recalls his unease at the spectacle of the boss ingratiating himself with the men at the printers' traditional autumn feast:[42]

> Somehow it generally happens that this brief moment of relaxation is immediately followed by a tightening of the reins of government and a rather rough assertion of authority. As if the employer were fearful that his previous sentiments of universal brotherhood with which the hearts of employers expand convulsively and regularly once a year should be mistaken for anything more than they are meant for – mere flowers of rhetoric – next day comes some Draconic enforcement of often obsolete laws. At the heels of the weigh-goose, too, there frequently comes 'the bullet' as it is termed, or the sudden discharge, which sends a third or a half of the hands adrift after a fortnight's notice.

Working-class disillusion in Bolton was fed by the shabby spectacle of the Peel Park scheme, whose erratic progress was sabotaged by sectional priorities among the local middle class.[43] Although the machinery and resources of the municipal government were sufficient to provide for such a park in 1850, public opinion decided that such an undertaking had to involve a positive act of will on the part of the whole town, in deference both to the memory of Sir Robert and to the virtues of self-help. A committee was struck to raise a public subscription and make an appeal to the working classes, who as the main prospective beneficiaries were expected to give the lead; once their interest in the scheme had been realised in hard cash, the middle classes, so it was argued, would come forward with a subvention. Workshop collections over the winter of 1850–1 mounted steadily, and the Treasury weighed in with a grant from the government. In the meantime the park committee's voice grew fainter, and workingmen's letters to the *Chronicle* asked if the committee had disappeared. It had certainly gone to ground, and surfaced only briefly in the spring of 1852 to announce the shelving of the park scheme in view of the inordinate expense of land. In the following recriminations the Radical manufacturer Thomasson accused the 'Tory' committee of bad faith; back came the retort that Thomasson was one of several employers who had refused to allow collections among their workpeople, for fear of the party advantage their opponents might derive from the successful promotion of the scheme.

Thomasson's alleged boycott was, however, less offensive to the popular mind than that of the clergy and Sunday school teachers. The defenders of the Star against the anti-singing saloon association raised the charge that the churches had sunk Peel Park (and other schemes) by reserving their funds for improvements of their own establishments rather than for projects of general public benefit – this allegation remained a staple of popular debate in Bolton for nearly twenty years.[44] Such charges undoubtedly killed working-class support for any later subscription scheme; when there was talk of a Public Institution in 1860, one workingman wrote to the *Chronicle* explaining that he and his father were both deaf to such appeals, having each lost half-sovereigns on a previous project.[45]

Compounding such antipathy was the distinct unease which character-ised the social exchanges between the classes on occasions when rec-reation was taken in common. As we have seen, the traditional social bridges which had been built by the church, the aristocracy and the gentry had either fallen into disuse or were maintained for the occasional rites of an obsolescent sub-culture; the middle-class employer or pro-fessional man had no habit of easy association with his workpeople, certainly nothing of the studied yet engaging social style of the eight-eenth-century country grandee or squire that E. P. Thompson has recently anatomised. 'The great practical education of an Englishman', so a Commons committee still felt it reasonable to maintain at the end of this period, 'is derived from the incessant intercourse between master and man in trade', but the social experience of the workplace was already becoming too discrete and limited to generate much common sociability in the more loosely structured milieu of leisure. A fundamental short-coming among reformers was that they had little real knowledge of the actual substance of working-class leisure and recreation; in an age of extensive social enquiry, the workingman was more studied, more understood and more respected in the setting of his work than of his play. At the end of the working day master and men parted, and from this fact a Sheffield MP felt obliged to inform a select committee on public walks: 'I am scarcely a competent witness to their [the working-men's] social habits.' William Sargant, a Birmingham manufacturer, recorded how he had deceived himself with the facile assumption that the steady habits he saw in his own workshop were consistently repro-duced in life outside work:[46]

Most of us know very little about what goes on among workmen in the evening. We see them in their places during the day, we find them always ready to labour when they are called upon, and we set them down as men of temperate habits; inferring from their regularity that they are not guilty of excesses in their leisure hours. It is sometimes startling to find that we are entirely mistaken.

Plebeian recreation was, therefore, an alien world, and the middle-class interloper was least unhappy in it when decorating a platform or standing at a lectern. The first stance served to emphasise social distance, the second made plain the didactic intentions of rational recreation – a further obstacle to its success.

Whatever its accessories, rational recreation was basically and relentlessly didactic. As Heywood had revealed, the entertainments at the Lyceums were devised to sugar the pill of instruction. Once the revellers were pinned to their seats by a great weight of tea and buns, they became a captive audience for lectures on political economy, or homilies on the virtues of a Christian home life. Yet it is important to realise that Heywood was a venturesome man in his day, for he was willing to allow that popular recreation could legitimately embrace pleasure, the pursuit of which was vilified in his own culture as the road to vicious sensual gratification – the mark of an unregenerate aristocracy and a recalcitrant working class. He was also (against the wishes of his fellow directors) prepared to serve beer ('the merry brown bowl') at the mechanics' parties. He was, in fact, prepared to meet working-class culture half-way. That this was exceptional may be judged by comparing Heywood's tolerance with the forbidding severity of correspondents to the *Bolton Chronicle* on this question. 'Pro Bono Publico', for example, advocated no amusements but such as would impart a high-toned morality and pure devotional principles. A letter from a tradesman on the Peel Park proposal went thus:[47]

> The proper park for a Sunday afternoon is a tastefully laid out modern cemetery, where a conspicuous tablet, to the memory of Sir Robert Peel, or any other great and good man would preach a sermon upon the reward of virtue in the future.

It may be objected that letters to the editor notoriously represent a sour sample of humanity but there is other confirmation of the discouraging burden that improving recreation was expected to carry. Henry Mayhew recommended 'wholesome amusements' to rescue the costermongers from 'the moral mire in which they are wallowing' but added:[48]

> The misfortune, however, is that, when we seek to elevate the character of the people, we give them such mere dry abstract truths and dogmas to digest, that the uneducated mind turns away with abhorrence . . . we strive to make true knowledge and true beauty as forbidding as possible to the uneducated and the unrefined that they fly to their penny gaffs, their two-penny hops, their beer shops and their

gambling grounds for pleasures which we deny them, and which we, in our arrogance, believe it is possible for them to do without.

By the early 1850s, when Mayhew was writing, there could be no doubt that big changes had taken place in popular recreation. The study of a society at play was held to be an especially revealing test of its moral character, and several commentators were comforted by England's record of improvement. But improvement was essentially a middle-class concept and applauding its progress was primarily an exercise in bourgeois self-congratulation. Rational recreation could claim its successes, but it had encountered a number of difficulties which would not admit of easy solution in a class society. Men in the field close to working-class life realised how formidable was the task of remaking a whole culture. As Tremenheere pointed out: 'To train a rising society in the right way, is a process of comparatively little difficulty, but to change a great uneducated mass requires the well directed effort of many years.'[49]

3

The new leisure world of the mid-Victorians: the expansion of middle-class recreation, its practice and problems

In the years around the mid-century the Victorians entered a new leisure world. The Ten Hours Act of 1847 and the Great Exhibition at the Crystal Palace in 1851 were both in their various ways the concrete and symbolic pivots of this change whereby leisure in its modern form became progressively more plentiful, more visible, more sought after and more controversial. Something of the impact of this phenomenon (and the tensions it generated) is well caught in a leading article in *The Times*, 20 June 1876, which remarked tetchily on the importunate demands of 'Modern Amusements':

> The space we ourselves are from time to time compelled to surrender to this class of subject is in itself not the least proof of the importance they have attained . . . a mingled mass of perfectly legitimate pleasures ever thrusting themselves forward in a variety of shapes, some known, some unknown, to our more easily contented ancestors, and all together making continually increasing demands upon our time, upon our money, and not least, upon our strength and powers of endurance.

As we shall see, the untutored workers whom Tremenheere had contemplated with such unease on the eve of this new era, were to participate in this 'mingled mass of pleasures', but it is a point of considerable importance that it was the middle classes who were the most substantial beneficiaries of the new bounty. Like their inferiors they were entering into the process of developing a new culture within the unique matrix of a maturing urban industrial society, and from the mid-century on leisure and its activities became a significant area of social innovation and fulfilment for the Victorian bourgeoisie. The increasingly prominent role of recreation in middle-class life, its effects upon the bourgeois identity, the debate which such changes generated – all these features of the new leisure world held important implications for campaigns to improve the recreations of the working classes.[1]

I

Leisure and its enjoyments were hardly a mid-Victorian invention, but contemporaries were frequently moved to draw a contrast between the more abundant leisure of their own day and the meagre commons of previous decades. The middle classes of the older provincial centres of England had enjoyed a cultural life of considerable vigour and sociability in the late eighteenth century, and many of its institutions, if not perhaps its original *élan*, had survived into the early Victorian period. In the new towns too, middle-class life had not been all jejeune: Bamford was as impressed by the literary and musical interests of the Lancashire middle classes in the 1840s as he was by those of the workers; a Bolton lawyer who took articles in the 1830s recalled that hard work had taken its reward in leisure hours enlivened by a constant round of amateur dramatics, discussion clubs, much dancing, singing and athletic exercise, together with the relaxations of fireside and garden. Such a life-style could not have been unique to Bolton's John Taylor, but the more general recollection of middle and late Victorians was of an immediate past which was grey and joyless. 'We must remember', wrote the novelist Walter Besant, 'how very little play went on even among the comfortable and opulent classes in those days . . . dullness and a serious view of life seemed inseparable.' It has been well said that the Victorian bourgeoisie had had their own 'bleak age' to endure.[2]

Relief came with greater economic security and the time, services and commodities that it could buy. Though the business world was still visited by periodic crises after 1850, fluctuations became less severe and the remarkable expansion of the economy in the third quarter of the century did much to cushion middle-class incomes against irreparable reverses; even when growth and prosperity seemed to suffer a more general contraction from the mid-1870s on, the finances of a substantial element in the Victorian bourgeoisie proved solid enough to resist serious curtailment of expenditure and consumption. Such good fortune was being actively enjoyed by the 1850s. Men who had weathered the various exigencies of previous decades could afford to rest awhile on a comfortable plateau of prosperity, accompanied by wives whose domestic duties were taken care of by a growing army of servants. Constant attention to business was no longer necessary for the successful, and a mellowing process suffused their lives. We may take the Ashworth brothers of Bolton as an example. In the 1840s they had struggled through a period of uncertain profits; in the 1850s they felt secure enough to delegate the running of their mill to subordinates and allow themselves a series of travelling holidays.[3] Relaxation also became easier with the easing of political pressures – the Ashworths had imperilled their business by their preoccupation with the Anti-Corn Law League and the *Saturday Review* interpreted the new taste for social pleasures as a reaction from the intellectual and political crises of the Great Reform Bill, the Tractarian movement and the fight for free trade.[4]

The pursuit of leisure was more widely remarked because it was becoming more widely spread; it was not only master manufacturers who enjoyed the new bounty, but the lesser lights in a middle class which was growing more numerous as well as more prosperous. Henry Mayhew sought to represent a new middle-class type in his account of Cockayne, a very minor captain of industry, but one whose thirty-five years in command of a soap factory in Clapham had earned him a trip to Paris. This was in the 1860s, by which time the process of bourgeois enleisurement was plain to all. Its reach continued to widen throughout the period and T. H. S. Escott gave this account of its operation in the 1880s:[5]

> A social movement quite as remarkable as that which has been going forward among the better portion of the English middle class, has been taking place, and is now steadily progressing on a lower social stratum. This class would once have been called the small shopkeeper class, and its present condition is almost the growth of yesterday. . . . Only the commercial prosperity of England could have generated the new order from which the chief patrons of theatres and outdoor amusements are drawn.

There were always new recruits for the single-minded pursuit of money, but the second or later generations of successful business families were less disposed to answer its imperatives. The younger Gurneys of Norwich were 'rather more inclined to stand before the fire with their hands in the fronts of very good riding breeches' than to attend daily at the bank. The *Saturday Review* remarked in the 1860s how rapidly the 'habit of enjoyment' had spread among the young. 'It is', the journal maintained, 'an axiom with many young people that they have a right to be always amused, or to be always going to be amused.' Certainly the middle-class young (of whom more were surviving into early adulthood) enjoyed more free time than their elders had done, for the increasing emphasis upon public school and, to a lesser extent, university education as indispensable requirements for middle-class gentility meant a prolonged freedom from the immediate pressures of earning a living. Eventually put to work in the family firm the son and heir often continued to exploit the generosity of the paterfamilias – 'stretching his legs under the governor's mahogany' – and apply himself more to play than business. This much is clear from a lively debate on the 'young man of the day' in the correspondence columns of the *Daily Telegraph* in the late 1860s.[6]

The 'habit of enjoyment' was diffused and encouraged through major improvements in communications. By the early 1850s the major lines in the British rail system were completed or under construction. Rail travel stimulated a general public curiosity and helped break down regional insularities of mind and practice. 'The typical John Bull', said the *Cornhill Magazine*, 'is fast becoming a legendary personage; his vegetative life and stationary habits and local prejudices are all disappearing beneath the stimulating influence of the railway, the telegraph and the great cities.' Of parallel importance was the growth of the cheap press and the increase in newspaper advertising: the tax on advertising was abolished in 1853, the newspaper duty of 4d a copy went in 1855 and six years later the duty on paper was removed. Escott recorded the effects:[7]

The cheap press, with its ubiquitous correspondents and historians of all contemporary ranks and occurrences in the body politic, has transformed the severely domesticated Briton of both sexes, of all ages, who belonged to a bygone generation, into an eager, actively enquiring, socially omniscient citizen of the world, ever on the outlook for new excitements, habitually demanding social pleasure in fresh forms.

II

What were the particular forms that social pleasure took? Certainly a great deal of it took place within the ambit of the home and family. The proliferation of newspapers was part of a general flood of literature which kept the middle-class public well supplied with its periodicals and three-decker novels, either for solitary reading (perhaps during the new 'enforced' leisure of the railway journey) or to be read aloud to the family group. Cheap sheet music was also published in increasing abundance from the 1840s; mechanical refinement and improved production methods provided suburban villas with moderately priced pianos upon which the ladies of the house could display their talents – music was a fashionable, indeed necessary, accomplishment for girls. There were many other new diversions for the drawing room besides reading and music. The *Saturday Review* found 'the cleverness and the laziness of the age aptly typified . . . by its ingenious contrivances for getting rid of an evening'. Within the home these contrivances might consist of private theatricals, quizzes and games newly devised for the middle-class family market, or older pastimes such as draughts and billiards – the latter now restored to respectability within the new canon of 'domestic athletics'.[8] Cheap service and gains in space and comfort in the middle-class home allowed of the increasing vogue for entertaining guests, particularly at the dinner party, whose growing extravagance was a prime indicator of rising consumption levels among a class increasingly divorcing itself from its heredity of thrift and frugality. Gardens were also part of the improved amenities of domestic life; here the family and its guests could play a set of lawn tennis (an invention of the 1870s) or take a game of croquet – as E. L. Woodward pointed out, *Alice in Wonderland* affords a convincing demonstration that every middle-class child could be expected to know the rules.[9]

The mid-Victorian middle classes were not, however, permanently home-bound in their recreations, though they did in general take their public pleasures *en famille*. The railway gave them in particular a new mobility in leisure, and the regular spate of advice and reports in the press in the summer months testified to the growing habit and ritual of the annual holiday. Old-fashioned watering places were neglected for the attractions of new seaside holidays resorts. Travel horizons broadened, and by the 1860s Thomas Cook was running excursions, not only to the Continent but to the USA and the Holy Land. 'The quietest sort of people', so the *Saturday Review* observed, 'are uncomfortable unless they, at least once a year, tie themselves together in batches and go prowling over the tops of unexplored Alps.'[10] Recreation out of doors was generally brisker than the gentilities of domestic leisure, as a London lawyer and socialite recorded in his diary in 1861:[11]

> Muscular Christianity, the Volunteer movement, and alpine climbing are in the ascendant. The affected Dandy of past years is unknown. If he exists, he is despised. The standard or average English gentleman of the present day must at least show vigour of body, if he cannot display vigour of mind.

Sport or, more specifically, organised games gave expression to this predilection for the physical. The newly codified games spread from the reformed public schools to the universities, and thence into adult life; national bodies for the supervision and co-ordination of the major new sports were formed in the 1860s and 1870s under middle-class auspices. The Volunteer force, established in 1859 in the face of threatening noises from the French, also contributed to this particular impetus and direction in middle-class recreation; the local corps promoted the cause of physical fitness and the sports meetings which enlivened the drills often became the basis for the formation of permanent athletics clubs. In addition the fund-raising activities of bazaars and fêtes gave an outlet for the leisure energies and talents of the womenfolk. Though middle-class involvement declined considerably after only a few years, the movement was an important leisure stimulus – one contemporary credited the Volunteers with 'fostering a love of outdoor life that has been utterly wanting among the great middle-classes for a century'. Certainly the strainings of amateur athletes and part-time soldiers provided occasions for new leisure festivals for middle-class families: the Oxford and Cambridge athletics meet, the Eton and Harrow cricket match, the Volunteers' annual reviews, rifle meets and sports tournaments at Brighton, Wimbledon and in the counties – all were significant additions to the social calendar.[12]

Public amusements of a less strenuous kind were also plentiful; so much so that Stephen Fiske, an American who worked in London in the 1860s, found the English at play anything but the traditional dullards that other visitors had judged them (Froissart's tag 'they take their pleasures sadly after their fashion' was another cliché of commentaries on national manners). Wrote Fiske:

> Taking the average Englishman and the average Frenchman, the former goes oftener to the theatres, has more holidays, laughs more, and spends more evenings where something besides a drink and smoke are to be had for his money, than the latter; and yet the average Frenchman is mistakenly held up to us as a devotee of amusement.

These conclusions were based upon Fiske's experience as a theatre manager in a capital city which was sucking up the theatrical talent of the provinces and thriving on a tourist traffic built upon the excursion boom of 1851. Providing one was not in search of diversion on a Sunday – Taine found himself ready for suicide after his first sabbath in London – there was no gainsaying the longstanding vitality of the metropolis as an entertainment centre.[13] But what of the provinces?

There are some forbidding memorials to the bleak tedium of provincial towns, most notably in Dickens's descriptions of Coketown and

Dullborough. In his archetype industrial town, 'You saw nothing . . .
but what was severely workful'; in his archetype small town, 'the preva-
lence . . . of putting the natural demand for amusement out of sight'
strikes a sour but resonant note. An Australian visiting England in the
mid-1860s offered further confirmation of the discrepancy between the
capital and the country at large. Only in London, he concluded, could
one find company in 'idleness and pleasure seeking'; he found life in all
the great manufacturing towns 'as busy and rather more anxious than it
is in Australia or the United States'; in the small provincial towns he
found 'too much exclusiveness for an Australian to penetrate into society
when on a short visit'.[14] It is obvious that there had long been a gap
between the compendious attractions of the capital and, say, the thinner
pickings available to the Mancunian; but none the less, with all deference to Dickens (who was often concerned over this question), the
natural demand for amusement was being met in the provinces, if only
yet in modest proportions. The sophisticated Londoner on his reluctant
prowl out of town could overlook much that served the function of entertainment or recreation, hidden as it might be, for example, behind the
deterring items on a lecture list.[15] Besides, provincials might save their
time and money for pleasures elsewhere: in its growth from a small
country town to a London suburb, Croydon lost its taste for its local
celebrations as its inhabitants sought their diversions in the West End by
cheap rail excursions.[16] Thus the Londoner travelling out to the provinces might miss his county cousins travelling in.

Mid-Victorian Bolton certainly provides clear evidence that the
middle classes in one large manufacturing town knew a real expansion of
leisure and recreation. Bolton's growing population enjoyed general
prosperity in these years – the relative diversification of her industries
and her specialisation in better quality textiles enabled her to survive the
cotton famine of the early 1860s better than most Lancashire towns –
and the middle classes showed a substantial increase in numbers and
wealth. The *Chronicle* in the late 1850s considered the local bourgeoisie
'scanty' compared with other large towns, but correspondents pointed to
the recent wave of professional and commercial men now assuming
middle-class status in Bolton, plus a disturbing new breed of 'fast' young
men. The *Chronicle* was pleased to see the leisure energies of these
novitiates absorbed by the new passion for outdoor sports and the pull of
the Volunteer movement, thus dispelling its fears that increasing affec-
tation of manners must lead to effeminacy. But refinement was as
fashionable as athleticism and found its expression in exclusive subscription concerts at the Baths Assembly Rooms and 'select and gorgeous'

dinner parties in private houses. Pub society had ceased to be respectable. John Taylor took the teetotal pledge and pursued his love of debate in a private club which met at members' houses – the pledge was hardly fashionable but the retreat to the drawing room was. Middle-class homes grew more palatial and one local builder at least made his fortune providing new residences for wealthy Boltonians at Southport on the Lancashire coast. Southport was the fashionable resort town for the north-west, but the biographies of Bolton worthies show how much further their excursions ranged, from Scotland to the Continent.[17]

III

Yet amid this vitality one soon detects a persistent sense of dissatisfaction and unease on the part of both observers and participants in this new leisure world. Analysing the palsied progress of a middle-class dinner party, Trollope concluded that the pursuit of leisure in England was as laborious, affected and dull as foreign observers persistently made it out to be, and it was the spectacle of bourgeois 'enjoyments' that moved Matthew Arnold to ask: 'Can any life be imagined more hideous, more dismal, more unenviable?'[18] By taking account of the problems of leisure as well as its gratifications we can more readily understand the fundamental novelty of its presence in Victorian life.

The problem of leisure for the Victorian middle-classes was a many-sided one. In the first place they were discovering that recreation in the railway age meant planning and preparation; time-tables meant an increasing preoccupation with time-budgeting and the co-ordination of people and services. In a moment of disenchantment with modern 'holy-days' *The Times* complained that the search for enjoyment was often fatuous: 'It is work, and it is tiring work . . . it involves a perpetual attention to time, and all the anxieties and irritations of that responsibility.' Even when the respite of true leisure was reached, its satisfactions were impaired by that compulsive regard for the precise and purposive ordering of time that nagged the creatures of an industrial society. 'There is', remarked the *Saturday Review*, 'a sort of mechanical style in our joys.'[19]

A further cluster of difficulties lay in the very nature of bourgeois culture itself. As a class whose immediate history celebrated the virtues of unremitting industry, the Victorian middle class had only an attenuated leisure tradition to draw upon, so that the new lifespace they had won for themselves was something of an embarrassment – 'We really do not know how to amuse ourselves', was the *Saturday Review*'s admission in an article on 'Pleasure Taking', 4 June 1870. The leisure of the aristocracy and the gentry – the aboriginal leisure class of history – was rooted in the husbandry of their landed estates and nourished by a high amateur tradition in the civilised arts; the leisure of the common people still echoed with the collective rituals of the folk community and the craft workshop, and envinced a ready taste for pleasure. Yet it was these associations which had made leisure such a suspect quantity in bourgeois ideology; in a work-oriented value system leisure represented the irresponsible preoccupations of a parasitic ruling class or the reckless carousing of an irrational working class. Though the bourgeoisie had none the less at times been enamoured of the aristocratic style, the clash of political and economic interests and the strictures of the evangelical revival had severely reduced its attractions during the early Victorian period. By the same process certain once universally honoured convivialities were also now disallowed, but the question of their replacement could no longer be ignored, as the *Saturday Review* explained in a piece on evening amusements, 4 January 1862:

> It is a very fine thing to have cured ourselves of the boosing [sic] habits of our ancestors; but there is no doubt that the moral conquest has left a formidable void in our social existence . . . the gentlemen used to be drunk, and are now sober; and the mistress of the house, who got rid of them in the drinking days, has to bear the burden of their reformation, and find amusements to beguile the weary hours of sobriety.

A wide range of modified or newly contrived recreations were pressed into service to fill the void, but it was difficult to infuse such ad hoc devices with much spontaneity, particularly since the exercise of choice was heavily constrained by that need for moral legitimation which characterised bourgeois leisure in these early years of new growth. As another commentator noted:

> A lingering asceticism of sentiment, a relic of the superstition which looked upon the body as the source of sin, still affects our modes of thought. . . . We do not proscribe amusement as previous generations have done, nor do we go heartily into them, as Paganism did and the Latin races do; but we indulge in them and apologise for them. We take some of our more pleasant and more needful recreations with a half suspicion that they are only half right.

A further discomfiture came from the apprehension that the freedoms of modern leisure might prove too great a test of the individual's capacity for responsible self-direction, in the absence of that mutual public vigilance that policed the life of the small community. The temptation to delinquency was thought to be most acute for the young, particularly among the army of rootless young office workers in the great urban centres. 'The immense size and total unlocalisation of life', wrote a correspondent to the *Daily Telegraph*, 'tends to make the career of a young man excessively individual . . . he loses the fear of censure that is the guiding idea of much life in smaller places.' Compared to the disciplined structure of the workplace and the home, leisure appeared to some a normative as well as a cultural void.[20]

As we shall see in the next chapter, there were other tensions which attended the middle-class pursuit of leisure, but enough has been said already to demonstrate its ambivalence in bourgeois life. Moral integrity and the code of respectability which defined its public face were essential constituents of middle-class identity and class consciousness. Resting on basically religious sanctions reinforced by the teachings of political economy, bourgeois morality had, in the first half of the century, provided its class with an effective platform from which to challenge the aristocracy and subordinate the lower orders. From the turn of the mid-century the new and extensive bonus of leisure time threatened to subvert the internal disciplines of the middle-class world by its invitation to indolence and prodigality. Unwilling or unable to deny the claims and attractions of leisure, yet anxious to maintain a sturdy and coherent code of values amid rapid innovation and social change, the Victorian middle classes sought a rationale which would relieve them of the need to apologise for their pleasures, yet still keep them within the bounds of moral fitness. 'Many people', observed the *Saturday Review*, 7 April 1877, 'are manifestly incapable of enjoying repose and light diversion except on the understanding that they have a right to do so.'

The question received considerable attention in the periodical press, particularly during the summer holiday season, when the correct disposal of such a conspicuous slab of free time called special attention to the ethics of leisure. A representative piece appeared in the *Cornhill Magazine* for September 1867, written by Peter W. Clayden. Entitled 'Off for the holidays: the rationale of recreation', it moved on from the usual breezy bon voyage to the summer holidaymaker, to a consideration of the nature, method and purpose of recreation, 'a subject only now beginning to be understood'. The author emphasised how modes of life had been transformed by Britain's industrial progress. In response to the demands of modern civilisation, Englishmen had developed 'magnificent nervous organisations' which gave them an expanded capacity for work. This enabled them to continue to exploit the opportunities of the nineteenth-century world, but the cost of the new regimen was high:

> Our great-grandfathers ambled along with an almost restful movement; we rush along at high pressure, with fearful wear and noise. Their work was almost play compared with ours. . . . A kind of necessity is upon us, even at home, much more in our spheres of duty or activity, and all continuous necessity is a strain.

Readers could therefore rest assured that holidays and recreation were necessary, as relief from this strain; they allowed 'the rebound of an elastic nature from the repression and constraint of civilised life'. The rebound was best absorbed in recreation which afforded a total change of pace, direction and environment, for 'work and play, like day and night, are opposites, and the widest unlikeness between them is the truest completeness of each.' According to this principle therefore, men were encouraged to seek recreations which provided the greatest contrast to their normal occupations, and the article sought to free holidaymakers of the oppressive fears of ridicule which too often confounded this stratagem:

> We are dreadfully afraid of making ourselves ridiculous before one another. Public opinion . . . persistently merges the man in his profession, keeps him perpetually on the pedestal of his status, and will on no account allow him to descend from it.

Such strictures could be safely ignored, according to Clayden's dispensations.

Thus did one writer try to relieve some of the misgivings which attended the modern pursuit of leisure; there were, however, some important qualifications to be made. Mere rest was not true recreation, neither was amusement: 'amusement merely occupies or diverts, while recreation, as the word itself indicates, renews and recreates.' Work and play were best dissociated in time, locus and content – 'renewal and recreation proceed on the principle of antithesis' – but their functions were complementary. In this way recreation was validated primarily as an adjunct to work and its ideal represented in terms of the vigour and purposiveness appropriate to work. Play, explained Clayden, was change of work as much as change from work. The sentiment became a commonplace under the imprimatur of Gladstone, who maintained that recreation was nought but change of employment, exemplifying the ideal in his retreat from the toils of office to the arduous pleasures of tree-felling on his estate at Hawarden.

For all his purposeful tone Clayden was alive to the potential of leisure for the intellectual and cultural enrichment of the individual, but many writers were only prepared to justify leisure in its utilitarian role. Writing in the *Nineteenth Century*, G. J. Romanes put the matter succinctly:

Recreation is, or ought to be, not a pastime entered upon for the sake of pleasure which it affords, but an act of duty undertaken for the sake of the subsequent power which it generates, and the subsequent profit which it ensures.

There were other tests of acceptability, as W. H. Miller outlined in his *Culture of Pleasure*. The proper recreation should, he advised, 'bring back body and mind fitted again for the business of life . . . and it should accomplish its objects with the least expense possible of time, strength and money.' Writing in the late 1860s, John Morley thought that considerations of time and cost operated as a more forceful limitation than religion:

Just as we have ceased to believe that pleasure is fatal to salvation people start up to persuade us that it is fatal to getting on in the world. The active worldling is as ready to call every kind of amusement by the evil names of frivolity and stupid self-indulgence as the converted saint used to be.

There was still a general suspicion of pleasure. 'As a legitimate object of deliberate pursuit', complained Morley, 'it is invariably disparaged.' Education, he maintained, taught that anything pleasant was wrong. Yet, significantly, Morley felt able to record that 'Even within the most contracted limits, the range of allowable recreations is being extended.'[21]

The churches were particularly sensitive to the expansion of leisure. An early note of concern was sounded at the Wesleyan Conference in 1855, which recorded 'with sincere regret, the existence in some quarters of a disposition to indulge in and encourage amusements which it cannot regard as harmless or allowable'.[22] By 1872, when the prominent Broad Churchman, Henry Haweis, gave his attention to the problem, it had become more alarming: 'Our streets are reeking with the abuse of pleasure; our society is rotten with it; our social fabric is crumbling beneath it; our best institutions are being shaken and paralysed by it.'[23] It must be noted that despite the apocalyptic tone Haweis was not condemning pleasure, but its abuse. 'Pleasure', he allowed, 'is a legitimate incident of life, but not a legitimate end', and he sought some middle ground between 'the lean ascetic and the bloated voluptuary'. While conceding the case for leisure in modern life, Haweis was above all concerned to impress upon his readers the need to subject its pleasures to the strictest tests of conscience. It was a weighty matter, of a piece with the great questions of biblical warranty and evolution. Here is Haweis writing on music and morals in a two-part article in the *Contemporary Review*, December 1870–January 1871:

> The enormous importance of the distinction between right and wrong has been so branded by fire and stained in blood upon the page of history, that everything in modern life sinks into comparative insignificance by the side of morality and religion. No art or science is allowed to pass the solemn sentinels of the nineteenth century without getting some answer to the momentous question – What in its own deportment is really right or really wrong?

Men looked to the churches for guidance. A Nonconformist minister noted how the young in particular sought answers to the moral problem of leisure: 'Where is the rule which settles where to conform and where to protest . . . this difficulty of adjustment meets us everywhere.'[24]

The question was a prickly one to judge from the trepidation with which clergymen embarked upon its public debate. In a sermon at Sheffield in 1860 the Reverend G. J. Chester maintained that 'The subject of amusement is of such importance and involves such tremendous interests that I might well shrink from bringing it before you.' This was obviously no imaginary fear, for another Sheffield Anglican minister, Samuel Earnshaw, came close to losing his living after delivering a sermon on the subject in the same year. Chester had moved gingerly, but Earnshaw had pressed a bold attack against the old evangelical proscriptions on games and sports, for which he could find no scriptural warranty. It was, he argued, in any case 'unnatural to resist the call of nature for exercise in honouring what were simply the commandments of mere men'. Earnshaw appealed for a more charitable attitude towards the theatre and other public amusements, endorsing the example of the Royal Family who, he said, 'openly do the very things which the arbiters of religious opinions and models of Christian practice have pronounced irreconcilable with a religious state of mind'. In all, Earnshaw was trying to reconcile the Church with what he obviously considered to be the tolerable peccadilloes of a modern society. 'Is anything,' he asked, 'permanently gained by increasing the burdens and restraints of a religious life?'[25]

Earnshaw was a minor, though significant, figure but the importance of this matter can be better appreciated when we consider the concern of the Birmingham minister, R. W. Dale, chairman of the Congregational Union, and one of the century's leading churchmen. Dale tackled the problem before a wide audience in an article on amusements in *Good Words*, a middle-class family magazine, in 1867. 'What amusements are lawful to persons who wish to live a religious life' was, he claimed, 'the question by which many good people are sorely perplexed'. Dale was anxious to redeem the old evangelical strictures from charges of casuistry, and to explain them in terms of common sense rather than scriptural sanction. He maintained that the proscribed amusements had been condemned because of 'the accessories with which they have been associated'. Thus, he explained, racing had been excoriated because of the gambling which was so much a part of it. At a less obvious level, bagatelle had been acceptable because the game demanded no expensive and therefore wasteful equipment, and was usually played within the family home. Billiards was condemned because the expensive equipment it required would usually only have been provided in a public house (Herbert Spencer, revealing his affection for billiards in his autobiography, remarked 'those who confess to playing billiards commonly make some kind of excuse'). Fishing was permissible because it was solitary and encouraged meditation and communion with nature. Shooting, interestingly enough, was suspect not because of any cruelty involved, but because it took place among groups, which usually led to the unseemly conviviality of the dinner party and heavy drinking. Dale was attempting to argue out a revised catalogue of permissible amusements, but in the last analysis he was not prepared to make many specific rehabilitations; he acknowledged that there were some honourable exceptions in a sea of otherwise perverse popular fiction, and condoned dancing provided it was not excessive or tainted by 'unsavoury social intercourse'. He remained opposed to the theatre. But he did emphasise that 'each generation must examine recreation anew', and urged a more charitable attitude towards the recreations of one's neighbours – 'That may be safe to them which is perilous to us.' Dale's church took some of his teaching to heart, for the problem of amusements was subjected to several re-examinations, the most notable being a Congregational symposium called in 1879. Here again there was evidence of an advance in tolerance, for none of the contributors favoured re-enacting the old discipline against amusements, though much of the hostility to dancing and the theatre remained. There was, too, a general feeling that amusements were best kept within the home.[26]

Thus the churches came to allow the legitimacy of leisure, but there were still many conditions they attached to its pursuit. 'Recreation', warned the Catholic *Dublin Review*, 'should be more than even negatively harmless, it should be positively healthy.' The Reverend Chester urged that, 'As when men work, they should work, according to Apostolic rule, with all their might, so when they play, they should play with all their might.' Pleasure-seekers were reminded that Christianity had a high sense of the value of time, and that duty to others should find a place in recreation:

> Thus the enchanting country walk may be rendered more enchanting still by the visit of mercy paid on the way to the cottage of the poor or sick; the trip to the seaside may be rendered doubly enjoyable by giving some invalid an excursion; and the ramble . . . can delight the memory by the useful book given away on its banks.

That the churches themselves should make direct provision for recreation was a point frequently raised in the 1870s and 1880s. A layman attending the Congregational symposium had urged that, 'it would be better to reclaim certain amusements than to abandon them to those who abuse them', and such remarks prompted the churches' considerable participation in recreation in the last quarter of the century. But it was not easy for churchmen to unbend on this matter and, as a Scottish minister observed in the early 1880s, 'The Church has still to set herself right with what is called "the world" in reference to her oversight of amusements and recreations, and her providing of such.'[27]

Entering into direct competition with the world of amusements marked a climax in the churches' mounting anxiety at the general erosion of their pastoral presence. Halting dispensations on the range of permissible amusements probably just added to this wastage for unless they controlled them the churches were thereby simply endorsing the counter-attractions to the religious life. William Thomson, Archbishop of York, in a sermon on sports and pastimes in 1874, spoke of his fear that the church was losing contact with culture at every level, and admitted that many Christians were failing to find relevant scriptural guidance on the proper conduct of their recreations. Perhaps many no longer felt obliged to look in the first place – it was in a sermon on leisure time that the Dean of Durham, while arguing that good works and self-improvement were the proper constituents of leisure, wryly noted 'the more common feeling that leisure is out of the pale of religion altogether, a sort of neutral ground which we may fairly call our own'.[28] Yet, though the churches were to lose their struggle for dominion over leisure, their caveats against unproductive or purposeless amusements reinforced a mid-Victorian rationale of recreation which bristled with the highest intentions.

Accordingly, the recreations which recommended themselves to respectable tastes were those with some manifest moral or improving content. Much that took place in the home was naturally so blessed, but the new family games on the market took care to combine 'innocent amusement with instruction' – a formula met with in Greenwood's Round Games (Questions For Our Sunday Tea Table, Bible Quartets, Scientific Quartets) which earned the endorsement of the *Bolton Chronicle*. The fusing of recreation with instruction had been exemplified in the Great Exhibition and the improving mixture was dispensed in penny packets in public lectures and readings across the country. Albert Smith drew huge crowds in the 1850s with his lectures on the ascent of Mont Blanc, illustrated with lantern slides and the equipment used on the expedition. The retelling of an heroic exploit, the information on a foreign country which was now within reach of the excursionist and the excitement of a night out proved an irresistible combination. Travel was generally regarded as wholesome: 'To have seen a mountain', averred the *Chronicle*, 'is a great step in a man's education.' There was thus a great deal of recreation that came within the pale by virtue of educational rather than spiritual content, though there was a felicitous combination of both in oratorios, whose considerable popularity in these years was attributed to 'the prevalent religious sentiment of the English middle classes'. Because of its non-representational character, music was generally thought to be the least corruptible of the arts; even so, we may recall that Haweis had warned of the need to refer it to moral touchstones.[29]

IV

The concern for moral legitimation remained a powerful determinant of middle-class choice in leisure, but it was not the only or necessarily the prime motivation, for recreations answered a variety of needs, and though the Victorian bourgeoisie plainly suffered under some vexing inhibitions in their pursuit of leisure they none the less proved capable of exploiting its dynamic properties. This is evident, for example, in their new enthusiasm for organised games, a set of recreations which met the tests of moral propriety while serving as an important medium for advancing middle-class social aspirations.

Charles Kingsley's exaltation of muscular Christianity provided the necessary moral gloss for organised games. As a country vicar in the 1840s Kingsley had championed physical health:

The body, the temple of the living God. . . . There has always seemed to me something impious in the neglect of personal health, strength and beauty, which the religious and sometimes clergymen of these days affect. I could not do half the little good I do do here if it were not for that strength and activity which some consider coàrse and degrading.

Thus he had done much to dispel the suspicions of the body as a source of sin, a staple of evangelical teaching which Clayden and others had identified as an impediment to physical enjoyment. Kingsley urged his young audiences 'to carry into them [games] the principles of honour and religion', declaring bodily health a matter of personal responsibility to God and duty to one's country. Neglect of what he came to call 'the science of health' would, he maintained, render Englishmen 'incapable, unhappy, like a Byzantine Greek, filled up with some sort of pap'. Herbert Spencer acknowledged Kingsley's leading role in registering the importance of bodily exercise, and himself used the language and imperatives of religion in emphasising that 'the preservation of health is a duty . . . all breaches of the laws of health are physical sins.'[30] Kingsley's novels gave currency to such ideals, and inspired a whole school of imitators who were, in the words of the *Saturday Review*, 'continually ready to build a model hero, very good and very strong . . . and free from faults and fat'. As *The Times* remarked drily of the spread of athleticism: 'When you can at the same time enjoy yourself and feel the consciousness that you are doing a moral action, it is difficult to refrain.'[31]

In games, the rhetoric of recreation and religion tended to become one. Charles Box, an historian of cricket, wrote 'sportsmen's homilies' to console athletes obliged to interrupt their games in observation of the sabbath. His *Musings for Athletes* consisted of biblical tales rendered in the language of the sports field, thus 'Jacob's Eleven versus The Stings of Defeat'. But in such stilted compounds it was the religious content which suffered, and the vocabulary of exhortations which emerged from the new athleticism furnished the sentiments of an increasingly secular morality. The ideal of muscular Christianity yielded to that of manliness. Manliness as a Victorian ideal derived in part from Coleridge, who conceived of it as that state of intellectual maturity which marked the passing of childhood. It also carried strong associations of physical courage and endurance in the sense of the old eighteenth-century virtue of 'bottom'. Kingsley in effect had combined the two usages and added a dressing of aggressive religiosity.[32] But it was Thomas Hughes rather than Kingsley who provided the most popular model of the manly hero in Tom Brown, the archetype public schoolboy.

In creating Tom, Hughes drew heavily on his own rural upbringing in Berkshire, and the boy represented qualities that the author much admired in the old squirearchy – accordingly Tom was jovial, gregarious and combative – but in his later writings Hughes was anxious to commend a manliness shorn of any suggestion of boorishness or animalism. Though the Rugby boys in the novel 'mixed it' with drovers at the fair and navvies from the LNWR (just as the Rector's son in *Vanity Fair* had slugged it out with the bargees at Oxford) Hughes remarked of such brawling that he had not himself shared 'this indiscriminate enthusiasm'. Thus he deplored the notion of manliness as mere brute force, and was much concerned to represent its essence as a moral action which could be found in the physically weakest of men. Hughes's own personal model in this regard was Christ, but he recognised the declining enthusiasm for this feature of his philosophy.[33]

Historically the aristocracy had a long claim to manliness, but in several instances their conduct was found wanting by the standards of the revised ideal. In 1854 a court-martial at Windsor broadcast an example of dangerous horseplay in the Guards officers' mess. Among the many censures on such behaviour, the *Era* for 10 September declared:

> In that great middle class who form the most important element of English society the feeling is one of unmitigated and contemptuous abhorrence of the coarse habits and disgusting language which prevail where we looked for elevated and chivalric notions of honour and the refined manners of a gentleman. . . . We shall nowhere in manufactories or workshops find such unmanly brutality.

In 1871 there was an outcry against the pigeon-shooting at the fashionable Hurlingham Club. It was, said *The Times*, 'practised by aristocratic amateurs out of mere wantonness and love of killing. . . . It betokens and encourages the restless levity and insatiable pleasure-seeking of our younger nobility.' Haweis offered this comment: 'With some illustrious exceptions there is not enough real education among our upper classes, or we should not find them gawping over sports that the middle class have long abandoned as brutal and undignified.' Vicious antics in the mess and the slaughter of captive birds were unmanly offences against the spirit of the new laws of organised games, and all the more offensive when practised by the aristocracy.[34]

The hostility is, however, misleading. There was a continuing radical animus against the aristocracy, exemplified in the campaign against the mismanagement of the Crimean War but, in general, hostility towards the old class enemy was diminishing. The guardians of the new morality of recreation had no wish to ostracise their betters, but sought rather to use the new code as a discreet vehicle for advancing their own class by redefining the qualifications of a gentleman more in terms of conduct than heredity. 'Manliness without coarseness, polish without complacency, nobility without caste' – under Hughes's definition, any public schoolboy might make himself a gentleman, though he owed his education to his father's trade in 'unmentionables'. And it was in the public schools, not in the officers' mess, Tattersall's or the Hurlingham that the new model gentlemen were being made, for the schools were at once dynamos of the new athleticism and hothouses for the precocious seedlings of a newly aspirant gentility. Contemplating the games cult, the *Saturday Review* contended:

> Very many parents consider that the first requisite to success in life is the habit of associating freely with millionaires and their sons. They would, if possible, get teaching too; but the first demand is that their boys should go to the same schools with the sons of men of wealth and rank . . . a boy is sent to keep company with lords.

At the local grammar school in Derby in the 1870s, so J. A. Hobson recalled, 'Sport was encouraged as a means of bringing us into the company of more reputable public schools on the basis of equality.'[35]

The attractions of status were an obvious element in the appeal of lawn tennis, an innovation of the mid-1870s. The game was promoted without any moral apologia, and its principal recommendation seems to have lain in the fact that it could equip the suburban villa with some of the resources of the country house, thus reconciling flights of social fancy with the measurements of the back garden. Major Wingfield, the game's inventor, advertised a list of noble clients who had bought the necessary kit, together with a letter of endorsement from a baronet; the *Sporting Gazette* predicted with confidence that 'having won its entrée into good society . . . it [lawn tennis] will be a popular pastime in every English home which can boast a level piece of ground twenty yards by ten.'[36] Looking back on the 1870s, Escott had this to say:

> In all things the accredited exemplars of the latest and most cosmopolitan mode were followed by the younger generation of the classes that conveniently were still regarded as strongholds of the ethical severity which Puritan ancestors handed down.

To the *Saturday Review*, commenting on the pathos of pleasure seeking, 29 August 1874, the 'eager attempts of persons to wedge themselves into a slightly higher stratum of the social formation by seizing on the favourite amusements of that higher level' constituted one of the more prominent features of contemporary leisure. In these circumstances, reprimanding the aristocracy was something of an anachronistic exercise, a ritual denunciation which hurt no one and cost little by fixing on antique stereotypes rather than personalities. It was mostly the reflex response of an older generation; in a new and ad hoc leisure culture, fashion rather than custom conferred its own legitimacy, and fashion was dictated by the rich and aristocratic – the magical 'upper 10,000' – whose appeal remained undiminished by the scandals for which a few of their number were still notorious.

But middle-class leisure time was far from being totally given over to the emulative strivings of so many *bourgeois gentilhommes*, however much the latter crowded the pages of *Punch* during this period. There was in English society a process of long standing whereby prominent bourgeoisie could be assimilated by their social superiors, but in the middle years of the nineteenth century there was a flood tide of middle-class men and their families who could not be similarly accommodated and, in many cases, were not sure that they wished to be. For this large group leisure provided an opportunity to confirm and consolidate their social standing rather than redefine it upwards.

Building a community was a task which went hand in hand with the confirmation of class identity, and helped determine the shape and nature of middle-class leisure in a changing environment. Urbanisation had herded the working classes into a gross proximity in the centre of the cities; the same process relocated the middle classes on the suburban peripheries. The once tight middle-class world comprising a handful of families with more or less permanent entrées into each other's company was multiplied, fragmented and flung outwards to crystallise into large numbers of discrete and insular households (lacking as yet the telephone, that great and in England almost exclusively middle-class instrument of social communication). The dislocation of old patterns of neighbour-hood intimacy was compounded by the growing practice of boarding out children at school age; young adults returned home to find themselves bereft of local acquaintances. The solitary family was inadequate for social fulfilment and the middle class, no less than the working class, had to build its secondary associations to combat the strains of the new environment. For recreation these might take the form of private house or garden parties among business associates or the extended family, but a major agent of regeneration was certainly the formally constituted club or society. These voluntary associations embraced a wide range of activities: sports, amateur soldiering, literary and scientific education and debate, the definition and promotion of professional interests, and the pursuit of reform – all, in varying degrees, performed an important social function. 'In the Volunteer corps', observed Hugh Shimmin, the Liverpool journalist, 'patriotism is a mask for social relaxation; not only is each company or regiment as distinct a section of English society as a club, but its most prominent features are those of club life.'[37] Contemplating the annual meeting of the Church Congress, 12 October 1863, *The Times* was moved to comment on congresses in general:

> They are great social meetings to which people go to see one another and become better friends, or to learn, in a genial, offhand manner, the general course their thoughts are taking . . . this is the meaning of the Social Science Congress. It is not scientific, and it is not a congress, but it is social.

By such means did the mid-Victorian middle classes sustain communities of interest which overcame the barriers of a cellular suburban society.

Recreation through association appealed on many counts. It appealed on practical grounds, since for every middle-class arrivist bent on raising his status with the cheque book, there were plenty with a nose for a bargain, in leisure as in business. 'Most roturiers [self-made men]', observed Escott, 'carry into private life the sound business capacity that has made them so successful in commerce.' Plainly, clubbing together spread the cost of facilities and equipment – the exclusive gentlemen's clubs of St James's were copied by rising professional bodies for their economy and convenience as well as their associations of gentility. A club atmosphere also afforded new opportunities for informal dealings in business and politics. All this suggests heavy male dominance, but the broadening choice of sports and outdoor activities provided increased recreational opportunities for the ladies as well. Games parties and sports clubs provided cover for courtship and flirtation, and the constant surplus of women over men during this period accounts for female enthusiasm for the mixed sports of lawn tennis and croquet – the latter, we are told, offered 'fresh air and flirtation in agreeable combination'. The ice-skating boom or 'rinkomania' of the 1870s was clearly attractive to young people anxious to escape the chaperone, as Escott also noted:

> Not without a shock to her sense of maternal propriety did the English Matron of old fashioned ideas see, or hear of, her daughter being twirled in the arms of some youth just introduced, or perhaps without even the preliminary of that easy form.

Even matrons bold enough to take to the ice themselves were no doubt easily out-skated, just as they were soon to be out-bicycled.[38] Yet there were also ways in which associations reinforced rather than slackened the bonds of orthodox morality. For good or bad, they reproduced the kind of mutual vigilance which acted as a social discipline in the small town milieu, but which tended to break down in the anonymity and disconti-nuities of a big city. One imagines that correctly ordered social clubs would have recommended themselves to such moral watchdogs as the journalist Ewing Ritchie, who was scandalised by businessmen who drank heavily in town but passed as models of respectability at home – the Jekylls and Hydes of suburbia.[39]

Voluntary associations in general, and those for recreation in particu-lar, met a variety of important needs in middle-class life. A perceptive French observer offered these remarks on this notable phenomenon:[40]

This tendency of the English to form groups through the attractions of certain pleasures, deserves our attention. . . . In France men like to meet for the sake of meeting; the Englishman is perhaps less sociable: he requires an object, a community of tastes, a peculiar tie, which draws him nearer his fellowmen. Does not this explain how a nation founded in great measure on the principle of self, maintains itself so firm, compact, and united, without calling on the individual to sacri-fice any of his liberties? The voluntary association in groups and series, is the great counterpoise of British personality.

There is a further point: in a literal-minded society with a taste for the formulas of constitutionalism, few associations were without their rules and regulations – by such proper devices the Englishman could choose who to join with or exclude from such associations.

The example of Bolton provides illustrations of several of these themes.[41] Here there was no resident aristocracy to turn the heads of the town's burgeoning middle class; but the new men abroad in business and the professions, many of whose grandfathers according to a disgruntled local informant 'had sold sand, boiled tripe, cobbled shoes, sold clogs, worked the traddles, or spun cotton', needed to find some corporate identity, some social expression for their new status. A correspondent to the *Chronicle* in 1865 declared the great need for a club for gentlemen (the term itself was almost a new designation in Bolton, for men like the Ashworths had been proud to style themselves 'manufacturer' or 'cotton spinner'). The town's gentlemen were soon accommodated in the suc-cession of associations formed in Bolton from the mid-1860s: a rowing club was in existence in 1865, the year of the foundation of Bolton's cricket club (whose membership grew from 30 to 220 in six years); an amateur athletic club formed in 1870, followed by an amateur swimming club in 1871. A public school man, trying to locate his kind in a town to which he was a stranger, wrote to the *Chronicle* in 1872 suggesting the formation of an association football club, and Bolton FC was born the following year. Subscriptions were beyond the range of any but a middle-class pocket, and there were several complaints about the exclusivity of the clubs, so much so that a Liberal parliamentary candidate in 1868 tried to make political capital out of the élitist pretensions of the cricket club and the Volunteer corps which, he claimed, were 'confined to a certain class' (mostly of a disappointingly Tory persuasion). We have seen how John Taylor, the Bolton lawyer (and sometime town coroner) no longer took his recreation in the pubs by the 1850s but entertained at home, and mention has been made of the town's 'select and gorgeous' dinner parties, but a good deal of socialising, for some perhaps even the greater part, took place in groups outside the drawing room. 'Home sweet home', lamented one Boltonian in the mid-1870s,

> does not form the centre of attraction it once did. . . . We do almost everything in public . . . every idea nowadays assuming the form of a society – and these of course must all be supplemented by their music, their eating and drinking, and the inevitable speechifying.

The process of adjustment to the greater incidence and opportunity of modern leisure was certainly more complex than we have been able to explore here, for the Victorian middle class was a social composite embracing men and women of widely differing conditions and experience. In general, however, the evidence does show the increasing facility with which the bourgeoisie learned to incorporate leisure into the normal pattern of their lives. Despite the admonitions of a rationale which subordinated recreation to the priorities of work and Christian duty, the old constraints were dissolving, and the public face of leisure grew increasingly unabashed, particularly among the young. Yet tensions between work and play, between moral glosses and social reality still remained, and were reflected in the dispensations of rational recreation to the masses, themselves enjoying something of a modest leisure boom in the less straitened circumstances of the third quarter of the nineteenth century.

4

Dispensing recreation to the masses in the new leisure world

From the mid-century, many among the English working classes found themselves sharing in the new bonus of leisure and the expansion and diversification of popular recreations. The middle classes had therefore not only to decide upon their own response to the invitations to worldly pleasure, but what to do and say about the multiplying pleasures of the masses. Social reformers gave more attention to monitoring popular amusements during this period than before, but though they increased the facilities for rational recreation they fell far short of the complete realisation of their schemes for improvement; among the various difficulties they had to contend with was that of a more competitive leisure market, and the refusal of the middle classes to play the regenerative role the reformers assigned to them.

I

The growth of working-class leisure in this period was facilitated by a complex of changing circumstances, the most dramatically felicitous of which were concentrated in the decade of the 1870s. First, the working-man (and his family auxiliaries) enjoyed more free time, as supplementary industrial legislation in the mid-1860s and trade union activism in the early 1870s brought a further reduction in working hours and the provision of a Saturday half-holiday in an increasing number of trades. In turn, the success of the Short Time agitation encouraged further campaigns to cut working hours, including that of the Early Closing movement for shop and office workers which continued to register minor local victories. Measured overall the gains were no doubt marginal; many occupational groups remained unprotected at law, and to one informed workingman the half-holiday meant a rearrangement rather than a diminution of hours. But the Saturday break seems generally to have been savoured as a real bonus. Certainly its increasingly common observance imprinted the pattern of *la semaine anglaise* with its fixed proportions of work and leisure more firmly in public habit, and though St Monday was not yet extinguished, it was Saturday night that was now installed as the ritual climax to the average workingman's week.[1] The working year also began to assume the familiar profile of the modern industrial society. The Bank Holidays Act of 1871 guaranteed modest annual holidays for bank workers and the dispensation spread to other groups. Commenting on the institution two years later, *The Times* noted: 'The result seems to have been not merely to increase the number of holydays, but to stimulate the observance of them.' If the paper correctly discerned a new trend, by the same token it was anachronistic in persisting with the old spelling, for the Bank Holiday was significant as a purely secular device with no counterpart in the liturgical (or agricultural) calendar. Company holidays also became more common: in the late 1860s bank clerks in the City could expect up to three weeks off after a certain period of established service, and railwaymen with the Great Northern in 1872 seem to have been the first workingmen to receive regular holidays with pay. Employers in the north increasingly conceded 'Wakes Weeks' as legitimate annual holidays which reinvigorated rather than debilitated their workforce.[2]

Improved communications broadened the horizons of working-class life. The cheap press expanded social consciousness here as it had done in higher levels of society; similarly, the working classes shared in the benefits of increased mobility conferred by the growth of cheap rail travel and the excursion business. Provincial workingmen and their families poured into London by train for the Great Exhibition in 1851. Sometime in the 1860s working-class families began to take breaks of several days at the seaside, where distinctively proletarian resorts were developing. A party of Bolton artisans went to the Paris Exhibition in 1867 and a London journeyman published advice on cheap continental holidays for workingmen in 1878 – vacations, that is, as distinct from the traditional working tours of the tramping artisan. Savings clubs assisted in financing the more ambitious trips, and the development of third-class rail travel in the 1870s increased popular traffic.[3] Robert Baker, factory inspector, noted approvingly:[4]

> The working class are moving about on the surface of their own country, visiting in turn exhibition after exhibition, spending the wealth they have acquired 'in seeing the world' as the upper classes did in 1800, as the middle class did in 1850, and as they themselves are doing in 1875.

There were other gains in space and facilities inside the towns and cities. As one observer recorded in the late 1860s:

The lavish provision of public parks, pleasure grounds, baths and free libraries in all the larger Lancashire towns, testifies that the corporate authorities are not unmindful of their obligations to promote the health, happiness and culture of the industrial orders.

In Bolton and district, municipal and private initiative increased the number of parks and indoor places of assembly. A vast new town hall, opened in 1873, looked down upon the Free Library, the Chadwick Museum, a new Co-operative Hall, a second Temperance Hall and a rash of different clubrooms, institutes and coffee taverns. Of course, what might appear lavish to a visitor may well have been so only in comparison with his preconceptions of the industrial town as a Dickensian wasteland; in comparison to local needs, proper amenities were still in short supply. In proportion to the number and density of population in many big cities the provision of open space, for example, was grossly inadequate, and modern research suggests that the 'civic gospel' of municipal improvement brought only modest recreational gains for the working classes before the 1880s. Yet it remains plain enough that the workingman had a wider choice of leisure resort than simply that between church or pub which had previously obtained.[5]

Though constraints on time and space were considerably eased, popular recreation could still not escape the rebukes of its old opponents. The sabbatarian lobby delayed the Sunday opening of art galleries until 1896, a stand which exasperated many working-class leaders though galleries may have been caviar to the general; more offensive in popular eyes, as we have seen, was the victory of sabbatarians in closing down Sunday band concerts in London parks and their threat to pub opening hours in the 1850s. There were several clashes in Bolton between a sabbatarian rearguard and a popular party led by the local secularists, who interpreted the issue of Sunday opening in terms of class discrimination. 'The question of the Sabbath', declared Simon Hilton, veteran Bolton radical, 'is never mooted but when the privileges of the humbler classes are concerned.' Hilton's party secured the Sunday opening of Peel Park in 1867; two years later Hilton led the fight to allow the sale of refreshments in the Park on Sundays – quoting John Stuart Mill to the hisses of the Sunday school claque – and there were other contests in later years. The Temperance movement developed a formidable national organisation in this period which secured various curtailments of pub opening hours, thus cutting back on recreational drinking. In Bolton, regular memorials from influential Temperance supporters to the annual licensing sessions cut off the grant of new pub licences; the same group, in alliance with the Sunday school lobby, also took advantage of new requirements in Bolton's Corporation Improvement Act of 1872 to pressure the magistrates into withholding a singing and dancing licence for the Museum Music Hall, the descendant of the Star. In the same decade, the increasing reach of licensing legislation also made fairs and race meetings more vulnerable to official closure, though it was the music halls where the clash of opposing interests was loudest.[6]

'The Battle of the Music Halls' made headlines in the 1880s, but there was another battle over popular recreation – the battle of the streets – which went on interminably, but whose communiqués were lost in the small print of provincial newspapers. From one of many similar reports from this forgotten front here is the case of a certain George Healey of Bolton, charged with indecent conduct on Chorley New Road in the spring of 1866. The principal witness before the court was a Mr W. H. Wright, a respectable tea dealer of the town:[7]

> on Saturday afternoon, about half past two, he was in his garden at Heaton, when he heard a noise in the road, and on turning round, he saw a man pass by wearing nothing except a pair of drawers; while directly afterwards he saw the defendant running along the road in a completely nude state, with the exception of a handkerchief which was wrapped around his loins. . . . Witness ordered the defendant to dress himself, and then brought him to the police office in a cab. There were about fifty men and boys on the road. Witness added that he had been very much annoyed by this sort of conduct lately. Defendant said he was only running for exercise. Mr Wright: He told me he was racing for 5s.

The police superintendent commended Mr Wright on his zeal and remarked on the frequency of such happenings: it was, he said, 'the same all round the town'. This, then, was an example of the 'Race Running Nuisance', as it was regularly characterised by the authorities; there were several other nuisances, some of which have been noted previously, which also gave rise to frequent arrests. The nuisances were often the desultory recreations of the loafers in the street, by many accounts a common, numerous and obtrusive constituent of the town's poor. On Sundays their presence was even more disturbing, and their contumely more offensive – 'crowds of men and boys', reported one observer, 'for the most part all in their deshabillé . . . applying the expression "bloody" to almost every person and thing that came in their way'. Such congregations must often

have unnerved the middle-class passerby and they most certainly out-
raged city shopkeepers anxious for respectable custom, but in the case
quoted above there was no threat to life, limb or property – a large and
interested crowd (some no doubt with money riding on Healey's performance) gathered together on a Saturday afternoon (a legitimate time-
off work for most) and watched without protest (there was apparently no
bad language) while Mr Wright made his citizen's arrest. Healey's
specific offence was that of indecency, a condition easily achieved within
prevailing definitions of nudity – police witnesses thought it worth while
to inform the courts whether or not defendants in such cases were appre-
hended with or without a jacket on – but his general offence was against
bourgeois respectability, and he was only one of the countless many so
indicted in this period. The police had not by any means abandoned
their attacks on the more publicised and sensational unruliness of certain
surviving traditional festivals, but it was in their more intensive surveillance of everyday life that their discipline of popular culture was most
felt. Police harassment of popular recreations was compounded by the
hostilities of petty officials: park keepers broke up games in the parks,
and library attendants became minor ogres in working-class folklore.[8]

Active hostility to popular recreation was therefore still very much a
reality in the mid-Victorian period, but on balance the working classes
enjoyed a greater freedom and opportunity in their leisure than previously, not only in terms of time and space, but in terms of spending
power, the greatest of emancipators. Average real wages rose gradually
from the mid-century, and there was a pronounced upward swing in the
1870s; since there was as yet only a restricted choice of cheap consumer
goods available to the working classes and few social incentives to save
for some progressive betterment of living standards, much of the extra
pocket money went on leisure. Though not all workers shared equally or
simultaneously in the advance, in general popular demand became not
only more numerous but more effective.[9]

Popular recreations in this period of growth often evidenced considerable improvement in terms of regularity, moderation and edification,
particularly in the north, where working-class life conformed more tidily
than elsewhere to the parameters of an urban industrial society. Such
trends were exemplified in the careful year-round saving which made the
seaside holiday a regular annual occasion for many Lancashire cotton
workers. A survey of Lancashire at play in the *Pall Mall Gazette* for
11 September 1884 reported that £60,000 had been paid out by
Oldham's works' savings committees on the eve of Wakes Week, adding
that holiday drunkenness had much abated. Choral and brass band

music flourished in the north and midlands, and armies of choristers descended regularly on London's Crystal Palace for the great choir festivals. The more popular and commercialised music hall that took root throughout the country never approached the respectability of these offshoots of orthodox culture, but its devotees were seldom profligates and several observers discerned a decent, humanising influence in this burgeoning institution. The Volunteer force was a patently respectable movement that was soon drawing a surprisingly large number of its recruits from the working class – by the 1870s young workingmen comprised the majority of members in a scheme originally conceived by and for the middle class – and the modern historian of the force makes it plain that it was the opportunities for recreation and camaraderie, rather than the appeal to patriotism, that pulled in these part-time soldiers.[10]

Thomas Wright, the 'Journeyman Engineer', also notes the popularity of Saturday afternoon volunteering in his 1867 description of a typical working-class weekend – typical, that is, 'among the general run of the real working classes, the steady-going, regularly-employed artisans and labourers, and their wives and families'. Other young men, observes Wright, who draws his illustrations primarily from London working-class life, spend their Saturday afternoon as members of workshop bands or rowing clubs, while their elders attend to a little domestic handiwork, peruse the newspaper or address themselves to some more solidly educational reading. For the womenfolk, routine shopping is enlivened by the purchase of some new finery or a piece of furniture for the parlour. After a substantial tea comes the Saturday 'night-out', spent most commonly in the theatre gallery, the music hall, the dancing saloon or the pub free and easy. On Sunday morning the men luxuriate in bed while the women dispatch the children to Sunday school. Then follows a large and savoury breakfast, after which the men climb into their Sunday suits and repair to the barber's shop, obviously a social institution of some importance in working-class neighbourhoods: here they gossip with their mates, discuss the previous night's doings, take a leisurely toilet and, if they are regulars, treat themselves to one of the barber's famous 'revivers' – a sustaining confection of spirits and other healing cordials. The day proceeds with the midday dinner, the most imposing of the weekend meals both in size and ceremony. This is a select family occasion, whereas Sunday tea (taken after an interim walk or nap) is a time for guests and hospitality, and significant in the furtherance of budding courtships among the young. For some, Sunday is given over to a special excursion or outing; for few is it the automatic occasion for churchgoing. The piece is not without a certain disingenuous cosiness, but in sum it carries conviction. There is incidental gambling on a fist fight, some clandestine tippling out of licensing hours, and Wright introduces us to the phenomenon of the proletarian dandy or 'working-class swell', but the general impression that he leaves is of the comparative seemliness and decorum of so much of this family-based weekend recreation.[11]

From elsewhere comes evidence of how workingmen with a literary or intellectual appetite made good use of the wider range of public resources. Tom Barclay, semi-skilled hosiery worker and self-styled 'bottlewasher', enjoyed a fair choice of recreations in late-century Leicester: dancing classes at the Spiritualist Hall, lectures at the Secular Club, Gilbert and Sullivan at the Opera House. From London in the 1880s we learn of a certain Edward Baker, 'who had a faculty for making the best of the various organisations created for the elevation of the working classes . . . a perfect directory of free and cheap concerts and lectures all over London'. From Leeds in 1870 a workingmen's institute reported the proliferation of cheap concerts, penny readings, church entertainments and public libraries in the town. Old showmen attributed the decline of their profession to, among other things, the modern appetite for reading; it was, they claimed, destroying the public credulousness upon which much of their business had been traditionally based.[12]

It was, of course, far from true that popular recreations had succumbed en bloc to a new sophistication, for many traditional styles and occasions retained their appeal. 'In most of our provincial cities and boroughs', so the *Saturday Review* maintained in 1869, 'the fair and the race-meeting are the two great festivals of the local calendar, the two seasons from which the mass of people date forwards or backwards.' Though fairs declined in number, recent research demonstrates how one at least – St Giles' Fair in Oxford – proved capable of enhancing its attractions, by utilising the modern technology that one may too readily assume to have spelt its doom. In Lancashire the term 'Wakes Week' was borrowed to describe the seaside holiday the workers increasingly preferred to the local summer fairs, but the spring fairs remained great occasions for neighbourhood visiting (though May Day celebrations seem to have been appropriated for displays of municipal pride – parades of corporation dust-carts and the like). Bolton's New Year's Fair was still a two- or three-day holiday, celebrated in more extensive fashion than Christmas.[13] The number of race meetings in the country actually increased, particularly in the vicinity of the larger towns; their provenance is clear from the disparaging label of 'publicans' races' awarded them by the racing establishment. The Turf was becoming more commercialised: admission charges were introduced as a growing number of courses were enclosed; more exciting programmes were devised to tempt spectators to pay for their pleasure; the bookmaker appeared in force, and gambling on and off the course was further serviced and encouraged by the cheap racing sheet and newspaper supplement. The sport at the minor tracks was still rough and ready and in general much working-class sport of the 1860s and early 1870s remained unreconstructed. Contemplating the sporting press of the 1860s, one journalist remarked:[14]

> *Bell's Life* tells us, not what ought to be done by Englishmen, but what, as a matter of fact, is done. It shows what a large balance there still is versus that crushing respectability which threatens to overwhelm us – it tells us how much of the animal pleasures of savage life survives in the heart of civilised life.

Animality, excess, certainly boisterousness – these were still notable features of popular recreation. Some of their typical manifestations had been driven underground, as in the cock and dog fighting which survived only in clandestine encounters, but a good deal of popular amusement in the old style could not be kept from the public eye. The Sayers-Heenan fight in 1860 offers a notorious case in point, and most historians of mid-Victorian England have their favourite horror stories of brutal or violent episodes which passed for recreation; public executions continued into the 1860s, and elections, despite reforms, were celebrated as popular holidays cum licensed brawls throughout the period. A Lancashire speciality was 'purring', a form of single combat by kicking, which still produced occasional fatalities.[15] The violent delights of Derby Day continued to jolt the confidence of the most generous anglophiles, and from the mid-century Boat Race Day occasioned similar popular bacchanalia. August Bank Holiday seemed to encourage more of the same – 'For days the streets are full of stragglers,' recorded a Frenchman living in England, 'it is a whole week lost, drowned in beer.' As suggested earlier, there was a certain rawness and urgency in popular recreation which marked the reflex action to the rigours and privations of much working-class life. Thomas Wright thought there were times when the London workman in particular was driven to a craving for excitement in his amusements by squalid and over-crowded housing, and Taine considered the licence of Derby Day 'an outlet for a year of repression'.[16]

But it was not all quite so manic: violence bespeaks frustration but prodigality answers to other less desperate explanations. From *Gammer Gurton's Needle* to Harry Champion's *Boiled Beef and Carrots*, the message of folk wisdom to those who lived near the poverty line was to put any extra money in the belly and not on the back. There were in any case still relatively few competing alternatives to food and more especially drink for the spare cash in the workman's pocket. The consumption of alcohol reached its highest level in Britain in the mid-1870s and it seems reasonable to assume that in working-class life this represented a considerable increase in social drinking in the pub rather than that done for physiological or dietetic reasons in the workplace or at home. Heavier drinking in these years may have been due to the shortage of other leisure-time commodities or things to do, but it must also surely have been an activity often relished in itself, and much of the drinking behaviour among workingmen that middle-class consciousness registered as excessive would have been well within their physical tolerance. Drinking was also part of the unique and continuing attraction of pub life; the licensed trade was still under attack and the number of drink outlets began to level off during the 1870s, but publicans and architects devised ways of making existing premises more commodious and their style and ambience yet more seductive.[17] Though certain ritual obligations to drink were declining, particularly in the workplace, the sentimental drinker might still be propelled by some powerful traditions, for great things were still claimed for beer, as this snatch of popular oratory from the 1860s reveals:

> Beer and wine met at Waterloo: wine red with fury, boiling over with enthusiasm, mad with audacity, rose thrice against that hill on which stood a wall of immovable men, the sons of beer. You have read history: beer gained the day.

Strong ale and its legendary compeer roast beef were not merely the stage properties of an erstwhile Merrie England, but sacraments in a continuing mythology of national superiority and class identity. The English workman was the great ale-swiller and meat-eater whose industry and stamina put the puny continentals to shame or flight, in work or war – thus was the lesson of Waterloo repeated in the prodigious exploits of Peto's navvies on railway construction in the Crimea and France in the 1860s and 1870s.[18]

Though not every day was Derby Day, there were a good many occasions for celebrating its minor relative the 'beano', the 'spree', the 'blow-out' – all terms of popular currency in mid-Victorian England. The national meeting of the Friendly Society of Ironfounders held in Bolton in 1866 provides an example. The society enjoyed a strong local following for iron workers constituted the town's second largest occupational group

next to textile workers, and though it was in the process of transformation from a trade friendly society to one of the new model unions, it
obviously retained a strong emphasis on good fellowship. The chairman
opened proceedings by declaring they were met for two principal objects
– 'enjoyment and pleasure, and to show the country that the ironfounders were not behind other bodies of workpeople in this age of
improvement'. Improvement here was measured on a different scale
from that used by politicians and reformers – it came by the bellyful. In a
pavilion in Peel Park a local publican provided the following spread:

> 1000 lbs. of beef, 400 lbs. of mutton, 500 lbs. of lamb, 300 lbs. of
> salmon, 100 rice puddings, 150 plum puddings, 200 cheese cakes, 200
> small and 100 large blackcurrant, damson, strawberry and gooseberry
> tarts; 6 loads of potatoes, 12 doz. of cauliflowers, 36 doz. of cabbage,
> 24 bags of peas, 150 4 lb. loaves, and 1200 cobs of bread, in addition to
> cheese.

To cater to the thirst of the 1,500 delegates 'the whole length of the west
side of the pavilion had been appropriated to a refreshment department,
in which were to be seen a multitudinous array of glasses, jugs and beer
barrels.' Afterwards the ironfounders and members of local allied trades
disported themselves with 'singing, dancing and reciting, and other
amusements which continued until the dawn of day'. The friendly
societies in general provide an interesting example of the continuing
strength of traditional recreational priorities in institutions which mostly
commended themselves to middle-class observers as improving agencies
in working-class life. 'After all their drawbacks', concluded the *Bolton
Chronicle* in a review of the Lancashire societies in the late 1870s, 'they
. . . provide an education in the duties of citizenship through the practice
of self-government.'[19]

Thus rationality and old-style conviviality were not necessarily irreconcilable qualities in popular recreation, a point given further exemplifi-
cation in a suggestive piece by Thomas Wright called 'Bill Banks's day
out', published in 1868.[20] Bill is a railwayman who goes 'St Mondaying'
with his wife and friends to Hampton Court. They meet outside a local
pub, admire each other in their best dress, and start the excursion with a
morning pint. They travel out to Hampton Court by hired van, complete with cornet player to enliven the journey. On arrival they tuck into
a dinner provided by the van-owner at 2s 6d a head – 'a first-rater; beef
and mutton and ham, and any quantity of rolls, and lots of fruit-tarts, in
the way of eating, and bottled ale and a small cask of porter to wash 'em
down'. The harmony of the occasion is disturbed when Bill, somewhat

flushed with drink, takes exception to the superior airs of a young shop-man in the company (Wright himself detested 'counter-jumpers'); after a scuffle, peace is restored and the party continues, finishing up in late evening back in town, at the Alhambra, the famous Leicester Square music hall. Bill and his wife together with two friends share the cost of a cab home, enjoying the prospect of scandalising the neighbours by returning in such style.

Retailed in the first person, the piece has an internal consistency which suggests how a workingman at play could move through several different roles, all reconcilable, but each in turn likely to be interpreted by an out-sider as the behaviour peculiar to a distinct, separate and exclusive type within the working classes. On the evidence of his home life Banks would pass as the self-improving artisan: he is a considerable and intelli-gent reader who borrows books from the local institute to supplement his own small library. Thus he belongs to the tradition recorded by Bamford and lauded by the students of working-class progress. In taking an excur-sion (albeit on St Monday) Bill appears at first to be a further credit to his class. His expenditure can be reckoned at between 10s and 15s for him and his wife, yet the day out is not the reflex action of a poor family gobbling up a sudden windfall, but the happy product of careful budget-ing which, so we gather, owes something to Mrs Banks's good manage-ment (Wright, in company with other commentators, attributed many of the miseries of working-class life to inefficient housekeeping). Hampton Court, an historic house on which Bill is well read, represents a 'rational' choice for a visit, and in their concern with their appearance the party display that 'pardonable vanity' which Slaney had once recommended as a tonic both for trade and self-respect. Thereafter, however, Bill Banks's respectable image disintegrates, as he regresses into the time-honoured role of the English workman on a spree. To a middle-class observer he would then appear drunk, gluttonous and unruly. Detected among the music hall crowd he would serve as an example of the feckless new breed of workingman who surrendered himself to the temptations of the 'fast' life. If Bill Banks is at all representative, the pattern of his day out can, at a latter point in this chapter, help us understand the gap between ideals and achievements in the work of those who worked to reform popular recreation. It is to their continuing endeavours that we now turn.

II

The concern to encourage rational recreation for the working classes which had awakened public attention with the passing of the Factory Acts in the late 1840s continued to grow in the following period, finding a firm place in the general vocabulary of most social reformers. 'There is', wrote Professor Stanley Jevons in a much-quoted article in the *Contemporary Review* for 1878, 'hardly any other method [of social reform] taken separately, to which greater importance should be attributed than to the providing of good moral public amusements.' This greater sensitivity to popular leisure clearly came from the growing realisation of its significance as the workingman's major area of free choice. As the Christian Socialists pointed out in the house journal of the London Working Men's College: 'Our work, whatever it might be, was for the most part assigned to us by circumstances over which we had very little control; but with respect to our amusements much more was left to our freedom of choice.' This fact gave leisure hours 'a value for the formation and development of character which cannot be estimated too highly'.[21] Since leisure was now assumed to be a common possession, the manner of its proper disposal was a frequent topic for debate at all levels of the press, from the detached commentaries of the critical reviews to the crusading journalism of men like Mayhew and George Godwin (editor of the *Builder*) in London, and Hugh Shimmin in Liverpool.

Working-class reformers and writers were generally more concerned with the achievement of the essential prerequisites for leisure – time and money – than with its proper content. They were, however, worried that immoderate indulgence in amusements and holidaymaking would reduce the political consciousness of the workingman. In a well-known commentary upon Lancashire in 1870, Thomas Cooper discovered that affluence had reduced many of the heirs of his unkempt Chartist heroes of the 1840s to political indifference, and he stood aghast at the spectacle of Lincoln workmen pawning their beds to take a railway excursion. Wright, too, had some misgivings about the Londoners' insatiable taste for amusements. The recommended corrective was that of rational recreation, both to continue the political and educational improvement of the class and, through public good manners, to oblige the other classes to respect the workingman.[22]

Faced with declining congregations the churches interested themselves more actively in the question of popular recreations. This was particularly noticeable in the Church of England which was shrugging off its discomfiture in the presence of the urban masses and moving in to tackle a wide range of social problems. The activists in recreational improvement were only a minority, but a very vocal one which pushed its case hard at the annual Church Congresses that met regularly from 1862. The Established Church also reassumed a prominent role in the

Temperance movement, which expanded its work of providing counter-attractions to pub-based recreations.[23]

The commonest platform for reformers of all stripes was that of the National Association for the Promotion of Social Science which met in annual conference from 1857. Meetings of its department of social economy received regular reports on recreational reform projects. The reformers in the field were mainly churchmen, local notables, occasional municipal officials, and a number of middle-class women. The audience included most of the leading contemporary 'friends of the working classes': new model employers such as Mundella and Morley, Christian Socialists such as Kingsley and Maurice, civil servants such as Chadwick and Tremenheere, reconstructed aristocrats such as Lords Shaftesbury and Lyttelton, reform MPs such as Slaney and Ewart. The tone of proceedings was earnest but non-sectarian, the rationale that of gradual-ist social engineering serviced by philanthropy. The association was a good deal less rigorous and hard-headed in its promotion of social science than its propaganda proclaimed, but it provided the most important single forum for middle-class recreational reformers.[24]

Rational recreation widened its brief in one important respect as reformers addressed themselves to the problematical social life of the young clerks and shopmen whose number increased dramatically in this period. Although concern for their welfare echoed something of the traditional concern for the town apprentice, this group constituted a new phenomenon, an overnight creation of modern urban society; the clerk, maintained Charles Kingsley, 'is distinctly a creature of the city; as all city influences bear at once on him more than in any class, we see in him at once the best and the worst effects of modern city life.' Clerkdom occupied a decidedly marginal and ambivalent position in society; from within its ranks one Liverpudlian wrote that it 'presents divergencies as wide, and peculiarities as interesting as does any other class of a great labouring community'. In Edward Hodder's cautionary tale, *The Junior Clerk: A Tale of City Life* (published in 1862 and recommended to employers for distribution among their young men), the hero is well educated and confident of an eventual partnership, but below the articled youngster with good connexions stretched an army of young men with careers ranging from middling to destitute – Shimmin, another practised observer from Merseyside, included clerks and shopkeepers' assistants in the working classes.[25] Generally, however, reformers defined the social problems of this group in terms of its urban environ-ment rather than its class identity. Young and impressionable, often living in lodgings away from the restraints and affection of home, 'their

hours of business constantly shortened and relaxed to suit faint inclinations for work', according to one sardonic but not untypical estimate
of the achievements of the Early Closing Movement, clerks were considered exceptionally vulnerable to the temptations of fast company –
juvenile 'swells' and 'cads' who had yielded to such corruptions figure in
most contemporary descriptions of music hall clientèle and the loungers
in city cigar-divans.[26] Organised rescue work had begun with the
founding of the Young Men's Christian Association in 1844 in London
and YMCAs multiplied throughout the country in the next decade.
Although at first these institutions were narrowly evangelistic – 'Amusements are not necessary to your happiness, religion is' – they began to
broaden their activities in the 1860s with cautious doses of recreation.[27]

As debate increased, the lineaments of rational recreation for the
masses became clearer. In the calmer climate of the mid-Victorian era
there was less preoccupation with recreation as a distraction from mob
politics. In any case, as we have seen, the idea of recreation as a safety
valve whose cathartic effect justified the suspension of normal social
disciplines was unacceptable to men primarily concerned to maintain
control and conformity. Play was not to be allowed any form of special
licence; rather it had to be firmly and unequivocally integrated with the
rest of life and securely anchored in orthodox morality. Ideally – rationally – recreation was an adjunct and complement to work. The literal
implications of the word itself were repeated: 'Recreation is the RE-
creation, the creation anew of fresh strength for tomorrow's work'; and
again, 'Amusement, to be legitimate, wholesome, innocent, must be
useful, in refitting the body or mind for its duty.' Accordingly it was 'of
WORKERS only that there can be RECREATION'.[28] In this prescription work and play were antithetical in form only; in purpose they were
part of a single natural process at the service of God and society. It was
however made clear that of the two constituents work was sovereign:
work disciplines had to be projected into play, not vice versa. As the
house journal of the Christian Socialists' London Working Men's
College put it: 'The question is not, are we to have all work and no play,
but what sort of work can we find pleasant enough to be made play of?'[29]
To invert the relationship would be destructive, as the Bishop of Win-
chester warned a workingmen's meeting at a Church Congress in the
1870s:[30]

We have been considering how best to get the workingmen leisure
hours and I myself am bent upon it. But why? That they may in their
leisure hours raise their own physical force – I don't forget that we

have a body as well as a soul – then their family, then their intellectual, and above all their spiritual being. That is the use of having these leisure hours, and if the additional hours should be spent by the work-ingmen of England in dissipation, riot and drunkenness – if they should be spent in learning himself and teaching others not to be satis-fied, not to understand that work is glory, and that doing the work he is set to do is the glory of man here, and will be the elevation of his faculties – then better by far that they should not have hours of leisure.

The address reveals the tension which attended most debates on the place of leisure in working-class life. Leisure was a necessary condition for physical refreshment and progress towards the good life, but without moral vigilance its practice would threaten the priorities of work and social discipline. The discussion of leisure was still characterised by the weight of cautionary advice it was made to carry. Leisure was time – ideally a third of men's lives, according to reformers in the Early Closing movement who resurrected King Alfred's formula of eight hours' work, eight hours' play, and eight hours' sleep – and time was valuable. Members of the YMCA (which was started by employers) were reminded that 'their masters would naturally be chary of curtailing the hours of labour unless they could see the leisure of their young men PROFIT-ABLY employed.' Profit was tangible in work, but how was it to be made a recognisable quantity in play? Young men at the YMCA were advised to apply a simple catechism to their recreations: 'Are they likely to make us better sons, brothers, husbands and fathers, better servants or masters, better citizens, and better Christians?'[31]
    At this point it might well be asked how the precepts outlined above differed from those urged upon middle-class audiences. The answer must be that there was little difference in basic teachings – the Victorian rationale of recreation was not in itself specifically discriminatory – but that the stronger tone employed in addressing the working classes betrays fundamentally different assumptions regarding the capacity of the particular classes for recognising and acting upon moral imperatives in recreation. A society based upon a paramount belief in the benevolent operation of free will had to concede the right and capability of the individual to practise and police his own leisure activities for, according to the commonest of contemporary analogies, 'Free trade, free religion, free art and free self-culture are all bound up in the same bundle, and stand or fall together.' Nevertheless, it was as yet only the middle classes who in the nature of things could be expected to apply the appropriate moral calculus to their pleasures. Reformers were generally agreed that

most workingmen still lacked the education and elementary accomplishments of 'social economy' – the proper management of time and money – which would qualify them to assume the responsible status of free agent in the dangerously open-ended world of leisure time.[32] Fears for the working classes' ability to apply the necessary controls in leisure grew sharper in the 1870s, when observers noted that gains in free time and spending power seemed generally to promote increased drunkenness rather than self-improvement. 'The period of transition from low to high wages, and from incessant toil to comparative leisure', warned Goldwin Smith, 'must be one of peril to the masses.'[33] Faith in the powers of formal education gave hope that the recent educational reforms would produce a better disciplined younger generation, but there were still wide areas of working-class life untouched by any effective control mechanisms. Education in the necessary leisure disciplines had to be taken to the masses. It was, declared Jevons, 'a positive duty on the part of the middle and upper classes to frequent the well-conducted places of popular recreation'.

The question of precisely who was to set the correct example was no longer contentious. Neither the aristocracy nor the bourgeoisie now contested for social or political leadership in the terms of a class dialectic; philanthropy in particular afforded opportunity for the middle classes both to savour the snobbish frisson of rubbing shoulders with nobility, and to advance their claims to share in the common gentility which identified a new composite ruling class. The agreed denomination for exemplar of rational recreation was that of gentleman. Example-setting by superiors and the common association of ranks in recreation was a formula well rehearsed during the previous period, but it was now being urged more forcefully. In the first place observers argued that the superior classes had need to be put on their best behaviour as a corrective to their own infatuation with the lure of worldly amusement and the seductions of materialism. Obliging them to fulfil their reform role would be mutually beneficial and arrest the degeneration which faced society as a whole in its transition to a leisure culture. 'Raise the workers', wrote one reforming journalist, 'and the masters will be shamed into morality.'[34] A further and more prevalent argument for securing an upper-class presence in popular recreation was that it would achieve a return to what many believed to have been a pristine state of fraternity among all the classes. The bitter alienations of the previous period seemed to have subsided but industrial strife still advertised the hostility between capital and labour, and urban dispersal and the physical segregation of the classes threatened general social disintegration.

Rational recreation could help rebuild a community of common sentiment and interest. This was the formula of the Christian Socialists, as explained by the secretary of their London Working Men's College to the Social Science Association. The promoters sought to overcome diversities of birth and education by appealing to

> the weight of common interests which bind together fellow strugglers in the race of human progress . . . they work on the principle of a direct personal relationship . . . on the principle, in short, that in order to do any good to or for a man you must first make a friend of him.

The Christian Socialist cultivated only a select corner of working-class company, but there was general agreement among reformers that some such exercise on a broad scale was necessary to integrate and humanise mass society.[35] As the *Bolton Chronicle* put it in more down-to-earth manner: 'If the working classes cannot have equality, they can at least have fraternity.'[36]

What was the best setting for this fraternal exercise, this restoration of a community of feeling? The semi-rural industrial colonies which had furnished the milieu for reform experiments in the previous era were mostly defunct; there were continuing experiments in building model industrial settlements – Titus Salt built Saltaire near Bradford in the 1850s under the spell of Disraeli's picture of Trafford of Wodgate as the ideal employer – but this form of patently proprietorial philanthropy carried less weight than previously in reform thinking, which looked now for something less isolated and more accessible to general membership.[37] The search passed by some seemingly obvious alternatives, for the middle classes were unwilling to throw open their homes or relax the exclusive regulations of their clubs and societies. There was a longstanding concern with the alleged breakdown of the working-class family in industrial towns and reformers urged the prior claims of home life as a salutary and necessary recreation for the workingman, but his home was too small and ill-equipped to afford a common meeting ground and homes in general were in any case becoming increasingly respected as desirable sanctums of privacy.[38] In this regard the home also lacked what reformers came to hold as a vital property of rational recreation – visibility or, in its contemporary usage, publicity, the condition or fact of being open to public observation or knowledge. Teaching by example was done most effectively and economically in open congregation. Public assembly under proper restraints and of the right social mix exerted a collective moral vigilance – 'the coercion of public opinion', 'a police of good understanding', as it was variously called by reformers.[39]

It was therefore of little use to clear the street of its various nuisances if the workingman retreated to the impenetrable bolt-hole of the home or, much worse, the pub.

There were suggestions for taming the pub (and other places of entertainment) by constructing the front entirely of plate glass so that its denizens would be visible to those outside and thus shamed into moderation and respectability, but reformers generally preferred that the milieu of improvement be of their own making.[40] In an age which remained awestruck by the scale, logic and success of the Great Exhibition's Crystal Palace, schemes for some kind of grand mechanical solution were regularly offered: People's Palaces – built at Muswell Hill in the 1860s and the Mile End Road in the 1880s – were attempts to provide a Great Eastern, as it were, of rational recreation.[41] There was support, too, for public gardens on the model of the German Volksgarten or Copenhagen's Tivoli. Foreign travel introduced an increasing number of middle-class reformers to the continental Sunday; its moderation and easy mingling of the classes in public promenade won many new converts and encouraged the growing opposition to sabbatarianism. A People's Garden Company issued a prospectus in London in 1870, and there were regular appeals in the press for the opening of the many private city squares to the public.[42] But the most favoured device for improvement was not the people's palace or the people's garden but the smaller association of the club or institute. Although the pub was still anathema to most reformers, its ubiquity and popularity in working-class life made it an inescapable model, and rational recreation tried in many guises to reproduce its human scale and convivial intimacy of spirit away from the contagion of strong drink and the corrupting benevolences of the publican. Accordingly it was the smaller institutions of rational recreation which grew considerably in number from the mid-century.

There was considerable debate among reformers as to precisely what fare these institutions should offer in the name of rational recreation. Given the moral purpose it was meant to serve it was, as one interested party neatly observed, a very difficult task to provide recreation that was 'pure, yet not dull; relaxing, yet not enervating; invigorating, yet not too exciting; popular, yet not vulgarising, and much more besides'. Since the early Victorian period improving institutions for workingmen had concentrated on solidly instructional fare. Where the pill of 'useful knowledge' had been sugared with entertainment, the more serious purposes had often been thwarted; this had been so with the Lyceums in Manchester, as we have seen, and it held true for the London Mechanics'

Institute in the 1850s.[43] But as popular demand for amusement rose steeply in the 1850s and 1860s reformers were forced to acknowledge it. In 1861 the London Working Men's College felt it necessary to hold a conference on the 'Amusement Question', although in this particular confrontation between the claims of seriousness and frivolity, as J. M. Ludlow chose to characterise it, seriousness prevailed. Three years later, at the YMCA's annual conference, workers in the field impressed upon senior officials how important it was that they offer amusement as well as instruction in order to boost the association's appeal. Temperance audiences demanded and got comic relief as well as exhortation.[44] British Workman pubs (dry facsimiles of the real thing, started in Leeds in 1867 and copied in many northern towns) and coffee taverns and palaces (offshoots of a movement established in 1874 with the formation of a London Coffee Tavern Company) from the outset placed a major emphasis on amusement and relaxation as well as the provision of cheap refreshments. By 1879 a People's Entertainment Society was in operation in London and within a year its example had been followed in three major provincial cities.[45] Such ventures were expected to pay their own way and met with mixed financial fortune. Their premises and fare varied considerably in attractiveness, but some of them clearly strove to give their message of rational hospitality a certain gusto, to judge from these lines written to celebrate the opening of a Birmingham coffee house of the period:[46]

> Throw open your doors with a flourish of trumpets,
> Let the generous tea urn run frothing and free.
> Oh! toast the rich muffins, and butter the crumpets,
> We pledge the promoters in mocha and tea.

Dating from the 1860s there was in fact a significant retreat from unrelieved didacticism in most schemes for recreational improvement. Reformers were learning that successful competition with the growing range of leisure attractions meant making some attempt to approach popular culture on its own terms, taking the workingman for what he was, rather than for what he ought to be. James Hole in Leeds had indeed arrived at this realisation some years previously:[47]

> It is no longer a question of social morals, but of supply and demand; not of the elevation of popular taste, but of gratification. . . . It is not drink, much as our people are given to drinking, which attracts the majority. The singing saloon supplies what neither the gin-palace, nor the beer-house supplies – amusement. . . . Exclude the workingman

from the opportunity of spending a leisure hour unprofitably if you like, and you shut the door of your institute on half of those who now enjoy its advantages. To raise the workman, we must take hold of him where he is, not where he is not.

As Shimmin remarked from Liverpool in the same period, 'An improvement of manners has been attempted without duly considering the man to be improved.'[48] Hole and Shimmin were men who knew working-class life at close hand, but the good sense of their message impressed itself on others further removed from its actualities. Explaining the Working Men's Club movement to the Social Science Association in 1865 Lord Brougham emphasised, 'Nothing can be more erroneous than the notion prevailing in some quarters that the object of these clubs is for education . . . the primary objects are relaxation and amusement.' Methods had changed, as another speaker impressed on a later conference of the Association; 'Their object', reported James Airlie, 'was to instruct through amusement instead of amusing through instruction.'[49] It is likely that this tactical volte-face was due to something more than a changing appreciation of the realities of working-class culture – due in good measure to the more relaxed mores of middle-class life. As Walter Besant remarked of this latter transformation, the days had gone when employers of leisure disallowed merriment among the poor because they themselves were content to be dull.[50]

It is obvious, however, that whatever the changes in style and method, rational recreation remained a very serious business for its proponents, who still spoke in a strongly missionary tone. The dilemma they now faced was that the admission of lighter and more entertaining fare would dilute or obscure the moral message which lay at the heart of the reform design. Churchmen were particularly sensitive to this problem. The churches' concern for recreation was partly a defensive operation against what the Dean of Manchester identified as a 'non-Christian humanitarianism', and partly a determination to rid the clergy of the kill-joy image which hampered the fight to hold and expand congregations. It was attended by a real effort to understand popular needs – to recognise, as Bishop Fraser of Manchester put it, 'the actual instincts and appetites of the human beings with whom we have to deal' – and Anglican reformers in particular (with the new wave of Christian Socialists in the van) moved forward in the 1870s and 1880s to endorse the claims of dancing, the theatre and even the pub as humanising institutions which might yet serve as proper vehicles for social and moral improvement. In such a spirit did a certain Canon Woodhouse propose to update John Wesley: 'If the devil ought not to have all the good tunes, why should he have all the popular amusements?'[51] But many clergy and lay workers were disturbed by the consequences of entering into competition with the outside world on its own terms. The Sunday schools enlivened their meetings with songs and sketches, but according to one Bolton minister, who claimed to detect the same syndrome in all the local churches and chapels, the additional recreation failed to hold young people for the senior church:

> Where are all the scholars that pass through our Sunday schools? How is it that they do not find their way into the church? My answer is, you have created in them an appetite for something else, and if you want to find them, visit our theatres and singing saloons, and you will find them there in thousands.

A lay worker noted that occasional booms in Sunday school attendance were directly attributable to the announcement of some treat or excursion and were never sustained beyond that date; 'Pleasure seeking', he concluded, 'is so rampant on every hand that it crushes out all desire for mental progress and produces indifference to religious matters.'[52]

Disillusionment and disappointment provided a persistent counterpoint to the reformers' faith in the ultimate efficacy of rational recreation. After the conclusion of a debate on recreational improvements in the Social Science Association in 1866, Lord Shaftesbury remarked wearily: 'It has exhausted the subject but it has devised no cures.'[53] A dozen years later Jevons was no more impressed with the progress of reform. Undoubtedly much of the reformers' disappointment can be attributed to the difficulty of realising expectations that were markedly at odds with the cultural process at work in urban popular society. Rational recreation was meant to supplant all 'irrational' recreation and thus establish a moral monopoly in working-class leisure. But in the absence of coercion the workingman still retained the right to choose his recreations, and on the evidence of Bill Banks his choice was indiscriminately rational and irrational. We are not told how Bill Banks spent his Sundays, but even though he may well have been no churchgoer he passed as a man of rational taste in respect of his intelligent literacy and the good management of his home – in several other respects he could be seen as a pleasure-seeking yahoo. Bill Banks reflects the nature of his culture, which was predominantly additive rather than substitutive, and exclusively responsible neither to fashion nor ideology. In an expanding working-class leisure world recreations were not all equally attractive, but they were all equally legitimate. In such circumstances it was most unlikely that rational recreation could effect total victory.

III

Other problems which the reformers faced in reaching and holding
working-class attentions are considered more fully in subsequent
chapters; this chapter concludes with a consideration of the middle-class
response to rational recreation, bearing in mind the important role
assigned to them in the reform design.

It seems clear that the reformers' propaganda did much to convert the
middle-class public to recreational improvement in the 1850s and 1860s;
recreation grew to be accepted as a necessary amenity, a basic overhead
in the maintenance of an industrial society. The opening of new facilities
were occasions for much official self-congratulation on the theme of
progress. The inauguration of Peel Park in 1866 moved the *Bolton
Chronicle* to recall how leaders of the people had once made the poor find
amusements for themselves, whereas now the poor were increasingly
well provided for in any number of schemes across the country 'which
may fairly be qualified by the adjective disinterested'. Editorialising on
the Working Men's Club movement of the same period *The Times* commented that 'such institutions stand upon the modest and unassailable
ground of simple convenience', opining that, aside from a little neigh-
bourly assistance, 'we see no necessity for a gentleman going much out of
his way or putting his hand very deep into his pocket.'[54]

If this was the language of encouragement it was also the language of
disengagement, marking a general middle-class reluctance to favour
popular recreation with anything other than an occasional subscription
or platform speech. Letters to the *Chronicle* in the 1870s pointed out the
still inadequate facilities for rational recreation in Bolton. There was,
remarked one correspondent, no shortage of moralising on the workingman's condition, but a real shortage of practical assistance: 'moralisers in
general never "knuckle down", that is, propose much more worthy
substitutes for recreating the plebeian order, seldom go beyond a sort of
Infirmary-recommend' (the latter was a sour local joke referring to the
long delay in building a much-needed hospital in the town). Bishop
Fraser assailed the Bolton middle classes for their neglect of what he
called 'the great question of the day', chiding them for their self-
righteousness as they sat over nuts and claret deploring the crudity of
working-class behaviour. They had, he said, no sympathy or interest in
the unfortunate yet remediable environment in which workingmen
lived.[55] Certain employers provided their workpeople with reading
rooms and sports facilities, but as the big masters withdrew to Southport
or farther afield class contact had diminished; the day-to-day running of

the mills passed to a new class of managers with little interest in the lighter side of industrial welfare, and the heads of firms only met their hands for celebration of the major dynastic events of marriage and majority, and occasional beanos in the run-up to elections. On the evidence of the factory inspectors' reports (which, with the increase in legislation, covered a greater number of establishments) the country's employers generally paid less attention to their workers' social welfare than in the 1840s.[56] Thus, with the exception of some sporadic largesse and the endeavours of a handful of local philanthropists and churchmen, the behaviour of Bolton's bourgeoisie conformed to what the reformer Ellice Hopkins identified as 'the selfish indifference of the higher and educated classes to the people's amusements'.[57]

Indifference might be better rendered as distaste, for the period witnessed a growing middle-class impatience with the workers. There had been something of a honeymoon period in class relations following recovery from the alarms of the 1840s: the working classes had distinguished themselves by their good behaviour on the 'shilling days' at the Great Exhibition, the workingman in arms had won admiration for his courage and steadiness in the Crimea and the Lancashire millhands had earned great praise for their stoic bearing during the cotton famine in the early 1860s. No doubt, too, others besides Mr Gladstone were heartened by the accumulating deposits of small investors in the Post Office Savings Bank. With the revival of reform agitation and the passage of the 1867 Reform Bill the working classes came under more critical scrutiny as 'Our New Masters' (a somewhat apprehensive designation), and it was discovered that the workingman was being paid too much, scamping his work, striking indiscriminately and spending his 'overplus' in reckless style. In 1873 *The Times* remarked tetchily that 'More wages and more idle time furnish this abundant leisure which is indeed the luxury of the so-called working classes.' 'Workingman worship', so the *Saturday Review* reported in the same year, 'has abated'; the workingman had become 'rather tiresome and exasperating'.[58]

The conspicuous pleasure of the masses gave particular offence where it was maintained in the face of financial exigencies in the business and professional world. The author of a theatre article in the *Daily News* in 1868, writing for an audience still presumably shaken by the collapse of the financial house of Overend and Gurney two years previously, confessed himself irritated by increasing working-class patronage of the theatre and music hall, at a time when 'the critical nature of commercial affairs demands that the middle-class man must ration the visits of his family in the interests of economy.' Such comparisons became more frequent and invidious as the economy met with later difficulties which threatened to halt the rising standard of middle-class living by the relative stagnation of their incomes. Reviewing the expenditure in an East End music hall in 1880, the journalist Ewing Ritchie was indignant that 'In these bad times, when people in the middle ranks of life are in despair at the hard prospect before them, here were these workingmen spending their two hundred pounds a night at least.'[59]

The offence was compounded when the workingman made his mass breakout from the urban ghetto and thrust himself in upon the privacy of his betters. After four weeks in Southend, reported Ritchie, 'I began to tremble at the very sight of an excursionist.' In the following childhood recollection of the descent of the 'townie' upon rural Derbyshire, the novelist Ouida expressed her repugnance more fully:

> The excursion trains used to vomit forth, at Easter and in Whitsun week, throngs of the millhands of the period, cads and their flames, tawdry, blowzy, noisy, drunken; the women with dress that aped 'the fashion', and pyramids of artificial flowers on their heads; the men as grotesque and hideous in their own way; tearing through woods and fields like swarms of devastating locusts, and dragging the fern and hawthorn boughs they had torn down in the dust, ending the lovely spring day in pot-houses, drinking gin and bitters, or heavy ales by the quart, and tumbling pellmell into the night train, roaring music-hall choruses; sodden, tipsy, yelling, loathsome creatures, such as make a monkey look a king, and the newt seem an angel beside humanity – exact semblance and emblem of the vulgarity of the age . . . vulgarity likely to live and multiply, and increase in power and in extent.

The magazine *Fun* provided regular graphic illustration of the boorishness of the workingman's leisure seen through middle-class eyes. In a representative cartoon on the rough's holiday, a suitably wart-encrusted blackguard confers with his mate:[60]

> Well, we ain't done a bad 'oliday 'ave we? We've broke lots of trees an' 'edges, an' spiled a luvley garding, an' trampled down some roses an' things, an' ruined all the lanes about here. Now let's set fire to a Common an' go 'ome to supper.

Yet, in one sense, reducing the workingman to this loutish stereotype may well have been comforting; a little gratuitous hooliganism was better than the fury of a Communard, and was small price to pay for its implicit confirmation of bourgeois superiority of manners and morals. The reality, however, was more insidious, for the broad advances in working-class leisure (in company with marked economic and political gains) threatened to obliterate the social differential between the classes. Contemplating the prospective 'plebification of art' in 1866, the journalist Matthew Browne remarked that 'social boundary lines are not so sharply drawn as they used to be. . . . In other words the old "cordon sanitaires" have snapped under the pressure of the multitudes, and we have not yet succeeded in twisting new ones.' This advance of the multitudes was more clearly defined by another writer, Keningale Cook, in a consideration of 'The Labourer's Leisure' in 1871:

> From being machines, fit only for machine work or inert quiescence, the masses are given the liberty of being men – gentlemen indeed, if in that term be applied the possession of leisure, the power of being 'at large' – a coveted attribute of gentility.

By the 1880s the implications of this development had made themselves very clear to the middle classes, for as Walter Besant noted,[61]

> they have perceived that their amusements – also, which seems the last straw, their vices – can be enjoyed by the base mechanical sort, insomuch that, if this kind of thing goes on, there must in the end follow an effacement of all classes.

In such circumstances the middle classes stood ready to defend the line of their own gentility with a judicious mixture of discrimination and neglect, and the reformers found themselves pulling against the stream. The latter were proposing to alleviate the tensions and degeneration in society through the fraternal association of all classes in leisure, at a time when the middle classes were acutely concerned to reinforce, not reduce, social distance.

5

Rational recreation in operation: the Working Men's Club movement

The Working Men's Club movement provides the most prominent example of rational recreation formally organised on a national scale. Fostered by the Working Men's Club and Institute Union, founded in 1862, the movement derived its momentum from middle-class initiative and support, yet by the 1880s the clubs had become exclusive working-class preserves, and the original designs of its mentors had been all but frustrated. The history of the movement provides further illustration of the social philosophy of rational recreation, while demonstrating the problems of putting it into practice.[1]

I

The idea of providing workingmen with social clubs which emphasised good fellowship rather than adult education clearly finds its antecedents in Heywood's Manchester Lyceums of the 1840s. Charles Knight, the publisher, also recalled a club in Birmingham in 1848 which was run by a hosiery manufacturer called Brookes, who advertised it as his own Ministry to the Poor, providing cheap food and reading rooms 'in an attempt to penetrate down to those classes which Mechanics' Institutes and Benefit Societies have never yet reached'. This sounds more like an exercise in relief than recreation, but the attempt to reach beyond the established working-class public for improvement and mutual assistance was one of the principal objectives of the Club movement as it developed. In Brighton in the same year, the Reverend Frederick Robertson founded a Working Men's Institute which, though short-lived, provided some early inspiration for Henry Solly, the subsequent founder of the CIU; its primary emphasis was on formal education, but Robertson's Institute has been awarded the title of the 'first recognisable workingmen's club'.[2]

Of the twenty or so clubs which emerged in the 1850s and satisfied the CIU's later search for a pedigree, the majority were rural. They were the

creations of paternalist landlords and clergymen anxious to counter the
beer-shops, whose spread had excited much more opposition from local
authorities in the country districts than in the towns. The Reverend
Sidney Godolphin Osborne, a shrewd observer of rural society (and, as
S.G.O., an indefatigable correspondent to *The Times*) wrote in 1852 of
the need for 'moral beer-houses', painting a picture of 'a simple retreat,
furnishing warmth and light, bread and cheese, baccy and beer under the
superintendence of a steward with no interest in beer sales'. Osborne's
description soon came to life in the establishment of Bastard's Club in
Blandford, Dorset (named after its founder and not its members, as Cole
and Postgate enjoy telling us) and several other clubs were in existence in
the southern counties by the middle of the decade. At Littlemore, near
Oxford, the local vicar formed a club for farm labourers which progressive
churchmen hailed as a timely experiment. At Rothamsted in Hertford-
shire, Sir John Lawes, the pioneer agricultural chemist, established a club
for the workers on his estate. The success of his experiment attracted a
visit from Dickens, who recorded his approval, noting that the sale of beer
in the new club – in limited amounts – had put the local village pub out of
business. Such a victory was the battle honour reformers were proudest to
display, but the mortality rate among these early village clubs was high,
and the few details of their careers which survive show clearly where
they were most vulnerable to working-class disaffection. The prohibition of beer which prevailed in most of these pioneer establishments was
much disliked, but the greater offence of the first club promoters in the
eyes of members was that of their intrusive supervision of club affairs, a
particular failing of the clergy.[3] These problems bulked large in the
history of the developing Club movement.

A handful of town clubs were also started in the 1850s. Temperance
was a common guiding light – literally so in the case of the Notting Hill
Workman's Hall where a working model of the Eddystone lighthouse
guided the converted to its doors – and clergymen were the commonest
promoters.[4] Among them was Henry Solly, who founded a Working
Men's Mutual Improvement and Recreation Society in Lancaster in
1860. The organised games at least pleased the local police sergeant – 'If
this thing goes on, sir, there'll soon be nothing for us to do' – but the
experiment was short-lived, and provided Solly with hard evidence of
the difficulties of establishing a constructive rapport between middle-
class patron and working-class members. He found the latter's behaviour
alternately encouraging and exasperating, as he reported to Lord
Brougham on the progress of his scheme; one week he was warmed by
their 'earnest, brotherly zeal', the next week, he was depressed by their

'miserable apathy'. Such vagaries no doubt bedevilled other town clubs, for they were not noticeably hardier than their country cousins.[5]

But Solly held faith with the club ideal, and it was largely through his energies that the CIU was founded in 1862, to encourage, supervise and co-ordinate the establishment of Working Men's Clubs across the country. Solly had found the ideal platform for propaganda in the Social Science Association, and it was in the course of its annual congress in London that year that his lobbying produced a meeting with other interested parties which established the Union.[6] The other founder members included philanthropic businessmen such as Edward Rathbone of Liverpool, the MP James Heywood, Edward Clarke, a young London lawyer interested in social reform, and the Reverend David Thomas who had pioneered clubs in the capital. Two workingmen were present among this predominantly middle-class assembly, one of whom, John Bainbridge, had been Solly's friend since the 1840s. Solly prevailed upon Lord Brougham to be the first president of the CIU, an early example of his success in attracting aristrocratic patronage. But the real work of the Union was done by a small secretariat, and its early history is dominated by successive secretaries. Of these, Solly himself, who held the post intermittently from 1862 to 1872 and remained an influential figure for several years thereafter, is most important. He embodied the CIU, and his credo exemplifies much that was common thinking behind rational recreation.

II

Solly's interest in working-class improvement was conditioned by his first-hand experience of class conflict in the 1840s. Born in 1814 into one of the well-educated and commercially prosperous London dissenting communities, Solly had been educated at London University and was destined initially for the family business; he chose instead to enter the Unitarian ministry, which took him to the West Country, where he became involved in the Chartist agitation. This was his first contact with working-class life and politics. He discovered a sympathy with the local Chartists who, as moral force men, impressed him by their intelligence and restraint as well as the basic justice of their case. It was in this company that he met Bainbridge, who later moved to London and served as something of a mascot for Solly in the early years of the CIU. Bainbridge clearly represented all that was best in working-class life for Solly, and was most likely the model for the eponymous hero of Solly's novel 'James Sandford, Carpenter and Chartist', a workingman who takes William Lovett for his hero and admits the good sense of working with rather than against middle-class reformism. After the excitements of the Chartist years, strenuous self-help brings Sandford the proprietorship of a small business, the happy-ever-after dénouement of the bourgeois prescription for working-class contentment. During the course of his progress, Sandford meets with and resists the appeals of the dark forces within the working-class community, represented by the physical force Chartists with their credulous infatuation with Feargus O'Connor. Thus for Solly the confrontations of the 1840s revealed two distinct and contrary faces to the working class.[7]

During these years Solly also learnt at first hand of the gulf between the classes; the elders of his church in Yeovil had been so affrighted by Chartism that they had threatened to withhold Solly's stipend when they learnt of his implication in the movement. Solly was a natural convert to Joseph Sturge's Complete Suffrage Union of 1842, which was formed expressly to effect a reconciliation between middle and working classes behind a reform programme free of all associations with O'Connorite militancy, and he enlisted as one of the movement's missionaries. His appetite for political reform subsided after the 1840s, and under the influence of Christian Socialism he turned to social questions. His continuing concern here was that the classes should work for improvement in concert, and thus preclude a return to the dangerous divisions of the Chartist years.

Solly's ambivalent attitude to the working classes persisted into the 1860s. At his most optimistic, Solly cast them as 'the new Greeks', whose genius for association would, when effectively released, renovate national life, which he considered dangerously decayed owing to the reckless competition and materialism of both the aristocracy and the middle class. But this same canker which was demoralising the upper levels of society was liable to disrupt those of the working classes necessarily cast as helots or worse:

Every advance in material prosperity presents increased temptations and facilities to the destitute and criminal classes for more DIRECT violations of the eighth commandment. What would a force of eight or nine thousand police be against the 150,000 roughs and villains whom, on some sufficiently exciting occasion, the metropolis might see arrayed versus law and order . . . we must not conceal from ourselves the possibility of Londoners having to live from time to time under the protection and even rule of the military; that again might raise the labouring classes throughout the country, and give us a civil or servile war.

The garotting scare in West End streets and a recent bread riot in the East End moved Solly to raise this spectre of insurrection in an address in 1868 to the Royal Society of Arts, and his warnings reflect the underlying nervousness among his class at the continuing combustibility of the masses, particularly in the capital.[8]

To Solly the achievement of a well-ordered and harmonious society depended upon educating the working classes to recognise that the existing system offered the best, and indeed the only guarantee that the interests of both capital and labour would be well and equitably served. The better elements among the workingmen would come to this realisation voluntarily if they could find sanctuary from the ignorant clamour of the pub and the baseness that lurked among their fellows; 'the more prudent, worthier members of the working class', noted Solly, 'are too often dragged down by their reckless, drinking, cowardly or dishonest neighbours.' The club was the right milieu within which the necessary education of the workingman could proceed; it provided firstly for recreation, which Solly recognised as a basic need of social welfare, but it also constituted an informal teaching situation into which more serious matters could gradually be introduced. The principle was explained in Solly's theory of the inclined plane:

> Begin by meeting the workingmen's humblest social wants for relaxation and amusement, and you may lift our hardworked brethren by degrees up to very respectable heights of knowledge and education. . . . You fail if you present the thick end of the plane first.

Accordingly, he explained, some incidental discussion on news of the day could lead to regular classes which, had they constituted the only item on the club programme, would have been impalatable to the average workingman. Head of the list of suggested topics was political economy. 'If they [workingmen] were asked at the outset to join such a class', Solly maintained, 'they would never consent; but if they once attended such classes, they would discover that political economists were not striving to enforce laws of their own or anybody's making, but simply seeking to interpret the laws of God.' Solly chose the word club for its associations of sociability and relaxation but the inclusion of institute in the Union's title was meant to indicate its serious educational intentions, and there was never any dissembling as to its ultimate purpose of social indoctrination.[9]

The success of the scheme was, in Solly's mind, very much dependent upon the participation of the middle and upper classes. They were to provide the initiative, the 'stimulus ab extra', as he called it. Working at the local level they would establish clubs according to the guidelines recommended by the CIU. The workers themselves were expected eventually to take over the complete management of the clubs, but the practice of social contact between the classes would by then be firmly implanted. It was an express purpose of the clubs: 'to form a centre of communication between men of all classes interested in the welfare of the people; to bring about a better understanding between men of different occupations and standings'. Communication would be facilitated by instructing workingmen in the proper forms of address and conversation – 'getting rid of that which makes men repellent in ordinary intercourse', as the wealthy Christian Socialist E. V. Neale explained in his club lectures on True Refinement. Cordiality and good manners would then allow such practical returns as the arbitration and conciliation of industrial disputes and 'the interchange of kind services'.[10]

Solly was indefatigable in pursuing his dream ('This is Mr Solly,' Henry Fawcett remarked drily to his wife, 'who thinks Heaven is made of working men's clubs') but his single-mindedness was a mixed blessing to the movement. Benjamin Hall, the CIU's first official historian, wrote that Solly had two jobs to do in his capacity as Union secretary: he had to obtain support, financial and moral, from non-workmen; and he had to interest the workmen themselves. He was more successful in the first task. Hall, who was not wholly uncritical of his predecessor, was none the less dazzled by Solly's skill in raising subscriptions, declaring that 'so comprehensive a list of distinguished men and women of the Victorian era, led by Lord Chancellors and Archbishops, was never before or since attracted to any scheme.' The tenacity with which Solly pursued aristocratic patronage bemused and ultimately exasperated Lord Lyttelton, who succeeded Brougham as president. Lyttelton confessed to the latter that he had allowed himself to succumb to 'our persevering friend', and be used 'as a jackal to get letters and opinions from the nobility'; he finally rebelled after 'ten years of ridiculous gyrations'.[11] There was something of the social climber in Solly which may have been anxious to compensate for the occasional ostracism he had suffered as a Unitarian, or may more simply have reflected the characteristic desire of his class for lordly contact and recognition; in any case, it is clear that he was more solicitous of noble than working-class company. Within the council of the CIU he rode roughshod over Thomas Paterson, the most prominent working-class member, and in 1870, when Solly was at issue with the council as a whole and attempted briefly to form a rival organisation, it is noticeable that though he contrived to redirect the subscriptions of most of the dukes and earls to his new scheme he was unable to command the allegiance of the rank-and-file club members. Paterson is an obscure figure and it would be too facile to interpret his clash with Solly in exclusively class terms, especially since the latter was told by James Hole that he was 'without exception the most deficient in tact of any man in a public capacity', a deficiency which, as we have seen, could exasperate an aristocrat as easily as an artisan.[12] But the court revolt against Solly was against his authoritarianism, and it is plain that this characteristic alienated workingmen with whom he worked in other improvement schemes. As one of them wrote:[13]

> Mr Solly's different attempts at similar movements have not recommended him to the working men. He has never worked unless allowed the entire lead as well as good pay. And has never been over-scrupulous in obtaining his ends.

It is doubtful if the lordly guineas that Solly attracted were always sufficient compensation for the ill-feeling generated by his often irascible missionary zeal.

III

The CIU grew but slowly during its early years and Hall identified various general difficulties that impeded its progress. Of these, 'The Great Beer Question' and the complications of patronage weighed heaviest. Beer was central to working-class culture but mostly abhorrent to middle-class reformers. Solly himself was an active teetotaller, and though the original prospectus for the CIU disclaimed any connexion with the Total Abstinence movement it recommended prohibition of the sale of liquor, and Solly mailed a copy of the prospectus to every Temperance society in the country.[14] Many of the clubs of the 1850s had been strictly teetotal and Hodgson Pratt, Solly's successor to the secretaryship, recollected that local cadres of Temperance workingmen, backed by discreet subsidies from wealthy sympathisers, had founded a substantial number of the new clubs following the inception of the Union in 1862. Pratt also recalled how unpopular these 'temperance shops' had been with other workingmen.[15] Brougham and Lyttelton of the Union council had from the outset advised Solly against enforcing prohibition. Lyttelton, who was an enthusiastic supporter of the CIU, took his model for the workingmen's clubs from the gentlemen's clubs of Pall Mall and St James's, and argued that drink in moderate amounts had a natural place in social life.[16] As a peer, he was more likely to prevail with Solly than other council members, but what seemed finally to effect the latter's

conversion to tolerance on the beer question was the respectable character of those clubs which had ignored the CIU ruling and sold beer to
their members from the beginning.

At several conferences in the mid- and late 1860s Solly heard the
workingmen's case: that they drank beer for the company rather than
from an unmanageable lust for beer; that tea and coffee were inadequate
refreshment after a shift down the mines or in the steel mills; and that the
clubs would foster moderation by moving men out of range of the publican with his encouragement of traditional customs of 'treating and
tossing'.[17] These arguments were not new – they were mostly common
enough counters to the Temperance case – but now they were proven in
practice, and were supported by club patrons who had been won over
from an initial hostility to strong drink. Union officials tried to promote
coffee as an alternative beverage and took club secretaries on tours of the
coffee taverns, but the clubmen were unimpressed by the 'black dose of
chicory soup' as a source of refreshment or good cheer, and by 1871
Henry Solly was to be found urging the Social Science Association to
recognise the fact that the great majority of British workmen were
'moderate drinkers' who would never join a club without beer. Thus the
CIU came to accept the sale of beer on club premises and, indeed,
yielded to another experiment in homeopathic therapy in these years by
allowing card games for moderate stakes.[18] The young Lord Rosebery
endeared himself to clubmen by delivering the final blow for tolerance at
the thirteenth annual meeting of the Union four years later. As guest
speaker he declared that each club 'should be free from all vexations and
childish restrictions on the supply of intoxicating drinks and all similar
matters.'[19]

The patronage issue constituted a more obstinate problem than the
Great Beer Question, though the two were closely connected, for the
prohibition of beer exemplified the tight control which most early
patrons considered appropriate for club members. Drawing on their
experience of other promotions, several speakers to the Social Science
Association had warned of workingmen's resentment of manipulation
and autocracy, but club patrons were confident that they knew best. As
Ben Hall remarked: 'It may be taken for granted that what took place in
the majority of clubs in the first year of our Union was not what the
members wished, but what was ALLOWED.' After ten years' acquaintance with the CIU an artisan reported to *The Times* that little had
changed; the clubs, he maintained, offered only a secular version of 'the
cup of tea and tract formula'. Solly was aware of the members' criticisms
and in one of the Union pamphlets explaining club philosophy to

prospective patrons he reproduced one of the workingmen's complaints: 'We have masters all day long, and we don't want them at night.' The motto of the movement, emphasised Solly, must be 'Supplement, not supersede'. The middle classes must prime the pump, but the workers were to be given every encouragement to work towards independent management, and Union policy recommended that at least half the members of any club's governing committee should be bona fide workingmen. Patrons, advised Solly, must conduct themselves as friends, not masters.[20]

Solly's own overbearing manner reveals how difficult it was to reconcile this prescription with existing class roles; moreover, however much confidence Union propaganda expressed in the workingman, Solly and other middle-class supporters of the movement had considerable misgivings about his ability to initiate or maintain an orderly and efficient organisation. As one otherwise encouraging article on the clubs pointed out when the CIU was formed: 'if such institutions are left entirely to the working classes they will be deficient in power, method and stability, and for want of the conservative element will be ever in danger of falling to pieces.'[21] At the inaugural tea party of the Bolton WMC Edmund Ashworth warned:[22]

> We shall always find a number of men, perhaps, whose education has been acquired in the pub, and the improprieties of such characters will be difficult to control, except you have a vigorous committee and an absolute authority to enforce good order. You may find sometimes a little difficulty but I suggest that absolute authority be placed in the hands of one individual and that the committee be always at hand to support his authority.

In recounting the history of the early years Hall confessed: 'As we know now, failure lay principally in the fact that the clubs were not spontaneously originated and democratically controlled.' In explanation he offered the standard apologia that workingmen then 'were little capable of the thought of, or the power to originate and manage clubs until taught and inspired by others.'[23]

Certainly, outside support was often invaluable in establishing clubs; granting premises, guaranteeing rents and mortgages, advancing loans, providing a legal umbrella – these were services the working classes could not easily provide for themselves. But members objected to the further tutelage they were obliged to accept, 'the cup of tea and tract formula' that included censorship of entertainments and a ban on all political discussion.[24]

The CIU oligarchy was particularly anxious to keep politics out of the clubs. Solly had promoted the club ideal as non-sectarian in matters of religion and politics – 'a green spot', as one of his supporters once put it, 'where all shades of opinion, creed, or calling can meet in harmony with one another'. Though he was sympathetic to the London junta of trade union leaders he shut George Howell out of the CIU council in 1866 as an undesirable agitator, and in 1870, when he was joint editor of the *Beehive* for a few months, he tried hard to counter-balance the radical views of George Potter, the founder of the famous working-class paper. 'Politics', Solly once declared, in a desperately ingenuous remark, 'should be studied without reference to politics.' He feared that the working classes would return to the political adventurism of thirty years before and destroy the likelihood of achieving the fraternal class consensus he yearned for.[25] W. T. Marriott, QC, a long-standing supporter and council member of the CIU, told a union soirée in the early 1880s that he would say nothing against political clubs, but he much preferred social clubs, because in the latter there would be more fair play (loud cries of 'No' and 'Yes')'. Fair play in the early years of the CIU had meant no play; in the 1870s, as middle-class control of individual clubs was supplanted, many of them provided strong political content, and by 1881 Solly estimated their number at between 500 and 600.[26]

Friction between patrons and members appeared least in small towns, and it was this type of club which fared best in the first years of the CIU's history. In a list of 103 clubs known to the Union in 1869 only nine were in the big towns or manufacturing districts; two years later, despite an overall increase in number, the proportions had scarcely changed. It was a small town which provided the Union executive with its model club – Wisbech WMC in Cambridgeshire. Hodgson Pratt awarded Wisbech first prize after a tour of clubland in 1870, and it represented the ideal to him and Solly for more than a decade. Its patrons were drawn from the prominent local Quaker family, the Peckovers, and in a town of 9,000 it enjoyed a membership of over 800 workingmen. It incorporated its own co-operative society, savings bank, library and allotment scheme; it stayed teetotal and, in Solly's words, 'eschewed polemics'. Strong traditions of deference and a marked community identity gave the club its stability. The other successful clubs which impressed Pratt during his tour were in Bridlington and North Ormesby, and one of the few enthusiastic reports from workingmen in these years came from Scarborough, another small urban centre.[27]

The halting progress of the movement in the large towns and cities reflected the tensions of a more divisive class society. CIU reports attributed slow growth in the capital to the fragmented nature of its working-class community and the abundant rival attractions of a great city. Solly felt that the root of the problem lay with the trade societies. The Union encouraged workmen to use club premises for their trades' and friendly societies meetings rather than the pub, but London trade societies' leaders feared the employer's hand in this, for during the 1859 builders' strike the masters had attempted to set up workingmen's institutes to supplant the existing houses of call and shelter and indoctrinate non-unionised labour. Solly met with the trades' leaders and went some way to appeasing their fears, but there were still considerable working-class misgivings about the motives of the Union patrons, and the annual meeting of 1866 remarked on 'the suspicion with which the great mass of workmen view the Union'.[28]

Just as the workingmen held back, so too did those 'men of higher social position' whose assistance the CIU considered so necessary to success. Few of the vice-presidents whose names adorned the Union's prospectus sponsored their own clubs. The treasurer of the Wellclose Square WMC in the East End of London reported on 'the utter indifference of most of the wealthy employers of labour who amass their money here, but spend it elsewhere'. The indifference was not confined to London, and appears as much a measure of studied retaliation as of insensibility, for the annual report of 1873 acknowledged that 'In several localities we have found a determination on the part of employers to refuse any aid towards the establishment of these clubs – the result of the unfortunate disputes which have arisen between them and those they employ.' When the first Working Men's Club in Bolton was in a state of imminent collapse in 1869, the *Chronicle* warned that its members could expect no subvention from employers while industrial relations were strained. Thus were the new clubs afflicted by the very problems they were supposed to remedy.[29]

But the club idea met real working-class needs and workingmen gradually overcame the problems of absent or overbearing patronage by founding their own clubs or discharging the original middle-class promoters as redundant. Some workingmen had formed their own clubs in the first decade of the CIU's history, but the practice became noticeably widespread in the mid-1870s; the annual report for 1873 which remarked on the hostility of employers also noted the increasing number of applications for CIU advice from workingmen – 'The idea of no patronage', it noted, 'grows fast.' As examples the report referred to the establishment of an independent WMC in St Austell in Cornwall, and the emancipation of the Wednesbury WMC in Staffordshire, where members had succeeded to self-government by kicking out their 'sluggish' gentleman patrons. Established clubs assisted their new neighbours, and members pooled their trade skills to convert and furnish premises whose amenities were often thus superior to those provided by patrons – as one observer remarked, 'Many friends of the working classes think that they have done all that is necessary when they have provided a building like a cab stable or a wash-house.'[30]

The sale of beer was of great assistance in the development towards worker control of the movement, for it provided valuable revenue. From Maidstone, the local Working Men's Clubs made the following report to the Union's house journal in 1873: 'The members have made the discovery that the profit on beer is about 30%, and brings them double what they have to pay for rent, though the quantity sold does not average two pints per person per week.' Once a club was self-supporting it could become self-governing. So went Maidstone WMC, and so went many others.[31] It should be noted here too that the sale of beer indirectly encouraged a greater responsibility among club members, for it obliged the clubs to fight a long defensive action against the publicans' trade protection societies which contested the legality of club liquor sales. Good order and scrupulous attention to the conditions of membership were thus necessary to assure the clubs of their continued status as private institutions exempt from official licensing requirements.[32]

By 1878 an outside observer estimated that 52 per cent of the clubs were wholly self-supporting, and five years later Pratt put the figure at 75 per cent. Membership figures indicate the overall growth in the same period: in 1874 membership was put at 90,000, in 1878 at 150,000, in 1880 at 320,000 and by 1883 was estimated to have passed the half-million mark. The expansion was particularly marked in the London area where the number of clubs rose from 82 to 120 between 1876 and 1882.[33]

It was the London clubs which took the lead in attacking the last stronghold of patronage. For though the clubs increasingly controlled their own affairs, they were almost completely unrepresented on the CIU council. A handful of the more politically minded London clubs began to protest the middle-class monopoly of council offices by refusing to contribute to CIU funds and forming a virtually independent London branch of the Union in 1881 (the forerunner of the Metropolitan Federation of Radical Clubs of 1886). The withholding of subscriptions hurt the Union. Solly complained to the Social Science Association that it was being 'mischievously crippled', and by 1883 the council realised that it could no longer survive on the hand-outs of honorary vice-presidents and agreed to a conference on the question of finances and club representation. Here the longstanding complaints of club members found full and forcible expression. One working-class delegate put it thus:

> The Union has reached a crisis in its history. It must either be patronising or self-supporting. It cannot be the former and must either become the latter or cease to exist. . . . A great deal has been said about abolishing class distinctions but under the present system these existed in the constitution of the Union itself.

Another workingman registered 'a strong protest versus patronage', before meeting criticisms which must have been used to block working-class representation before:

> The working men have a right to work out their own aims. It is absurd to say they cannot maintain and work the Union – they must take it in hand at once, for at present there was no faith in it.

Council members repeated the Union's aims of eradicating class feeling, talking bluntly of the need to deflate the bigots in fustian as well as in broadcloth. Solly was afraid that a sudden working-class takeover would alienate subscribers to Union funds. But the working-class delegation claimed that such dependence was not only demeaning but unnecessary if the CIU could command the complete allegiance of its members, and, following a series of meetings in committee, the delegation carried the day with the passage of New Model Rules, which secured direct club representation on the CIU council. J. J. Dent became the Union's first working-class secretary on the resignation of Hodgson Pratt.[34] In Manchester there was to be a similar victory over the class exclusiveness of the district headquarters, and at the annual general meeting in 1884 Thomas Brassey pronounced the Union justly democratised.[35]

IV

Who were these first generations of clubmen and what was club life like? Hard evidence is difficult to come by, but it seems that the movement attracted members from across a wide range of working-class society. The CIU had never recommended imposing any test of membership (or conditions of dress) and advised only a lower age limit of eighteen years. Henry Mayhew, whose categories are generally reliable, visited London clubs where membership comprised 'lower middle class', well-to-do artisans and petty tradesmen', others where membership was 'confined to the labouring rather than the artisan class'. Some club secretaries agreed in recognising a caste distinction between mechanics and labourers which determined local membership, but the majority of references suggest a broad mix of members within each club. The Scarborough club reported that its members included 'the better class of workmen, the indifferent, those who spend their spare time in drinking and loose company, and some of the offscourings of society'. The Leeds club ran the gamut 'from respectable artisans to the low fellows who may be seen leaning against the walls of public houses'. On the evidence of the minutes of the Newcastle upon Tyne WMC it may have been true that it was the skilled craftsman who dominated the club committees, but it seems likely that in general the clubs recruited by neighbourhood rather than particular trades.[36]

The self-evident fact of the clubs' exclusively male membership should not go unremarked, for it seems to have been a matter of popular preference within the movement as much as it was part of the original design of the middle-class founders. Union officials do appear to have been somewhat embarrassed on this point; they justified the exclusion of wives and families on simple logistical grounds, claiming none the less that in insulating the head of the family from bad company and raising the moral tone of his recreations they were contributing indirectly to the improvement of home life among the working class. The membership in general does not seem to have been anxious to reverse official policy, for though the question of the admission of womenfolk was raised at two successive annual conferences in the mid-1870s it provoked little in the way of popular response.[37]

There was some adverse comment on the quality of club membership. Hodgson Pratt complained in the 1880s of 'the lack of some sort of intellectual or educational backbone' to the movement, and was disturbed at what he felt was a 'complete separation' between the clubs and other working-class organisations such as the co-operative societies (of which he was himself an active supporter). Frederick Rogers, in what seems to be the only contemporary working-class autobiography to record club life in any detail, maintained that 'the clubs did not attract the more intellectual of the working classes; these were in the trade union movement or the co-operative world.'[38] Such comment is not to be disregarded – particularly since this kind of charge became more common by the 1890s – but neither should it be left unchallenged. At Newcastle and Wisbech, for example, local co-operative societies used the Working Men's Clubs' premises, which argues some mutual acquaintance, and during the campaign for the Third Reform Bill in 1884 the *Club and Institute Journal* reported that 'the affiliated clubs formed no mean part of the procession, although somewhat short of numbers through the fact that many of their members fell in with the various trades unions.' James Beal, the middle-class chairman of the Metropolitan Municipal Reform Association, found that the clubs in Chelsea at which he lectured were composed of 'the most intelligent workingmen of the district in all cases', and Stan Shipley's researches into metropolitan club life reveal programmes of lectures and discussions which fulfil his claims that certain of the clubs constituted an artisans' university.[39] The vigorously intellectual club was no doubt an exception in the movement as a whole, and would have been too iconoclastic in the content of its debate to recommend itself to Pratt and the Union council, but the weekly reports in the club press record a regular diet of literary and scientific talks, dramatic readings and discussions, which demonstrates that club life was far from mindless. Perhaps it was the unabashed informality of the clubs – the constant traffic, the cries of the pie-boy and the pot-boy, the smoking and bantering – which produced a bad press among middle-class visitors. For Rogers, fired with the enthusiasm of the working-class auto-didact, disenchantment came in the middle of his Sunday morning lecture on Shakespeare, when the club chairman called a break to let the man come round with the beer.[40]

Certainly in these years the clubs were not passive institutions, and as patronage receded they made themselves heard on an increasing range of public questions. The Newcastle upon Tyne club petitioned Parliament on several occasions in the 1860s: on the franchise question, the Alabama Dispute and the Contagious Diseases Act. Several clubs in London and the provinces applied for membership of the republican-flavoured Land and Labour League in 1870, and there was considerable protest from metropolitan clubs at the grant of funds to the Prince of Wales for his Indian trip in 1875. The London clubs also spoke out against sabbatarianism and the anti-music hall lobby, and took a considerable interest in local municipal politics. There are echoes of this kind of activism in Lancashire.[41]

But the main function of the clubs was to provide for 'the humbler wants' of its members, and this they did admirably. They provided a set of permanent premises for recreation to an extent which no other organisation or movement could match. Illustrations of club interiors seem cheerless to us, but the rooms were kept clean, well-lit and warm, a far remove from the condition of much working-class housing. They were genuine recuperative refuges, free from commercial pressures, ritual drinking, police harassment, district visitors and the wife and family.[42] With their lectures, concerts, indoor and outdoor games, excursions and picnics, Christmas clubs, coal clubs and sick clubs, they provided, at modest cost, the facilities of the public library, music hall, pub, playing field and friendly society combined.

The spare and functional aspect of the clubrooms was relieved by the feeling of community generated by the members, a factor that impressed otherwise critical visitors such as Rogers and Walter Besant. This had not been an instant accomplishment. In the early years members had missed the commanding central figure of the landlord and the familiar atmosphere of the pub – one man complained that he missed the pot-boy in particular, for here at least had been someone he could order about after a day of taking orders. When drink was introduced the Union urged club stewards to play the part of the host, but as simple dispensers of beer they lacked the traditional substance of the publican.[43] The style of the Working Men's Club as it evolved was much less monocentric than that of the pub, and management by committee made authority more self-effacing. Something of the essence of club life and of the typical clubman is conveyed in this character sketch by Rogers of James Lowe, the greatly respected president of the Hackney WMC:[44]

> He was a man with a good fund of general information but was not in any large sense an educated man. He was not a great orator; he was a moderately good speaker, and that was all. . . . He had the frank geniality which the workman loves, knew his own limitations and never presumed on his position, devoted himself absolutely to the well-being of the club and its ideals, and in his interpretation of them was only just a little ahead of his followers.

Club government was none the less forceful for being by committee. Mayhew had remarked on the perfect decorum in the clubs he visited on his London tour. He had, he said 'witnessed NOT ONE single case of drunkenness, nor riot, nor coarse language'. At the Newcastle upon Tyne club, which was self-managed, the committee appointed a super-intendent who patrolled the clubrooms, alert for drunkenness, 'ungentlemanly language' or petty corruption on the part of the bagatelle marker. The club hired up to a dozen policemen to keep order at the annual picnic. Members who were expelled or suspended for some breach of the regulations anxiously solicited for reinstatement, for membership was obviously highly valued and the rules generally respected. This concern for good order and good manners fulfilled something at least of the original intentions of Solly and his friends.

How close had the CIU come to realising its founder's designs? The clubs' historian provided one answer: 'The sphere of the workman's club, wrote B. T. Hall in 1912, 'is smaller in circumference than was at first projected by the Pioneer, and immeasurably smaller in its results.'[45] Measured against Solly's expectations, this would also stand as a fair judgement of the reach and progress of the organised Club movement in the first twenty years or so of its life. The good order that obtained was obscured by the fug of tobacco smoke and the clatter of glasses, and if club members were not barbarians they would hardly yet have passed as the new Greeks. The workingmen who gradually assumed control of the clubs were bent on improvement, but though they moved up Solly's inclined plane they were bound for a different destination and – most disappointing of all – they expressly rejected the guiding hand of their social superiors. The resolution of class differences through 'the friendly discussion of capital and labour' clearly begged too many questions about the outside world of the 1870s and 1880s, and in struggling to construct their own life within the clubs the members revealed the instincts of an authentic class consciousness and the continuing strengths of an independent culture. Yet in their willingness to allow beer in the clubs Solly and other bourgeois patrons had come closer to an informed and committed tolerance of that culture than the great majority of their fellows, for they had after all been prepared to modify social patterns to accommodate behaviour that others tried simply to eradicate. It was ironic that it was this concession which gave the working-class members the economic self-sufficiency that enabled them to unship their mentors.

6

Rational recreation and the new athleticism

One of the more remarkable features of the expanding world of mid-Victorian leisure was the innovation of organised and codified athletic sports – a broad category of activities which comprised primarily the athletics of track and field events, as the term is understood today, together with a reconstructed version of football, and the previously reformed game of cricket. In the 1860s public school men began to carry their enthusiasm for the reformed canon of athletic sports through into adult life, and by the Jubilee year of 1887 Gladstone was pointing to the popularity of these sports as a measure of the nation's improved taste in recreation. 'For the schoolboy and the man alike', he observed, 'athletics are becoming an ordinary incident of life.'[1] Thereafter the practice spread still more widely and moved one reputable historian of the period to contend that 'the suburban middle class made organised games rank among England's leading contributions to world culture.'[2] In today's world sport is recognised as a powerful instrument for commanding social conformity, with a unique role to play in counteracting divisive forces such as class and race.[3] How did it commend itself to the Victorians, and what part did it play in the prescriptions of rational recreation?

I

There were those contemporaries who were persistently hostile to the growing cult of organised games, but they need not detain us long; the intellectual strengths of their case could do little to check the tide of popular enthusiasm. John Ruskin, Matthew Arnold and Wilkie Collins were among those who attacked the worship of athletics as boorish and dehumanising. In 1869 Collins enjoyed considerable literary success with his novel *Man and Wife* in which the central figure, Geoffrey Delamayn, is an athlete whose life is brutalised by his sport. In the preface Collins makes it quite clear that Delamayn represents a new type, 'the rough in broadcloth', who constitutes a serious menace to society.[4] Recalling this indictment some twenty years later, Montague Shearman, barrister, athlete and author of discerning and respected handbooks on sport, commented that the English public had admired the story but refused to swallow its message; to Shearman it was by then self-evident that 'the athletic movement has benefited the people at large.'[5]

For the most part the new-style athleticism won a good press and recommended itself as an eminently rational, even spiritual, recreation. In mid-Victorian England, in particular, the preoccupation with the maintenance of national military preparedness led to a new respect for physical education. In the 1830s and 1840s reformers had talked of the Health of Towns; the capitalised imperative in following decades became the Health of the Nation. The shift is significant. The previous concern had been that the disease and misery of the new manufacturing towns would demoralise the working classes, make them easy prey for the political agitator, and lead them to subversion and revolt. After 1848 the fear of the governing classes was of assault from without, more than from within. In 1850, contemplating the welter of self-congratulation at England's escape from the fires of the continental revolutions, John Stores Smith, a Manchester businessman, declared England 'the forlorn hope of European life'. Smith was impressed less by the fact of her survival than by the extent of her vulnerability which, in the light of his study of other once-great nations, suggested the danger of immediate decline. This theme gained currency. In 1852, in the course of reviewing the activities and publications of the growing number of vegetarian and homeopathic societies, the *Westminster Review* – while enjoying itself a little at the expense of the 'potato gospel' – pointed out 'how unfailing an accompaniment of the decline of empires is the depreciation of the national habit of body'. A proper concern for the nation's health, continued the journal, came 'just in time for that great contest with European tyranny during the remainder of the century, which is apparently to be the part of England and America'.[6] The Crimean War, the invasion scare of 1859 and the dramatic rise of Prussia increased alarm at the imminence of such a contest, and gave new emphasis to the traditional utility of sport in preserving the fitness of the nation's physical stock. Thus the Volunteers played their games in the service of England's security.[7]

The call for effective exercise was addressed to town dwellers of all classes, for the debilities of city life seemed to threaten rich as well as poor. Of the former, Leslie Stephen noted in 1870:

The class which does not live by manual labour, and which at the same time has very little opportunity for hunting and fishing, has increased

in an enormous ratio, and is still increasing. We are living more and
more in towns and treading closer upon each other's heels.

Though he was apprehensive at the dangers that the popularity of
athletic sports posed to intellectual life at the universities, Stephen
allowed that they met the need for physical recreation ('some good
stupid amusement') for the urban middle classes. Some traditional prescriptions were in any case now simply impractical – as John Morley
pointed out, 'the persistence of doctors in urging horse exercise is, to
the majority, absurd.'[8] Among this majority were the clerks and shopmen, whose work, according to *The Times*, demanded only the slightest
of physiques: 'Civilisation wants light men – they don't want six feet to
vault over counters and run up steps at a draper's shop.' At the time of
the Crimean War the paper warned that the nation could not rely upon
such insubstantial material to win future Inkermans, unless nimbleness
was reinforced with muscle and stamina. Thirty years later, in a survey
of modern English sport, Frederick Gale concluded that only organised
games had saved the 'counter skippers' from effeminacy.[9] The working
classes were never in danger of effeminacy, but city life blighted their
health to an extent which alarmed doctors and disappointed recruiting
sergeants. William Hardwicke, medical officer for health in Padding-
ton in the 1860s, urged the case for state promotion of games and
gymnastic exercises to halt this degeneration, and Lord Brabazon,
chairman of the Gardens and Playgrounds Association, moved the
same case twenty years later on the evidence that nearly half the
recruits seeking enlistment in the services were rejected for physical in-
capacity.[10]

Physical recreation received further endorsement from major contemporary figures. We have seen in a previous chapter how Charles Kingsley imparted a spiritual gloss to sport and bodily exercise. His emphasis
upon their necessary practice as a duty to one's country became more
insistent after his conversion to Darwinism (an ideology whose popularity increased the general concern over national health). Another
Darwinian, Herbert Spencer, maintained that 'the contests of commerce
are in part determined by the bodily endurance of the producers.'[11]

Under the influence of such teachings sport became a medium for
training the young to meet with the diverse challenges of a naturally
harsh and competitive world – 'Games', declared the physician to Rugby
School, 'produce a just ambition to excel in every phase of the battle of
life.'[12] The language of games became the language of adventure and the
highest endeavour, designed to sustain the young under fire, whether

from fast bowlers or insurgent tribesmen. A Scottish divine expressed his delight at a youthful game of cricket in the following terms:[13]

> How I love to mark the quick, watchful glance of the eye as the ball comes speeding on which will decide for 'our Club' the honour of the day, and to mark on the faces of those who go out, the look which was on that of François I as he wrote to his mother after the battle of Pavia, 'Tout est perdu hormis l'honneur.'

In Newbolt's popular poem *Vitai Lampada*, it is the voice of a schoolboy that rallies the ranks during some desperate desert action: 'Play up! Play up! and play the game!'

The public school was the principal laboratory in which the young were exposed to sport as a test for greater things to come, and it was here that the games ethos was refined. Men like Dr Arnold at Rugby had promoted organised games to instil discipline and self-government in schoolboys who, in the unreformed public schools of the early nineteenth century, had often sought their recreation in organised riot.[14] The full returns on this practice stood out clearly by the 1880s when Edward Lyttelton considered the merits of public school athletics:[15]

> Firstly by being forced to put the welfare of the common cause before selfish interests, to obey implicitly the word of command, and act in concert with the heterogeneous elements of the company he belongs in; and secondly, should it so turn out, a boy is disciplined by being raised to a post of command, where he feels the gravity of responsible office and the difficulty of making prompt decisions and securing a willing obedience.

Personal courage tempered by the team spirit, and a respect for authority under the governance of fair play – these were the key values in the new rationale of sport, and also served as important social controls off the field. Devotees of sport internalised its values: N. L. Jackson, a prominent and influential athlete of the 1880s and 1890s, decorated his memoirs with an ample definition of sportsmanship, to which he attributed lessons in self-control, compassion and honesty, maintaining in conclusion that 'it unconsciously directs every action of your life.' 'Athleticism', asserted Charles Box, cricket writer and popular philosopher, 'is no unimportant bulwark of the constitution. . . . [it] has no sympathy with Nihilism, Communism, nor any other "ism" that points to national disorder.' Contemporaries felt too that the values of the games field could be fed back into business life to correct the unrelieved materialism and excessive appetite for speculation that seemed to have superseded what were represented as the essentially moral endeavours of the pioneer heroes of nineteenth-century capitalism.[16]

Sport could be effective in indoctrinating hoi polloi as well as public schoolmen. A testimony on this count comes from H. B. Philpott, an early historian of the London School Board:[17]

> It is as true for the children of mechanics and labourers, as for the children of merchants and professional men, that manly sports, played as they should be played, tend to develop unselfish pluck, determination, self-control and public spirit. Observe a group of Board School cricketers after they have undergone a period of friendly supervision. . . . No one quarrels with the placing of the field . . . the young captain does not bawl 'butter fingers' or 'silly fathead' whenever a catch is missed . . . the batsman bowled for a duck neither shouts that 'it ain't fair' nor punches the umpire. . . . No, they have learned to 'play the game'. And the change is not a matter of cricket only; in becoming better cricketers they have become better boys.

Philpott also remarked on the 'moral salvation' effected by football, but it is significant that he should pay most attention to the social therapies of cricket, for it was this game which was constantly made to serve as a metaphor for the ideal society. Although there was a thoroughgoing commercial sector in cricket, the general banishment of gambling from the game recommended it as a reformed sport. It carried with it long-standing associations of a bucolic, pre-industrial society; it was in fact a perfect vehicle for the myths of Merrie England. Cricket, wrote one representative commentator in the course of a political reform tract of the late 1850s, afforded 'a happy and compendious illustration of English characteristics and English social institutions . . . the truly English republican element of a mixture of classes with the right man in the right place, is nowhere better exemplified than in the cricket field.'[18] The game was applauded as a civilising influence in the new towns, not least because it was credited with disciplining the spectator as well as the participant. Recording progress in Yorkshire, John Lawson observed that 'it is not uncommon now [1887] for the people of Pudsey to be seen applauding their opponents by clapping hands' (the reactions of sixty years previous had been somewhat more curmudgeonly).[19]

Thus the new model athletic sports boasted some impeccable credentials: they provided a regimen which brought physical fitness to the individual, toughening him against the debilities of city life and maintaining his readiness for armed service; they also provided an education in self-discipline and team work which acted as a moral police over the individual's life at large; adapted to the new circumstances of modern society they yet retained sentimental historical associations of social harmony and the fraternity of all classes in sport. At the very least they were recommended as an antidote for what, by all accounts, seems to have been the common complaint of Victorian town dwellers – indigestion.

II

Given then the patently 'rational' nature of athletic sports or organised games we would expect them to have been widely promoted among the working classes. Yet such was not the case. As H. A. Butler-Johnstone, MP, pointed out to the House of Commons in 1875, 'it is no answer to the complaint that large classes are deprived of the advantages of athletics and outdoor sports to say that other classes are devoted to these exercises.' It was only in the late 1880s, and then with doubtful enthusiasm, that Shearman could record: 'The athletic movement which commenced with the "classes", and first drew its strength from the Universities and public schools, has finally, like most other movements and fashions, good or bad, spread downwards to the masses.'[20] The story of the cultural spin-off during these years records the obstacles in the way of achieving in sport the social liaison which had long been preached by those interested in the reform of recreation.

First, there was little provision or encouragement for athletic games in the educational world outside the public schools. Clearly one of the problems was lack of space. An assistant commissioner enquiring into popular education in the 1860s deplored the absence of playgrounds and organised games in working-class schools, and Thomas Okey, who was a boy in Spitalfields at this time, echoed the complaint of many a working-class autobiography in recalling that the streets were the only playing fields of his youth – as athletic practice he swam in the canal, for there were no games at his National School. The Education Act of 1870 did little to remedy such deficiencies. Philpott, whom we have quoted on the beneficent effect of properly supervised sport on board school boys in London, nevertheless found physical education 'one of the least satisfactory features of the Board's work' and described some of the problems impeding its progress. The children's interest in and capacity for playing sport was restricted by deficiencies of diet and of pocket money, and in the long absence of playing fields their cultural traditions stopped short with the games of the street. Some teachers had worked hard to promote sport, said Philpott, but most of them were too intent on the struggle of bringing each scholar up to the point of passing the government inspector; under the system of payment by results it was difficult for them to introduce anything not encouraged by the official code.[21]

The neglect of games in elementary schools was not, however, due simply to the dearth of play space but also to the specific social function assigned to these schools in educational policy. The Clarendon report on public schools in 1861 had recognised the value of sport in character training, but in terms of the State's provision it was training reserved for society's leaders, not the led. Physical education for working-class children meant not games, but drill. Edwin Chadwick was prominent among those who made a strong argument for drill in the 1860s and pressed their case upon Forster, the author of the 1870 Act. Drill would provide industrial training for each new generation of the labour force and paramilitary training for a potential citizens' army. The economics of the scheme were spelled out in detail – with such training, claimed Chadwick, three might eventually do the work of five and, if a boy was taught to walk with a more even step, he might do with one less pair of boots over the year. Drill found its way into the schools' curriculum and, unlike sport, qualified for a grant. The school boards welcomed drill: it helped control unruly classes; it made efficient use of limited space (drill could be practised in the classroom gangways if there was no playground at all); the children often enough enjoyed it, and it was not unpopular with parents (a man who was in school in Swindon in the 1880s recalled forming squares and doing elementary rifle drill with broomsticks – 'My father, a John Bright liberal, didn't object'). Gymnastic exercises provided an occasional supplement to drill but there was no teaching of athletic skills which might later enrich the adult life of board school children. Indeed, one authority talked as though physical education during schooldays was the only such training most working-class children would receive, 'in as much as, after an early age, they have little or no time for recreation like those socially above them.'[22]

In the adult world, even where time was available, working-class participation was limited by the restrictive rulings of the new governing bodies of the various athletic sports. As an example we may take the policy of the influential Amateur Athletic Club, formed in 1866 'to afford as completely as possible to all classes of Gentleman Amateurs the means of practising and competing versus one another without being compelled to mix with professional runners'. For the AAC an amateur was further defined as[23]

Any person who has never competed in an open competition, or for public money, or for admission money, or with professionals for a prize, public money or admission money, and who has never, at any period of his life, taught or assisted in the pursuit of athletic exercises as a means of livelihood, or is a mechanic, artisan or labourer.

The barring of mechanics, artisans and labourers was also standard policy for the Amateur Rowing Association and the Bicycle Union. The justification for this common barring clause was that those whose habitual mode of life involved physical labour would enjoy a built-in advantage in athletic contests which would preclude genuine competition. We may recall too the principle of antithesis in the Victorian rationale of recreation which maintained that the most appropriate recreations were those which provided the greatest contrast with a man's work. By this test it could be argued that the leisure needs of the muscular workman were best served by mental rather than physical exercise.

Some members of the new athletic clubs were anxious to keep out the lower orders to spare themselves the embarrassment of an unwonted physical intimacy in the dressing tent – 'a matter of some importance to a sensitive person'[24] – but a more basic explanation for the discrimination against the mechanic, artisan or labourer lay in the fundamentally new attitude of the middle class to the practice of sport. This gave a further emphasis to the distance between bourgeois and popular cultures, and is exemplified in the contrast between the new model athletic sports of the AAC and the popular athletics of 'pedestrianism' – the sub rosa world of professional running and walking races.

Pedestrianism was eccentric and undisciplined. Its contests were frequently bizarre – walking backwards, racing in heavily weighted clogs, picking up stones (or eggs) at regular intervals over a long distance, trundling barrow loads of bricks – and often seemed little removed from traditional rural feats of brute strength and endurance.[25] The sport had a long previous history of gentlemanly patronage – masters had chosen footmen for their running prowess, and backed them against those of rival households in matches which they themselves had often joined[26] – but upper-class interest and participation had waned considerably by the 1850s. In an article on gaming, betting, lotteries and insurance, 4 December 1852, *Chambers's Edinburgh Journal* reported:

In pedestrianism . . . we occasionally hear of gentlemen whose emulation impels to a contest, which they may spice with a bet of 100 guineas or so; but the competitors, in most instances where money passes, are poor men, who literally walk or run for their bread; the match is generally concocted by a tavern-keeper, who plans it so as to make it a matter of business. The individuals who outrage nature by walking 1000 miles in 1000 successive half-hours, and such like feats, are mostly publicans' protégés.

While shedding its old patrons, the sport had become extremely popular. The élite among the professionals, bearing heroic and flamboyant names – the Gateshead Clipper, the Norwich Milk Boy, the Crow Catcher, and the like – raced for championship cups and belts before crowds of several thousands at major pedestrian enclosures in the big cities. It was an unruly business, to judge from the notices of pedestrian meetings appearing in the sporting press of the period. From a match promoted by the landlord of the Yorkshire Stingo at Mr Roberts's ground in West London, the *Era*, 5 January 1862, reported: 'The betting was heavy, the sport admirable, the management insufferable . . . not until half the proceedings were over did the Proprietor send for the police to keep order, as is usual on all running grounds.' As we have seen, pedestrianism was a sport of the streets as well as the running grounds – an 'indecent nuisance', condemned by respectable citizens, harassed by the police and punished by the courts. The world of its champions was recorded in the pages of *Bell's Sporting Life*, the principal organ of a great underground of popular sport. A contemporary acknowledgement of the paper's significance is worth requoting:[27]

> *Bell's Life* tells us not what ought to be done by Englishmen but what, as a matter of fact, is done. It shows what a large balance there still is versus that crushing respectability which threatens to overwhelm us – it tells us how much of the animal pleasures of savage life survives in the heart of civilised life.

Supporters of the new athleticism would not have represented their games as celebrations of the savage life; in many ways they were institutions abstracted from life, whether savage or civilised. Despite the aggressive style of language which coloured debates on health and athletics in the context of social Darwinism and national survival, there was a sense in which the games field served more as a refuge from the competitive strains of real life than as an extension of it. The doctrine of fair play provided for competition, of course, but suspended the absolute judgements of success or failure, affluence or bankruptcy, which could befall commercial or professional life. The vindictive laws of Nature which were judged to govern a man's working life were to be barred from his play. Sport was now a laboratory in which men could test themselves under precise and uniform rules, not an arena where, to recall the phrase in *Chambers's Journal*, men were incited to 'outrage nature'.[28] The old

sports had about them the flavour of gladiatorial contests (in pedestrianism as much as the prize ring) and were reported in an arcane vernacular
of epic and arresting style; the new sports had their heroes, and the
heroic style of reportage survived in modified form in the flourishing
world of boys' periodicals, but the typical sporting paper which appeared
in the 1860s and 1870s to service the new athleticism was a journal of
record, rarely an essay in melodrama. Thus was sport represented as a
neutral, scientific exercise, an alternative world of physical improvement
and achievement which could be exactly measured, safe from the harsh
and often adventitious sanctions of working life; the members of its
fraternity enjoyed a sense of competitive striving which stopped far short
of self-destruction. In team games in particular, reckless individualism
was restrained by the insistence upon team spirit and co-operation. Sport
was not, however, to be allowed to engross life; a magazine article in
1881 which criticised the proliferation of prizes in amateur athletics did
so because they tended 'to exalt recreation above its limits into a substitute for work', leading to a situation where 'selfish competition
prevails rather than the sense of wholesome membership in sports.'[29]
Thus pedestrianism was abhorrent to amateurs because it was professionalised and therefore a kind of work. It was on such grounds that
the governing bodies of the reformed sports contested the participation
of professionals in their meetings, in a running controversy which dominated the athletic world from the 1860s onwards.

Also central to the case against professionalism was the contention that
it encouraged gambling. Gambling was reviled by middle-class opinion
on several grounds. It was a matter of perpetual scandal to the man of
business that the society gambler would honour his gaming debts though
scorning to the last the claims of the honest tradesmen among his credi-
tors, while betting among the lower orders was regarded as a constant
threat to property and social order. Young gentlemen were advised that
'The moral healthiness or unhealthiness of any recreation may generally
be estimated by the extent to which it has become the subject of bets.'[30]
The gentleman patron of traditional sports had backed his protégés as a
matter of course, and *The Times*, 30 May 1868, could still defend betting
in the 1860s with the argument that, with a few reckless exceptions, the
nobility knew how to bet; their vulgar imitators, said the paper, should
be cautioned but not proscribed. But the railways and telegraph had
produced a national sporting market in which the aristocratic backer had
been superseded by the bookmaker; the presence of a gentleman had
allegedly ensured fair play, whereas the bookie provided no such guarantee.[31] The 'roping' or rigging of contests by the gambling interests was

notorious at pedestrian meetings, and as far as the amateurs were concerned such chicanery distorted the neutral frame of reference within
which sports should ideally be conducted. 'The pedestrian circle',
asserted one of the new wave of athletic papers, 'is too much surrounded
by a halo of beer and skittles, and amenable to the low art of the bookmakers to make it either a healthy or an improving place of resort, or a
reliable gauge of man's physical powers.'[32]

Such associations were to be avoided at all costs if the new sports were
to be made socially respectable. The enthusiasts who founded the AAC
and like bodies had some initial difficulties in persuading their elders
that the practice of athletic sports outside the confines of public school
and university was not vulgar and morally ruinous – Walter Rye's
fiancée was forced to break off the engagement when her mother discovered that he took part in athletics, 'sharing with my own parents, as
she did, the then prevalent idea that athletics meant pot-housing'. It was
to avoid such opprobrium that early amateurs wore masks and competed
incognito. Even in 1868, Anthony Trollope considered modern football
and athletics too parvenu to include in his survey of British sports and
games, explaining that 'we have felt that they have fallen somewhat short
of the necessary dignity.'[33] Once such prejudice was dispelled, everything was done to maintain a respectable tone by securing amateur
athletics against interlopers from lower stations in society.

The new world of amateur sport was therefore an exclusive one. Discrimination against the older sport and its practitioners was based on
rational and moral grounds – what could be more irrational than walking
backwards, or more immoral than gambling? – but the concern for
respectability emphasises the strong element of class discrimination. In a
review of the amateur versus professional controversy on 26 April 1880,
The Times noted that

> artisans and mechanics have, by almost general consent, been shut out
> from the privileged inner circle, and have been counted as in every
> case, professionals. . . . Their muscular practice is held to give them
> unfair advantage over more delicately nurtured competitors.

The Times thought such an argument had become rather obsolete but
spoke up for discrimination on other grounds:

> The outsiders, artisans, mechanics, and such like troublesome persons
> can have no place found for them. To keep them out is a thing desir-
> able on every account. The 'status' of the rest seems better assured and
> more clear from any doubt which might attach to it, and the prizes are

more certain to fall into the right hands. Loud indeed would be the wail over a chased goblet or a pair of silver sculls which a mechanic had been lucky enough to carry off. The whole 'pot-hunting' world would be simply so much the poorer, to say nothing of the ridiculous nature of such a defeat, and of the social degradation which the contest would have implied, whatever its results had been. . . . No base mechanic arms need be suffered to thrust themselves in here.

The most difficult problem in maintaining exclusivity lay along the margins of the class line; it was, presumably, fairly easy to distinguish and therefore exclude the base mechanics or professionals – even though the latter occasionally adopted false whiskers and false names to plunder a few cups[34] – but in large metropolitan communities with a high rate of social mobility the screening capacity of the ruling cliques was severely reduced, and the ex-public school and varsity men faced a takeover by the lower middle-class tradesman and clerk. This situation produced a further refinement of the definition of amateur in an attempt to reserve the higher social reaches of sport for the 'gentleman amateur', as a letter to the *Sporting Gazette* in July 1872 serves to emphasise:[35]

Sports nominally open to gentleman amateurs must be confined to those who have a real right to that title, and men of a class considerably lower must be given to understand that the facts of their being well conducted and civil and never having run for money are NOT sufficient to make a man a gentleman as well as an amateur. They have a hundred and one tradesmen's meetings to fall back upon, and what more can they want?

Nor was it to be expected that sporting skills would secure an entrée where civility and good conduct on their own were insufficient credentials; as an editorial in the *Referee*, 27 January 1878, laid down, 'The fact that a man is exceptionally brilliant as a player is in no way an excuse for the assumption of unwarranted social rank; quite the reverse.' It appears that those most recently qualified as gentlemen were the most assiduous in pulling up the ladder behind them; as one observer remarked, 'From enquiries I have made I find that nearly all the members of the athletic clubs calling themselves "Gentleman Amateurs", and who exclude tradesmen are, IN REALITY, TRADESMEN'S SONS.'[36] If sport was indeed the great leveller, its social utility to the established or aspiring bourgeoisie was that it might level up, not level down.

III

Given then the limitations on working-class participation in the new games in the schools and those associations best equipped to provide for and encourage athleticism, by what process did athletics 'spread downwards to the masses'? In particular, what role did reformers allot to sport in their promotion of rational recreation?

Reformers certainly recommended physical exercise to the working classes. Samuel Smiles advised 'abundant physical exercise' in his programme of self-help. William Lovett prescribed the same in proposing a physical regimen which he believed would assist the improvement of his class, and other working-class reformers contributed to the delineation of a new model physique – trimmer and more ascetic than that derived from the publican and the prize-fighter.[37] The preservation of open spaces attracted attention among reformers in the 1870s: trades union leaders and middle-class friends of the working classes formed the People's Garden Company in London in 1870, and by the middle of the decade Octavia Hill and other philanthropists had established the Open Space movement, whose manifestoes emphasised the common man's need for healthy outdoor sports. As we have seen, Lord Brabazon and others urged the same case in the interests of national military preparedness.[38]

A growing number of athletic churchmen urged their colleagues to develop games skills as a means of reaching and extending their working-class congregations. As noted previously, Kingsley's teachings had helped to make sport more respectable (though Kingsley himself kept to fishing and leap-frog rather than football and cricket) and the new-style sporting parson was well enough known to suffer Dickens's mocking attentions by the 1860s.[39] The cricket field was the most frequently recommended setting for the clergyman's exercise in fraternity – in Bolton by 1867 about a third of the cricket clubs were connected to a religious body[40] – but he was active in other sports too. One knowledgeable modern historian of British football finds that 'the curate, and often the vicar, inspired by his own early education, frequently set out to claim souls with a Bible in one hand and a football in the other.' There are some well-known examples of this provenance in the histories of today's major football clubs, and the contention receives further support from another detailed local study of the period – about a quarter of the clubs in the Birmingham area in the 1880s had some connexion with religious organisations.[41]

The Church was one of several institutions that provided physical facilities for sports (the most welcome form of assistance) such as changing rooms and playing fields. In the 1870s and 1880s young workingmen (and such clerks and shop assistants who shared their enthusiasms) were able to meet together in YMCAs, friendly societies, Working Men's Clubs, public houses, schoolrooms and the workplace to form their various sports clubs. In Bolton in the 1860s a number of local employers provided their workers with a cricket ground; many of the clubs formed in this way followed the common national pattern of fielding a football side in the winter to maintain their association, thus further extending the practice of organised sports among workingmen.

But Butler-Johnstone's statement to the Commons, quoted above, should alert us to the extent to which active encouragement and provision by the wealthier classes was the exception rather than the rule. The Open Space movement provided a standing acknowledgement of the chronic shortage of playing room in the towns. Where public parks existed sport was often prohibited – Farnworth Park near Bolton was not unexceptional in banning cricket and allowing games 'of a quiet nature only'.[42] Church patronage in sport was not yet convincing enough to dispel the image of the clergyman as kill-joy, and the sporting churchman was in a minority in a profession which remained generally suspicious of popular sport as a corrupter of morals, despite the new and respectable models. 'Despite all the talk, fashionable as is the so-called muscular Christianity,' complained W. T. Marriott, 'still little is DONE for their [the working classes'] improvement.' In any case, according to some observers from within the Anglican Church, athletic clergymen often used their games skills to ingratiate themselves with the upper classes rather than with workingmen.[43] Moreover, church-sponsored sports clubs were subject to built-in limitations on membership, for the latter was often made conditional upon church attendance. Similarly, some business firms restricted passes to recreational functions to 'reputable' employees.[44]

Yet the role of the upper classes must still be recognised as an important one. Despite the reservations which some of their number continued to hold, the simple fact that athleticism was practised by the respectable made it legitimate practice for the lower orders. Certainly there was a new tolerance for sport which had not existed in the 1830s and 1840s. The new codes of play and conduct were the work of middle-class administrators who could secure them almost immediate national recognition through that intimate community of interest which the English know as the old-boy network, an institution for which there was no good working-class equivalent. There is some indication too that working-class boys absorbed the new teachings of fair play and good sportsmanship from reading schoolboy papers written for the middle-class market (though the new code must often have sat uneasily beside the laws of survival learned in a slum culture).[45]

What the substantial middle class did not provide in any abundance was a direct presence. Even in the case of the many football clubs associated with church or chapel, it is clear that in several instances the initiative came from within the church membership rather than from the church officers. The latter were often of less assistance than other members of the community, and once established the teams seem to have quickly severed the religious connexion. The original members of Aston Villa (a club referred to as a church team in standard histories of the game) were 'connected with' the Bible class of a Wesleyan chapel. Their playing field was provided by a local butcher and their dressing room by a local publican. Members of a Church of England school team in Wolverhampton, later the Wolves, derived more support from the publican father of one of the boys than from their clerical headmaster, and themselves took the initiative in approaching a local industrialist for his backing. Members of the Christ Church Football Club in Bolton deserted their mentor, the Reverend J. F. Wright, four years after he had formed the club; they walked out of a meeting in the church schoolrooms, crossed the road to the Gladstone Hotel and reconstituted themselves as the Bolton Wanderers. Tottenham Hotspur was a team originally associated with the YMCA, but it was formed by a small group of enthusiasts who approached the Association for assistance, rather than responded to any initial lead from that organisation. In the practical and eclectic fashion of their culture, workingmen used such institutions as a socially neutral locus for the formation of their clubs and teams; the function of institutions was more one of convenience than of direct encouragement.[46]

The popular expansion of the new sports in the 1870s and 1880s derived a great deal of its impetus from below; workingmen generated their own encouragement, and showed also how little they were deterred by explicit discouragement. There had always been a considerable popular appetite for sport in England, and it had been far from extinguished by the deficiencies of diet, income and space, and the attenuation of cultural continuity that Philpott later remarked. As Will Thorne recalled of Birmingham in the early 1870s: 'One of the remarkable things about those times was that, no matter how hard men and boys worked, they were whenever possible always anxious to take part in sports.'[47] Such was the pressure of popular interest in athletics that it became difficult for governing bodies to enforce any distinction other than the basic one between amateur and professional, where the former was defined simply as a competitor who was not dependent on the sport for his livelihood (the matter of legitimate expenses for the amateur was an early problem which did, however, continue to obscure the issue). Some officers in the London hierarchy had begun canvassing for the deletion of the clause excluding mechanics, artisans and labourers in the 1870s, though the appeals were sometimes less than gracious. Arguing that 'The common republic of sport does not admit of such invidious comparisons', H. F. Wilkinson of the London Athletic Club went on to instance examples from other sports of the happy combination of 'the lord, the lout, and the merchant'.[48] The lout was in fact turning out to be less of a threat to the new sporting ethics than had at first been feared. The Northern Counties Athletic Association, formed in 1879, dropped the mechanics clause and threatened to boycott the AAC championships which were traditionally held in the spring. The timing here was made to fit in with the university calendar but caught the bulk of working-class entrants unprepared; they could not train during the day and needed the long summer evenings to reach optimum fitness. Faced with this crisis the AAC went into dissolution, to be replaced by the more democratic and less élitist Amateur Athletic Association in 1880 which followed the provincial associations in deleting the mechanics clause and recognising athletics as primarily a summer sport.[49]

The popular participation which opened up the amateur running tracks to all comers was not, however, of such a volume to provide the regular market opportunities for commercial speculation which might have led to eventual professional domination of the sport. For some time the pedestrian world continued to co-exist with amateur athletics, still attracting large attendances on occasions, but otherwise alienating its supporters by the overt corruption of the 'gaffers', the backers who put up the stakes and manipulated the betting.[50] In any case the big crowds were being lured away by football, the most dramatic in growth of the new organised games, and a mass spectacle by the mid-1880s.

The middle-class officials of the Football Association, founded in 1863, had at first felt no need to stipulate the status appropriate to those who wished to play. The old game of football was an occasional and irregular affair, and there was no flourishing professional sector of the game to threaten the new code as had been the case with athletics. Moreover, the nature of the game itself allowed for a covert and largely inoffensive form of discrimination. Athletic clubs received entries for their meetings from individual competitors rather than from clubs en bloc, and then more often by post than in person, so that comprehensive screening was very difficult; football clubs could choose their opponents at will. For almost the first twenty years of its life, therefore, major wrangles within the FA centred on differences over the rules of play, as the administrators sought to reconcile the several variations emanating from the key public schools which had fostered a revised version of the game – the issues were those of technical, rather than social, discrimination.[51] But the early enthusiasts were mindful of the need to give football a respectable tone, for it was but a few years previously that the headmaster of Shrewsbury had dismissed the game as 'fit only for butcher boys', and we have noted above Trollope's misgivings about the lack of dignity in football. In Sheffield, an early stronghold of the game, the managing committee of the first established football club in 1854 stated its intention to confine activities to gentlemen, an intention echoed in the following advertisement for the post of secretary to the local football association in the 1880s: 'Besides possessing great educational ability, the secretary should be a gentleman of good position, with whom distant officials would not deem it derogatory to correspond.' Frederick Wall, secretary of the FA from 1895, recalled the game in its early years as 'a joyous revel for the middle classes', and so it remained with little need to police its boundaries until the mid-1870s.[52]

It was the inception of the FA Cup competition in 1871 which opened up the game, simultaneously disarming the freedom of preference the early clubs had been able to exercise in selecting opponents and inducing a cumulative excitement throughout the season which multiplied popular interest. The Cup competition was conceived initially as an extension of the system of public school house matches, but its subsequent history rapidly dissolved this recherché image. Northern clubs with a predominantly working-class membership and following entered for the Cup, and thus broke into London and the south where the idea of football as the gentleman's game was strongest. To travel to the south, the northern clubs were often obliged to raise a public subscription, and the problem of meeting their players' expenses grew as the range and frequency of matches increased. Competition in the north, particularly in Lancashire, became so intense that the leading clubs began to import players from Scotland, already productive of notably gifted 'professors' of the game.[53]

The signs of incipient professionalism were soon noticed – the sovereign in the boot, the mysterious deliveries of free coal, the easy tenancy of a pub – and the FA moved to defend the amateur status of the game. The debate between supporters and critics of professionalism had grown heated by the early 1880s, and the football world was convulsed in the autumn of 1884 when the governing body introduced a ruling effectively banning professionals from playing in the Cup competition.

The Lancashire clubs saw themselves as the principal target of such a move and expressed their resentment in class terms. The football correspondent of the *Bolton Chronicle* put it thus:[54]

> In the South the players are mainly of the 'upper ten'. They can afford time and money for training, and travelling, and playing. In the North the devotees of the game are mainly working men. They cannot play the game on strictly amateur lines. . . . They cannot afford to train, or to 'get in form', or whatever other name you like to call it. Besides, they command big 'gates' and they naturally think they have a right to a trifle from it.

A Preston official writing to the *Athletic News*, 29 October 1884, voiced the popular opinion that the covert professional was a workingman denied the full fruits of his labour. Those who paid to see the game were willing to pay its players and abhorred the system which sought to preserve the fiction of amateurism; it was absurd and unjust to reward the coal miner with a talent for football with 'the occasional supply of a set of dessert cutlery' when the man would be better served as an open professional in a new and superior employment. 'To the "upper crust", no doubt', concluded the correspondent, 'it is annoying to see "cads" attaining excellence and equal powers to themselves.' Class resentment was compounded by a provincial hostility to the metropolis, from where, in northern eyes, the game was being manipulated by 'a few mashers who wish to have the English cup back in London'.[55]

The north formed its own British Association in November 1884, announcing it as a democratic alternative to the peremptory oligarchy of the FA, and promising to regularise professionalism within the game.[56] Faced with the open secession of Lancashire and considerable disaffection in the midlands, the FA executed a remarkable volte-face and gave official sanction to professionalism in football in the summer of 1885.[57] Though the northern clubs were thus prevailed upon to accept the continued jurisdiction of the FA, the mood of grass-roots assertiveness persisted in the local Lancashire Football Association where there was an outspoken campaign to remove Lord Hartington as president – 'the day of ornamental officers', said one critic, 'has passed.'[58]

Professionalism did not, however, mean the end of patronage, but rather a change in its pattern and provenance. Professionalism, increasing gates and the inception of a national league in 1888 brought new problems of management without necessarily guaranteeing financial viability for the clubs. Men with longish pockets were needed in these years when professionals were contracted to individual members of club committees rather than to a club itself. Such men could provide jobs and housing for the pros, as well as stand as trustees for club grounds with expanding amenities and services.[59] The early enthusiasts who had encouraged workingmen to take up football had been men of a solid middle-class background or above. Probably fewer in number than has previously been allowed, they were none the less moved by considerations of social and moral responsibility and, in many cases, a player's love of the game. The new patrons who fastened on the sport in the 1880s seem more likely to have been marginal or self-made members of the middle class: successful tradesmen, small businessmen, aspiring publicans. William Sudell of Preston North End was a mill manager. William MacGregor of Aston Villa, the instigator of the new Football League, was a prosperous shopkeeper of humble origins. John Davies, who at a later date rescued Manchester United from bankruptcy, was a publican turned brewer.[60] Few clubs could have been without one of their kind. In one sense they represented a traditional source of support, heirs to the countless publicans and other middling men who had encouraged the new game of football as they had previously encouraged all manner of other working-class games and contests. The new patrons revealed much the same motivation as their forerunners – serving sport won prestige in the working-class community, a prestige flattering for men who still regarded themselves as of the people, and useful too in local council elections. But though often fanatical in their enthusiasm for their teams and football itself, the institutionalisation of financial control in the game made these men more hard-nosed and proprietorial than their predecessors from either their own class or the public school élite.

At the top, the FA continued to be officered by gentlemen, but in general the middle class withdrew from the game which they had once proclaimed an instrument of moral salvation and social order. The practice of professionalism, the related growth of mass spectatorship, and the growing commercialisation of the game made association football (soccer, as it became known) increasingly distasteful, and the middle class retreated to the more select world of rugby football. By the 1890s, commentators were attacking soccer as 'a moral slough' and 'the acme of athletic horrors'. The top players were, it was claimed, the objects of extravagant popular adulation and were better known than local MPs. The professional game generated 'an epidemic excitement' among the crowds. 'As a rule', remarked one observer, 'they do not go to see football; they go to see their own side win, and that is all they care about.'

The referee was an immediate ritual scapegoat in the working-class game, a symbolic proxy for the rent collector or school board man who suffered frequent abuse and assault. Reports of brawling in the crowd and altercations on the field were common, and seemed proof that ideals of fair play and gentlemanly conduct had given way to 'a fashionable brutality'. 'Football', concluded another disillusioned witness, 'is a passion, not a recreation.'[61]

Herbert Spencer crystallised much respectable contemporary opinion in representing football as a prime example of what he termed the 're-barbarisation' of society.[62] The modern game was in many ways far removed from the hectic clashes of its folk predecessor, but those of its features which excited the adverse comment of middle-class witnesses were strongly reminiscent not only of the older game but of much un-reconstructed popular sport in general. The occasion of modern football was now strictly limited in duration, and regularly scheduled within the legitimate free time of Saturday afternoon; players and spectators were clearly segregated, and the activities of both contained within purpose-built stadia, admission to which was governed by turnstiles and entrance charges; play was limited to a small, fixed number of participants policed by a referee in common acknowledgement of a standardised code of rules. Yet the fierce expressions of group or neighbourhood loyalties conveyed in the crowd's partisan identification with team and players, and the general function of spectatorship as an act of collective partici-pation showed how, even within its new structure, the sport retained much of the emotional temper and spirit of an earlier society.[63] For such manifestations was association football generally disqualified from the canon of rational recreation.

In contrast, cricket maintained its respectable image. Professionals had been an accepted part of the game since the early years of the century and, though cricket expanded greatly from the 1860s onward, they continued to play alongside the amateurs without corrupting the equable spirit of the game. (This held good despite occasional strikes among the top professionals in the 1880s and 1890s and the emergence of the more highly competitive and professionalised game of League cricket in the same decades.)[64] Professionalism in county cricket, argued the latter's many champions, did not produce the vicious rivalry and bad sports-manship which had marred pedestrianism and now corrupted football, because control rested firmly with the gentleman amateurs; their presence carried a traditional authority derived from that of the landowner in the rural society whence the game had originally sprung. Furthermore, the good manners on the field communicated themselves to the spectators, whose conduct was irreproachable beside that of the football crowds. There was something in this. The nature of the game was less combustible than other sports, and the absence of physical contact meant that to a large extent the normal terms of social address could be maintained at play. Patrons of the game no longer recruited professionals exclusively from the workers on their estates, but they clearly did regard the pros as servants who were assigned functions within the game appropriate to their station. Thus the pro would spend most of his time fielding – the chore given to fags in public school cricket – and bowling in the nets to give the gentlemen practice. The professional with Bolton Cricket Club in the 1860s bowled in clogs as if to acknowledge his status, and the distinction between amateur and professional or Gentlemen and Players (after the famous annual match inaugurated in 1806 and played until 1962) sat so easily on the game that it impressed itself upon the national vocabulary as a synonym for mutual and amiable discrimination. A Tory politician seeking to specify Disraeli's status within the Conservative party concluded thus: 'We know he does not belong to our Eleven, but we have him down as a professional bowler.'[65]

Much of the practice of sport in England remained segregated along class lines. The new athleticism had provided sport with credentials which gave unprecedented emphasis to its capacity for imparting the highest moral and social values. Despite these recommendations, there had been no extensive move to propagate the new games codes among the masses. The middle-class enthusiasts of the new athleticism mostly discouraged working-class participation, in order to prevent contamination from the corrupt practices attributed to popular sport, and to reserve the new games as a medium for defining class status. In the much vaunted 'republic of sport', only cricket received special dispensation as the one game whose mystique resisted popular corruption and kept the base mechanics in their place; otherwise, the working classes were to be left the basic commons of military drill and callisthenics. Despite the antipathies of its self-appointed governors, the working classes took up the new athleticism with avidity. The process of diffusion needs further research and explanation, but it seems clear that reformers played a more limited role than has previously been suggested. There was a strong appetite for sport among English workingmen and, while they took readily to the new models, they showed in the case of football a determination to adapt them to the circumstances and needs of their own culture.

7

Rational recreation and the entertainment industry: the case of the Victorian music halls

While organised sport increased its following among the working classes, it was undoubtedly the music hall which dominated popular recreations in the second half of the nineteenth century.[1] Developed from the singing saloons by a new breed of publican entrepreneurs, this prototype modern entertainment industry provides a strong example of the capacity of working-class culture to meet the leisure needs of its constituency. Middle-class observers reacted to the demotic vigour of the halls with mixed feelings: some derived a measure of encouragement from the new phenomenon, but the bulk of reformers were disturbed by the halls as a further manifestation of the generally debased tastes of the masses. Next to the pub the music halls became the most embattled institution in working-class life, as reform groups strove variously to close them, censor them or reproduce their essential appeal in facsimile counter-attractions purged of vulgarity. Though the halls proved remarkably resilient, they did yield some ground to the pressures of rational recreation; significantly, the more effective pressures came from within the industry itself.

I

The take-off in growth for the music halls came in the 1850s. In recognition of a growing popular demand for entertainment, some of the more enterprising publicans expanded the operations of the singing saloon. They abolished the refreshment check in favour of a straight admission charge thus de-emphasising the trade in liquor, and relying on the pulling power of the entertainment and the superior appointments of the new establishments – the music hall label was meant to indicate an advance in taste and amenities upon the singing saloon. A certain

Thomas Harwood (member of a family later prominent in East End music hall management) explained to a government licensing committee in 1852 how realisation of the potential of this new formula had prompted him to open a new concert room:[2]

> I was about leaving business, and it always struck me that the working classes could have a better description of recreation, supposing a person could speculate sufficiently largely, and give the recreation at a low price.

The smell of big money was in the air in the licensed trade; increased business in the 1840s had accelerated capital accumulation, and the publican was well placed to subsidise his ventures into music hall proprietorship from other enterprises such as sports promotion or outside catering in food and drink.[3]

The best known of the new wave of publican entrepreneurs ('caterers' in contemporary jargon) was another Londoner, Charles Morton, who opened his Canterbury Hall in 1851 in Lambeth. Originally an annexe built on the site of his pub's skittle alley, the hall proved such a profitable success that Morton reconstructed the whole premises in 1854 at a cost variously estimated at between £25,000 and £40,000. The new hall had a capacity of over 1,500 and boasted its own library, reading room and picture gallery; admission charges started at 6d. In 1861 Morton duplicated his success when he opened the Oxford in Oxford Street, the first purpose-built music hall, complete with a fully equipped stage and fixed stall seating (the latter a significant change from the free-standing tables and chairs of most halls). The lavish appointments of the Oxford were the talk of the West End; not the least attractive feature was its bevy of remarkably handsome barmaids.[4]

But the leading showpiece of the new era was the Alhambra in Leicester Square (the choice of Bill Banks and his party for their night out in the late 1860s). Converted from the Panopticon of Science and Art into a 3,500-capacity music hall in 1860, the Alhambra eventually outdid the Oxford in the scale and spectacle of its productions and the range of its amenities, and claimed a yearly attendance outstripping South Kensington Museum or the Zoo. It retained the patronage of a solid core of working-class Londoners, but also benefited from the capital's increasing tourist traffic (there was a further Exhibition in 1862). In 1864 it became the first music hall operated by a limited liability company, and proceeded to pay handsome dividends.[5]

Though most of its capital was still raised informally, music hall promotion boomed in the early 1860s, encouraged by the flourishing examples of the Oxford and Alhambra. By 1866 when the boom seems to have levelled out, the solicitor to the London Music Hall Proprietors' Association could list thirty-three large halls in town with an average capitalisation of £10,000 and an average capacity of 1,500.[6] The existence of such an association is a further indication of the success of the halls, for it was founded to protect proprietors from legal actions brought by theatre interests in central London who were suffering from the competition of the new entertainments (informers laid information that the halls were offering episodes of straight drama which encroached upon territory reserved for the legitimate stage under the Theatre Act of 1843). At the hearings before the select committee appointed to reconsider theatrical licensing in 1866, it became clear that the music halls were incomparably better appointed and better run than the theatres. From his experience of theatre management in London, Stephen Fiske, the American, concluded that 'almost the only managers who display extraordinary enterprise and ability are those of the music halls and east end theatres.'[7]

There was also considerable growth and enterprise in music hall promotion outside London (though this has been mostly ignored by historians of the halls, past and present). There were, it seems, problems of under-capitalisation, but the number of provincial halls more than doubled during the 1860s, and the big establishments in the midlands and the north rivalled those of the metropolis in size and popular success. Indeed it was the provinces that produced entrepreneurs like Moss, Stoll and Thornton who built up the big syndicates that began to take over the London halls in the 1890s.[8]

Below the larger halls stretched a dense undergrowth of smaller establishments, mostly pub music halls still operating by refreshment check, many of them probably without the necessary music and dancing license. The Licensed Victuallers' trade paper, the *Era*, calculated that there were between two and three hundred small halls in London in 1856. Figures derived from a sample of entries in Howard's inventory of London's halls indicate that their mushroom growth ended in the early 1860s when they went into a general decline; the great number of entries of only two to three years' operation suggests an extremely hazardous and competitive market. There was a further abrupt fall-off in the late 1880s when the London County Council began the rigorous enforcement of safety requirements under a Board of Works act of 1878 and the concert areas in many pub music halls reverted to billiard rooms. Municipal improvement also threatened the small fry in the provinces.[9]

The big establishments consolidated their grip at the expense of their smaller rivals, and the opening of the rebuilt London Pavilion in 1885 signalled a new bout of investment in music hall properties. The *Financial News* recommended the music hall for those investors recently frightened off the foreign market and confided that:

> wherever it has been decently and prudently managed, it has yielded large fortunes. If it paid well ten years ago it should pay much better today, for many more people now frequent it and people of a better kind than formerly – if it continues to refine itself and to heap novelty on novelty as it does, it will go on growing.

Given such encouragement the money poured in, and within a decade or so the publican and his check-taker were finally superseded by the theatrical capitalist and his accountant.[10]

II

The Victorian music hall qualifies as a prototype modern entertainment industry, not just because its capital investment allowed economies of scale which secured it a mass paying audience, but because of the thorough-going commercialisation which accompanied its growth and affected all facets of its operation. Commercialisation had, for example, important consequences for the performers, who were reconstituted as a fully professional labour force. At the top were the stars, already by the 1860s earning some extremely handsome salaries, and enjoying some useful perks – allowances from wine-shippers for the champagne which was the indispensable fuel of the 'swell', free suits from tradesmen in return for a mention in the act and royalties from publishers' agents anxious to push a new song.[11] Among the lower ranks of performers, rewards were often niggardly and the competition much more severe. The pub music halls provided a constant flow of aspiring talent which kept the profession permanently overcrowded. Though the halls paid better than the theatres, performers found themselves increasingly squeezed by managements. One example of the monopoly effect exerted by the big halls was the turns systems, introduced by Morton when he opened the Oxford. He filled his bill with artists already employed at the Canterbury who thus played in Lambeth and Oxford Street on the same night, crossing the river by cab. It became customary for an artist to do four or five turns a night, and the system played into the hands of the big proprietors and agents who could secure exclusive control of performers where they enjoyed an interest in more than one hall. Artists had to meet their own expenses for costume and transport between turns, and the practice of matinées (legal after 1866) and twice-nightly performances (introduced in the 1870s, though the early history is obscure and contentious) increased the workload without any guarantee of a proportionate increase in earnings. Growing alienation within the profession produced spasms of militant trade union activity among performers in the 1870s and 1880s. The unions proposed to by-pass the much detested agent (another product of the commercialisation of entertainment), end the turn system, control entry to the profession and, in one case, open their own co-operative music hall. But these occasional essays at organisation and protest left the exploitative grip of management unshaken.[12]

The increased scale of operations and the pervasiveness of market values under the authoritarian control of the caterers affected in turn the nature of the entertainment offered by the halls. As the simple platform of the singing saloons was gradually superseded by the full theatrical apparatus of a stage and proscenium arch, the big halls were encouraged to introduce greater show and theatricality into their programmes – lavish tableaux of famous battle scenes, hundred-strong corps de ballet, troupes of Can-Can dancers from Paris and Blondin cooking omelettes on the high wire. The *Music Halls' Gazette*, 29 August 1868, detected 'a feverish excitement abroad . . . which sacrifices everything to sensation, a constant hankering after something, not only novel but more or less terrible', conditions bred by the hectic pace of change in modern city life; Louis Blanc, in less charitable mood, implied that dangerous trapeze acts met an English taste for violence which could no longer be satisfied with blood sports.[13] Whatever the source of the audiences' apparent needs, the caterers, by their increasing use of publicity and show business hyperbole, sharpened the demand for spectacle and novelty.

This manipulation was applied not only in production techniques but in the making of the stars. The distancing of the performer from the audience, one of the essential conditions of star appeal, began with the introduction of the formal stage at the Canterbury. The turn system further removed the performer from his original place among the audience for, with the need to keep to a strict schedule, there was no time to spend hob-nobbing with the groundlings by the singers' table (a hangover from the singing saloons which, together with the office of chairman, gradually disappeared from the halls).[14] Morton began the projection of the star performer as something larger than life with his promotion of the Great Mackney. Another leading London proprietor, William 'Billy' Holland, the 'People's Caterer', took the process a step further and persuaded the star to live the role he had created on stage. Thus he insisted that George Leybourne ride everywhere in his personal brougham, displaying his fur-collared coat, a fistful of gold rings and a glad hand with the drinks, as befitted the style of 'Champagne Charlie'.[15] As a star, the performer became more important than his material; he was the agent who transformed the dross of a prolific cheap sheet-music market into gold for, as the *Music Halls' Gazette*, 27 June 1868, advised, 'a good song must be written, not for its own sale, but for that of the singer. . . . It must simply be a vehicle.' Moreover, once the leading performers took care to copyright hit songs under their name, and the Performing Rights Society proved capable of prosecuting infringers among even the minor professionals in the back rooms of pubs, songs ceased to be common property and the star's position was reinforced.[16] At the same time the spread of the railways and the cheap press opened up the provinces to the touring London star and company. There was still a distinctive topography of regional, indeed parochial, taste in entertainment (which comedians, in particular, could ignore only at their peril), but much of the style and content of music hall performance was becoming standardised across the country.

III

The modernisation of popular entertainment taking place in the music halls in this period was remarkable; yet just as remarkable was the extent to which the gregarious congeniality inherited from the antecedent singing saloons remained unimpaired. Only gradually did fixed seating facing the stage become the norm, and many halls continued to seat their public at rows of tables which allowed easy access for waiters and customers alike; thus for many audiences the music hall remained a face-to-face encounter – drinking, smoking, eating and general good fellowship went on unabated during the performances. As the comedian Arthur Roberts recalled, 'It was all uproar whether they liked you or not.'[17] Moreover, only in a few of the very largest halls such as the Alhambra could spectacle eclipse the appeal of the individual artist as the staple attraction; all the accretions of the new show business mystique had not yet removed even the most exalted of these from active contact with their public, for the essence of music hall entertainment remained the dialogue between performer and audience. Several middle-class visitors noted this, for it stood in marked contrast to the conventions of the legitimate theatre. At a Bradford music hall, the northern writer James Burnley was struck by the way artists would single out individuals in the crowd for particular attention, and was critical because they played so directly to the audience, 'instead of trying to be natural'. An American, Daniel Kirwan, reported that everyone in the audience at London's Royal Victoria 'seemed to be on speaking terms with each and all of the performers'.[18] The dialogue was robust, as Edgar Jepson recalled:[19]

> The old music hall was a place of freedom and ease, and I have heard a soprano, when her accompaniment was bungled, pause in her song to curse the conductor, the orchestra, the manager, the proprietor and his hall, and the audience, with a brilliance of invective never attained on the legitimate stage.

In similar fashion the stars themselves were not immune to the traditional sanctions of a dissatisfied audience. Charles Coborn muttered darkly about certain halls in Liverpool where 'the customers were as rough as the furniture.' At Glasgow the locals dispatched the Great Vance from the stage by hurling handfuls of rivets; at Harwood's in London's East End – 'the Sods' Opera' – the favoured missiles were trotter bones. Popular control did not stop short with the performers – at Chester Music Hall in the 1870s, the audience proceeded to dismantle all the stage machinery when a dioramic entertainment of the Zulu War failed to please and they were refused a refund of their admission money. Audiences could of course be extremely generous in their attentions, cheering the favoured artist on into innumerable encores, and in some halls the performers were wired in to prevent the audience from jumping on stage and dancing with them.[20]

The point in any performance at which the audience asserted its presence came with the chorus singing. Then the songs of the music hall would be reclaimed as common property; often the audience would alter the words to their own liking and the revised version would supersede the original. One common type of song demanded audience response: the Great Vance enjoyed considerable success with his number 'Is He Guilty?' into which he would introduce topical events and personalities, and refer such subjects to the cheers or hisses of popular judgment. Stephen Fiske recorded this phenomenon in the 1860s:[21]

> at a music hall the singer turns the news of the week into rhyme. Nowhere can you hear the Duke of Edinburgh more heartily cheered, the opinion of the people in regard to the disestablishment of the Irish Church more frankly expressed, the bills before Parliament more freely criticised, the general national feeling more truly manifested,

than at the music halls. Public sentiment is often better represented there than in the newspaper. The applause and hisses are surer criteria of popular favour or disfavour than the cheers of packed meetings, or the groans of suborned disturbers of the peace. Disraeli, Gladstone, Bright and Beales go for precisely what they are worth at these places of amusement.

A modern student of music hall entertainment has argued in persuasive fashion that there was little in the way of active political conviction in the crowd's response. We may allow that this ritual antiphony is unreliable as an accurate register of popular political opinion, but it undoubtedly met the expressive needs of an audience for whom demonstrative involvement in the performance was a fundamental and powerful attraction. Recalling the halls before they succumbed to the respectable programming of the 1880s and 1890s, one music hall regular put the matter succinctly: 'We went there not as spectators, but as performers.'[22]

Despite some contemporary contentions to the contrary, the music hall public remained predominantly working and lower middle class. Addressing the audience at his annual benefit night – reported in the *Era*, 23 March 1862 – John Wilton, proprietor of Wilton's Music Hall in Whitechapel, apostrophised on the great social and moral improvement that the halls had wrought among the working classes, 'for it is the working classes alone', he concluded, 'who are the great support of them.' A decade or so later, in a novel by Walter Besant, Emmanuel Leweson, owner and manager of the North London Palace itemised his clientèle thus:

City clerks, dressed a la mode, young shopmen, making half-a-crown purchase nearly as much dissipation as a sovereign will buy in the West; with a good sprinkling of honest citizens, fond of an evening out, neither they nor their wives averse to the smell of tobacco and the taste of beer.

The weight of other evidence confirms this picture of an audience largely comprised of the better-off artisans and tradesmen, together with the sprigs of clerkdom from office and shop; in the provinces we can note more of the same.[23] Women were in a minority; the number of wives was relatively small, though the complement of single working girls in the cheaper upper reaches of the hall could be considerable and was probably increasing. Particular note should be taken of the gallery – 'the top shelf' – for in this period few observers paid it a visit. The composition of its audience comes to us via the casualty lists of music hall fires and crowd disasters: of twenty killed in a crush at Dundee in 1865, the greater number were male and female factory hands between twelve and eighteen years of age; of twenty-three killed in a fire panic among a similar audience at the Victoria Music Hall, Manchester three years later, few were more than twenty years old.[24] The frequency of attendance is difficult to assess. Admission prices were comparatively low, the most commonly quoted ranging from 6d for the main body of the hall to 3d or less for the more cramped and distant accommodation. Thomas Wright complained in the late 1860s that 'vampirish' waiters who pushed the drink could drive up the cost of an evening's amusement, and critics pointed out how the lure of the halls drew in those who could ill afford it in the first place, but the logic of the market operation seems to have kept the basic cost of the entertainment within fairly regular and manageable reach of a substantial number of working people.[25]

The major caterers did strive to draw in a higher class audience. Morton had intended that the superior amenities of the Canterbury would lure the fashionable supper-room set from the Strand across the river to Lambeth. The price differential at the Oxford advertised his continuing bid for the quality, and the newly emerged music hall press of the 1860s regularly trumpeted the halls' breakthrough to respectability – 'audiences', announced the *Music Halls' Gazette* in 1868, 'are in the main formed of the middle-class members of society.'[26] These claims were a public relations fiction. The novelist James Greenwood saw through the caterers' myth on a visit to the 'Oxbridge' in 1868. He concluded,[27]

> The bulk of the people there were mostly people not accustomed to music halls, and only induced to pay them a visit on account of the highly respectable character the halls are in the habit of giving themselves in their placards and in their newspapers.

Fifteen years later *The Times* remarked that no gentleman would wish to patronise the music halls by choice; a cartoon of this time showed a middle-class couple deciding to risk a visit, but only after the close of the London season, when none of their friends would be in town to catch them slumming. In the suburbs large new halls began to provide proper resort for the respectable bourgeois and his family, but not much before the 1890s.[28]

The halls in the big city centres had always attracted certain fringe elements from the middle class and above – journalists, bohemians, officer cadets, undergraduates, medical students, foreign tourists, sprigs of the nobility – and in London the West End halls such as the Empire came eventually to cater predominantly for this clientèle, but in general it was the working class whose presence set the common tone of the halls, not the glamorous interlopers. At the Oxbridge, Greenwood noted the stalls full of champagne-swilling men about town and their painted ladies, but awarded greater significance to the more numerous complement of workingmen and their families in the 6d seats in the body of the hall:[29]

> Not but that the frequenters of the sixpenny part are very useful; indeed, to speak the truth, the Oxbridge could not get on well without them. They keep up appearances, and present a substantial contradiction to the accusation that the music hall is nothing better than a haunt for drunkenness and debauchery.

The smaller halls were often well meshed into the fabric of the local working-class community. Artists who worked the provinces in the 1860s and 1870s reported sharing the bill with tests of local skills: a bootmaking contest in Northampton, netmaking in Grimsby. Prizes were practical – blankets, bags of flour, buckets of coal – and often constituted thinly disguised hand-outs to the needy; in the same spirit, benefit nights brought in cash for local families hit by death or injury.[30] Some music hall managers in the East End gave workingmen's trade and philanthropic societies special rates for their meetings, and Crowder of the Paragon in the Mile End Road received a special presentation from the unions for allowing them free use of his premises during trade disputes in the 1880s.[31]

Even if they chose not to visit them, the inhabitants of the Victorian town or city could hardly have remained unaware of the music halls and their popularity. Built on the main thoroughfares and emblazoned with posters, they ranked second only to the new town halls in size and capacity as places of indoor assembly. Music hall advertising was ubiquitous – Morton even succeeded in placing copy with *The Times* – and the barrel organ and the whistling errand boy brought the hit songs out on to the streets. Those with first-hand acquaintance of working-class taste knew well the extent of the music halls' appeal: 'One place of its kind', reported a rueful James Hole from Leeds in the early 1860s, 'has a larger nightly attendance than the evening classes of all its seventeen Mechanics' Institutes put together.'[32] The report of the select committee of 1866 made the statistics of success better known, and received considerable attention in the press.[33] (Most periodicals of the period, whatever their leanings, carried occasional reports from correspondents who had seen the inside of a music hall and lived.) Fires, accidents to trapeze artists and the patronage of the Prince of Wales kept the halls in the news, and the mounting hostility of reform interests captured wide public attention in the mid-1880s with the cluster of demonstrations and court actions which the press declared the 'Battle of the Music Halls'.

IV

Though the most publicised reaction, hostility was far from being the sole or necessarily the commonest response to the rise of the halls. The magistrates, for example, when not under immediate pressure from reform lobbies, were generally tolerant. In the mid-1850s, the *Era* reported: 'The magistracy of the metropolis and districts have relaxed their former stringency in respect to the music licensing system and, with a liberality highly to be appreciated, regranted all the old licences and acceded to new applications.' William Lovett, whose Chartist National Hall in Holborn had been repeatedly denied a licence for music and dancing, noted that the local publican who evicted him and opened Weston's Music Hall on the premises met with no licensing problems; in Lovett's opinion the bench was facilitating the spread of cheap entertainment as an antidote to political excitement.[34] Further evidence from Liverpool in the 1850s suggests that magistrates were also becoming aware of the efficacy of the halls as a brake upon intemperance. This estimation certainly confirmed itself to the chief magistrate at Bow Street, who told the 1866 committee that he received 'scarcely ever a case of drunkenness from any of the music halls'. Similarly, chief constables had few complaints about the conduct of the halls, and caterers could often be sure of police testimony to the good order of their establishments when their licence was challenged.[35]

Some observers saw more of value in the music hall experience than the negative controls discerned by the harder-headed members of society – they saw the halls as valuable new socialising agencies for the city dwellers. In the first place, they accepted that the logic of an industrial society honouring free trade principles meant that entertainment, like any other commodity, was subject to the dictates of a self-operating market. Accordingly, the halls were a legitimate operation, sanctioned by popular demand. What was encouraging was not just the good order and temperate thirst which marked these mass assemblies, but the flux of direct and open social intercourse maintained within them. Furthermore, the halls were not exclusively male territory, as the pubs and clubs tended to be; some workingmen went there with their wives, and sometimes families, and as the journalist Matthew Browne remarked, 'with wives there come the first lessons in courtesy.'[36] Might not the halls serve as a milieu for repairing the estrangement of the classes and the isolation of the individual which disfigured modern city life?

The proposition appealed to the Christian Socialist leader, the Reverend Stewart Headlam, who attempted to convert churchmen from their general abhorrence of the stage, and sought to encourage the attendance of clergy and the respectable classes at the theatre and the music hall. Headlam founded the Church and Stage Guild in London in 1879 and lectured regularly on this theme, drawing upon the evidence of his own frequent visits to popular entertainments, where he met and talked with artists and managers. He was dismissed from his curacy for publishing his lectures, and the Guild was never a very effective body, but Headlam continued as an outspoken defender of the halls, and in this role he became one of the few clerical speakers welcome to the East End radical Working Men's Clubs. For Headlam, the music halls brought pleasure into a brutal industrial society: 'Those who work on the music hall stage are', he contended, 'genuine servants of humanity.'[37]

Stewart Headlam was no doubt exceptional in the intensity of his support, but there was a sizeable body of opinion which was generally sympathetic to the music halls, yet found certain features of their operation disturbing. The principal misgiving was that the halls were being run primarily as speculative ventures by men whose avarice led them to corrupt the popular taste. Headlam himself was disquieted on this point, and attacked what he called 'the plutocratic evil – the power which money had in comparison with worth and talent'.[38] Similarly, Hodgson Pratt, among others, complained that the halls had 'been started and managed by men who cared only for bringing money into the till': 'They have only thought of what would "take", whether it was bad or good, false or true in taste, refined or coarse; idiotic or indecent stuff.'[39] The caterer was cast as the villain of the piece, a gross and insidious mutation of the publican. Distaste for this despicable new archetype of capitalism was combined with another, older prejudice in the picture which Walter Besant drew of Emmanuel Leweson, music hall proprietor, in the early 1870s:[40]

> He was gorgeously attired in a brown velvet coat and white waistcoat, with a great profusion of gold chain and studs. . . . His features were highly Jewish. . . . His hair, thick and black, lay in massive rolls. . . ..
> In his hand, big in proportion, was a tumbler of iced soda and brandy.

Leweson supervised performances from the wings, 'contemplating his patrons with an air of undisguised contempt'.

Disclosing the cynical manipulations of the caterer could not, however, explain away completely what seemed to many to be the lamen-
tably low nature of music hall entertainment. Most disquieting were the
frequent charges that much of it was morally offensive. Observers
objected to the semi-nude tableaux or 'poses plastiques', and the
'indecent elevation of the leg' in the Can-Can; there was, reported one
witness, 'a predominance of "fleshings" and female shamelessness'.[41] It
is less easy to discover the specific offence in other features of the entertainment for, though many writers did their duty under fire by recording
the alleged indecencies on the halls, they were seldom explicit. Charac-
teristically, Henry Mayhew contained his distaste long enough to record
a song sung in a London penny gaff,[42]

> the whole point of which consisted in the mere utterance of some
> filthy word at the end of each stanza – 'Pineapple Rock' was the grand
> treat of the night and offered greater scope to the rhyming powers of
> the author than any of the others.

There were other occasions for vulgarities, as had once been explained to
a parliamentary committee: 'There are certain things which, in technical
phraseology, are called "gags", and in which there are often vulgarisms
and lewd expressions.' A later committee risked defilement and asked for
an example; E. T. Smith, the unlikely son of an admiral, and a music hall
proprietor who had once fitted his barmaids out in the unholy bloomers,
obliged:[43]

> Perhaps a man comes on stage, and he has a clock under his arm, and
> he says 'This is the way I wind the old woman up on Saturday nights',
> and all kinds of allusions and bestialities in a mild way. Sometimes
> they have an organ, and make the same remarks.

Given the low threshold of moral indignation which obtained among the
Victorian bourgeoisie, such repartee must clearly have put the halls
beyond the pale for the respectable middle-class family. It was this
failure of propriety which *The Times*, 15 October 1883, identified as a
kind of class discrimination in reverse, when it charged that the halls
'intensify the tendency of the nation to become two'.

Almost as affronting to the well-disposed outsider was the inanity of
many music hall songs. Middle-class critics applied their own standards
of literary judgment in separating the song from its performance, and the
unadorned lyrics were dismissed with disdain in the periodical press –
'arrant nonsense', was the verdict of the *Saturday Review*, which otherwise looked kindly if condescendingly on the halls. Working-class writers

who thought the halls represented some advancement in popular manners were embarrased by the low intellectual content of the entertainment,[44] and respectable opinion in general was discouraged by the halls' unedifying repertoire – all the more so because the Victorians believed music to be the least corruptible and most civilising of all arts. An article in the *Dublin University Magazine* of 1874 expresses the disillusionment with the halls in this respect:

> At the time when Music Halls were first started, high expectations were formed of their capabilities in this direction. It was thought that, by coming within the reach of the general public, instead of being a luxury confined to the favoured few, good music and true art would flourish more widely and beneficially than ever they had done before. Literature, which has on the whole done such immense good by becoming cheap and universal, afforded a parallel instance, giving substantial grounds for this hope. . . . We cannot but lament especially the disappointment of the expectations that were once entertained of the Music Halls as means of elevating recreation for the people.

Thus were erstwhile friends of the halls reduced to accepting them on sufferance.

Declared friends of the halls were fewer in number and quieter of voice than the root and branch men of the religious and temperance groups to whom the halls were anathema. Their principal objection to the music hall was the sale of strong drink. The association of drink and public entertainment confirmed the publican as the controlling interest and, it was claimed, fatally sapped the work of moral improvement. Songs which extolled the attractions of drink, and the extravagant wages paid to those who sang them, encouraged prodigality in the audience. On this point, we may recall the indignation of Ewing Ritchie (an inveterate music hall hater) at what he considered the excessive expenditure of an East End working-class audience, 'when people in the middle ranks of life are in despair at the hard prospect before them.'[45] Opponents of the halls were particularly worried by the susceptibility of shopmen and clerks to the temptations of the fast life as extolled by the star in his recurrent role of the Swell. Contemplating the rootless army of young lodgers who aped the manners and style of Champagne Charlie, one critic fulminated against the halls for promoting 'a sham gentility among the striplings of the uneducated classes'. They should, he recommended, 'be stripped of the sham finery and sham jewelry they wear on their indifferently cleaned fingers . . . and sent to serve a couple of years before the mast'.[46] Predictably offensive were the sexual innuendoes of music hall entertainment, which were alleged to corrupt working-class girls and make them easy prey for prowling roués; the enemies of the halls were generally convinced that, in the words of one of their number, they were mostly 'anterooms to the brothels'.[47]

The opposition drew little comfort from evidence of good order and incipient respectability. A Liverpool vicar confronted by singing saloons in which all was drunken confusion, found such scenes 'too disgusting to be very dangerous', maintaining that 'the best conducted of the rooms I fear the most . . . where there is more attention to appearances, and a thin gauze of propriety is thrown over all.' Another reformer, who recorded an increase in the number of respectably dressed women going in to the halls, found this disturbing testimony to the latter's ingenuity in the refinement of old temptations, rather than evidence of real improvement upon the gin shop. This witness drew his conclusions from vigils passed outside the music halls. Few reformers felt the need to go inside in order to prove their case; as one of them remarked: 'One does not want to taste poison to know that it exists in a chemist's shop.' Prejudice against the halls was served by imaginations well practised in discerning the worst – reviewing hostile evidence to the 1866 select committee, Browne remarked shrewdly: 'Good people have too often an exaggerating pruriency of their own.'[48]

The major strategy of the reform lobbies was to contest the annual renewal of music hall licences on the grounds of the moral dereliction of the proprietor. The strategy grew more menacing as the number and scope of licensing regulations increased. Before the 1850s it had been only in London and the area within a twenty-mile radius of its centre that a music and dancing licence had been required in addition to a liquor licence. In 1851 Birmingham introduced music licences, and the rest of the country gradually followed suit. Bolton's magistrates received the new licensing powers in 1872 as a result of a Corporation Improvement Bill. Faced with a petition from the town's Sunday school leaders they refused a music licence to the Museum Music Hall, the descendant of the famous Star, and thus reactivated the controversy which had split Bolton twenty years earlier. The magistrates recanted in the face of public protest meetings, but imposed a form of censorship on all music hall entertainment in the town.[49] Proprietors who learned to negotiate the hazards of the magistrates' sessions faced new difficulties as the administration of music licences passed to elective town and country councils which were more sensitive to organised public opinion.[50] The London County Council in particular won itself a reputation for the stringency of its licensing committee; it had a further powerful sanction to hand in its fire and safety regulations which, as noted previously, caused the closure of many smaller halls unable to afford the alterations necessary to meet them.

In London in the 1880s certain reformers went further than petitioning licensing authorities. For Frederick Charrington, scion of the famous brewing family and convert to Temperance, the road to Damascus lay past the door of his own pubs; shouting 'This way to Hell', he carried out a personal campaign of picketing East End music halls. Hired mobs pelted him with salvoes of flour and pease pudding, but he stood his ground, and was eventually taken to court by one proprietor for injuring his trade. Though found guilty of libel Charrington was undeterred, and his concern to mount a sustained offensive on the halls found ready support from the *Methodist Times*, which called on the LCC for a general purge of the halls as part of the programme of a new Social Purity movement. Stewart Headlam mounted a counter-attack with some support from the working men's clubs. This was the Battle of the Music Halls (which opened well in advance of Mrs Chant's more famous attack upon the Leicester Square Empire in the following decade).[51]

Frontal assault did not, however, recommend itself to all reformers, and the same decade witnessed an attempt to defeat the halls by providing rival entertainment of an improved nature. In 1880 the Coffee Music Hall Company was founded in London, as an extension of the Temperance-based coffee public house movement.[52] A company circular explained its intentions to provide several large music halls in various parts of London to which workingmen could take their wives and children 'without shaming or harming them'. No intoxicant drinks were to be sold. The company's first (and only) venture was to rent the famous south London theatre, the Royal Victoria, which after extensive redecoration and heavy advertising opened as the first Coffee Music Hall in December 1880. The company was meant to pay its own way, but within seven months it was badly in debt, and the counter music hall only survived through the generous subventions of Samuel Morley.

The faltering career of the Victoria Coffee Music Hall illustrates the growing difficulty of effective direct competition with an institution as commercialised as the regular music hall; it demonstrates too how authentic reproduction of a vigorous popular ritual eluded outsiders whose principal concern was control and dilution. 'In the first place', to quote one of the post mortems of the Coffee Music Hall's initial collapse, 'there was an evident want of real, bona fide commercial energy in the management.' The promoters shied away from engaging professional expertise; John Hollingshead, a respected theatre manager with considerable knowledge of the music hall business, was approached for his advice, but was obliged to stay in the background because of doubts about the 'safeness' of his associations. The promoters claimed that they were unable to afford top artists because, unlike the regular halls, they did not enjoy the substantial additional revenue which came from drink sales. This claim, and the assertion that managements elsewhere were warning their artists off the Royal Victoria, may have been true, but it is at least as likely that the coffeemen refused to pay what they condemned as 'reckless wages' on principle. (Arthur Roberts, the comedian, recalled how he got 1s 6d, a cup of coffee and a piece of cake for performing at a Temperance music hall, compared to the half a guinea he had made as a beginner on the regular halls.)[53]

The entertainment was as unsatisfactory as the management, and attendances were often poor. Friendly critics pointed to one familiar failing: 'There was an air of patronage about the place, which the Briton, even in his most unpolished condition, will at once detect; and woe then to success!' Then too, the Temperance propaganda which alternated with the regular acts was too obtrusive: 'At the Victoria', said one complainant, 'you were likely to get, not art, but a huge illuminated diagram of the liver of a Drunkard.'[54] In the further interests of improvement, the artists were obliged to submit to censorship of their material by rehearsing their acts in private for the manager. On stage restraints vanished, and the popular voice broke through:[55]

> Yet, in spite of all these precautions, let there come a chance such as an encore verse, such as some slip or stoppage in the stage machinery, and out will come something, not in the programme and never heard or seen before, which will bring down a thunder of enjoyment from the audience, and at the same time fill the manager's box with sorrow and humiliation.

Audience and performers were never completely tamed, but the music halls were reformed none the less; the industry had little to fear from the inept experiments of the Royal Victoria, but it did respond to the pressures of hostile opposition as the caterers discovered that improvement made for better business as well as sound defence.

V

Music hall interests had from the outset sought to disarm their critics by advertising the moral superiority of their operations to the older tavern entertainments. The *Era* became well practised in defending the licensed trade's new offspring, declaring in effect 'We are all Improvers now.' Speaking up for Sharples against the opponents of the Bolton Star in the 1850s, the paper argued: 'Public amusements must be left to individual knowledge and private enterprise, where they will be well directed and controlled by wholesome competition and authoritative public opinion.' Stewardship was safe in the hands of the responsible publican like Sharples because of his proven competence in a field best left to professionals. 'Public amusement', continued the *Era*, 'is a trade and a mystery and requires to be learned like any other trade . . . no amateur ever ventured into it without damaging its character and injuring its professors.'[56] Charles Morton had been the prime example of the modern reconstructed publican. Although an inveterate gambler, he maintained an impressively respectable front. As one music hall habitué recalled: 'No man was ever half so respectable as Charles Morton looked – his sense of decorum would have done credit to a churchwarden.'[57]

But this kind of protective colouring was poor defence against the intensified attacks of reformers. Alarmed at the threat to their licences and livelihoods, the major London proprietors reconstituted their Protection Association in 1876, and memorialised the Home Secretary with a scheme for an official censor for the halls. At the same time the proprietors asked again to be allowed to play the legitimate drama so that they might introduce dramatic (and improving) sketches. This concession, so it was claimed, would lessen their dependence on the comic singers, who could not be effectively controlled under the current state of the law.[58] When the project collapsed, the proprietors cast themselves as moral vigilantes. House rules of the 1880s warned 'Any artiste giving expression to any vulgarity, in words or actions, when on stage, will be subject to instant dismissal, and shall forfeit any salary that may be due for the current week', and programmes on sale in the halls invited the public to inform the manager of any suggestive or offensive word or action that might have escaped his notice. The *Era*, 28 November 1885, lent its weight to the internal improvement campaign with a progressive editorial which identified a further matter for reform:

It is one of the greatest nuisances possible to sensible people who go to places of amusement to divert their minds from politics and business alike to have the opinions of the daily papers reproduced in verse and flung at their heads by a music hall singer . . . persons who go to a place of amusement to be amused, and these we believe, form the steadily paying class, are too sensible to care to proclaim their private opinions by applauding senseless rubbish with a political meaning.

Proprietors who cater (as it is in their interest to do) for the tastes of the general public would do well to keep the political song nuisance decidedly in abeyance, and we do not despair of the day when such allusions shall be as severely reprobated as, from the manifesto now so often to be read on music hall programmes, we see that impropriety is.

Such proscriptions were soon in practice. At the New Sebright Wholesome Amusements Temple in London, artists were warned to observe the following house rules:[59]

No offensive allusions to be made to any Member of the Royal Family; Members of Parliament, German Princes, police authorities, or any member thereof, the London County Council, or any member of that body; no allusion whatever to religion, or any religious sect; no allusion to the administration of the law of the country.

The give and take between the performer and his public continued to pose a challenge to house discipline. Some managements obliged artists to sign contracts forbidding them to 'address the audience'. Just as the entertainers and the entertainment had been censored, so too did the audiences themselves eventually come under restraint: encores were limited, chorus singing was discouraged and uniformed commissionaires policed the auditorium. Will Thorne recalled proprietors in Birmingham who refused entry to any man not wearing a collar, and the Order and Decorum which became the cliché of every music hall advertisement were so rigidly enforced in Collins Music Hall in Islington that it became known locally as the Chapel.[60]

Despite this conspicuous concern for respectability, the music hall proprietor still remained vulnerable in his role as drink seller. Although, from the 1850s, entertainment had revealed itself as a potentially marketable commodity in its own right, drink seemed essential to the commercial success of the halls. At the Canterbury, Morton had kept a sharp eye on the flow of 'wet money'; when the volume of female attendance (another much advertised guarantee of respectability) had seemed to inhibit the sale of drink, he had been quite ready to turn the ladies away. The trade claimed that ginger beer sold better than the intoxicants, and that door rather than bar receipts provided the greater part of their revenue,[61] but it was not until the 1880s that music hall managements began to phase out the sale and consumption of strong drink in the auditorium. By then, changes in the domestic economy were affecting traditional consumption habits in such a way as to displace strong drink as the prime commodity of working-class leisure time, and the modest but significant increment of a more respectable clientèle also seemed to allow a safe retreat from the previously considerable reliance on liquor sales. As the solicitor for the London proprietors' association explained: 'Every year we find that so soon as we raise our prices and increase our better class accommodation, so soon does the drinking go down.'[62] Thus the phasing out of drink in the auditorium is not to be solely explained as a nervous reaction to the increased militancy of reformers.

The caterer's concern to qualify the music halls as a rational recreation was variously motivated. He was, it is true, anxious to disarm his reform opponents, and the protestations of respectability can be interpreted most obviously as a defensive response. Some of these protestations were undoubtedly disingenuous and misleading, of a piece with the hyperbole of showmanship – on this count we may adduce the trade papers' unsubstantiated claims for extensive middle-class patronage in the 1860s – yet, for the most part, the caterer was a man of honourable intention in his courtship of respectability. Despite his frequent occupational posture of man of the people (an initially valuable role which he derived from his antecedent office of publican) he was pricked by bourgeois ambition and keen aspirations to gentility, and respectability was a necessary condition for their achievement.[63] That the caterer's affirmations of respectability involved the enforcement of operational controls of the music hall more far-reaching and stringent than either the threat or calibre of the reform opposition necessarily justified or the traditions of its antecedent institutions sanctioned, gives the measure of the caterer's maturation as dynamic entrepreneur. Respectability served as a defensive umbrella for the music hall industry and a status lever for its tycoons, but its practice also made for the more efficient and profitable management which was necessary to realise the spectacular new growth opportunities of the mid-1880s.

Applying the disciplines of respectability to audience and performer was part of a general rationalisation of music hall operation. Banishing drinking from the auditorium – 'Abandon hops, all ye who enter here' was the wag's lament – made it less visible and therefore less offensive,[64] but it also facilitated the replacement of free-standing tables and chairs with fixed stall seating facing the stage which made for more efficient logistics: stall seating brought higher audience capacities, allowed for more effective price differentials, encouraged the habit of seat reservation and simplified the running of twice nightly houses. Diminishing the flow of drink may also have had some effect in controlling the volatility of the audience and its random interruptions of the performance. Censoring the artist and restraining the audience was meant to purge the halls of vulgarity, but in cutting down ad libs and encores it also helped ensure the predictable time-tabling of acts. This was important, for the development of the turns system and twice-nightly and matinée performances indicated a managerial concern for the maximum exploitation of time and resources which demanded their efficient scheduling and co-ordination. Eschewing the controversial as well as the vulgar also affirmed the respectability of the reformed music hall (or variety theatre as it was now styled), but it marked, too, the entrepreneurs' bid for the patronage of 'the general public', a clientèle more passive, more predictable and more numerous than that defined by the categories of class.[65]

The credo of the new regime was put by John Hollingshead, dramatic critic, author and sometime music hall manager, in contemplating the formation of the Moss Empires music hall syndicate in 1900 with a capitalisation approaching £2 million:[66]

> This interest has been created by commercial instinct for the supply of wholesome amusement for the people. Its work, without any false veneer, is entirely commercial. Its first duty, which it strictly observes, is to conduct its business according to the rules of good citizenship; and its second duty, which it performs to the best of its ability, is to earn a satisfactory dividend for its shareholders.

Thus by the late Victorian period it could be claimed that the music hall had been assimilated to the cultural apparatus of a capitalist society. In reality the conversion was far from complete. The particular chemistry of artist and audience which characterised the essential music hall experience was, for example, not easily extinguished, and the greatest of all music hall stars, Marie Lloyd, derived no little of her popular success in these years through flouting the new proprieties, and maintaining the traditional flow of ribaldry.[67] But many knowledgeable contemporaries recorded distinct changes in tone as well as those of scale and lay-out in the music hall of the 1880s and 1890s.[68] Managements had succeeded in impressing something of a more compliant manner upon the members of this robust institution. In a sense, big business had succeeded where the social reformers of recreation had failed. The improvements fell far short of the grand designs of the reformers, and proceeded from motives less scrupulously high-minded than theirs, but the manipulations of the music hall entrepreneur manifested a potential for defining and enforcing socially appropriate behaviour – 'the rules of good citizenship' – which identify the emergent mass entertainment industry as a conscious and effective agency of rational recreation. Addressing the Public Morals Conference in London in 1910, the Reverend Thomas Phillips remarked, without flippancy, 'If you bring a puritan saint and a music hall manager into contact, it is wonderful how well they get on together.'[69]

Conclusions

The control of leisure was a serious matter. Not everyone would have followed Bishop Fraser in adjudging it 'the great question of the day', but the debate it generated, if not the actual support it won, testified to a general acknowledgement of its importance to social reform in Victorian England. Traditionally, a nation's recreations were taken as a test of its people's character: 'when we follow men into their retirements', pronounced Joseph Strutt in 1801, 'we are most likely to see them in their true state, and may judge of their natural dispositions.'[1] Most observers who applied this test in the 1830s and 1840s found the recreations of the working people in a general state of physical and moral degeneracy. This state of affairs reflected poorly not only on the natural dispositions of working people, but on the general ability of the nation to match its astonishing material advances with commensurate social improvements. In repairing popular recreations, therefore, reformers were engaged in the responsible tasks of servicing national self-respect and demonstrating the efficacy of human agency in broadening and accelerating progress.

Contributing to the renovation of society was an exciting undertaking which encouraged, and indeed demanded, bold and sanguine expectations; yet it was characteristic of the propaganda of rational recreation that it produced no extensive scenarios of the future society that would reap the benefit of its endeavours. Visionary indulgence was limited to the occasional invocation of a bowdlerised Merrie England. We can understand why the reform literature produced no new Cockaigne, but why, from among ruling classes raised on a classical education, were there so few glimpses of the Good Life, of any modern equivalent of the *otium cum dignitate* of antiquity? This deficiency (for which, for example, one could not chide free traders) suggests how strongly the prospect of an increasingly leisured society was a matter of disquiet rather than gratification.

In the bourgeois ideology of the reformers, leisure was less the bountiful territory in which to site Utopia, than some dangerous frontier zone beyond the law and order of respectable society. Traditionally it dispensed its own licence, and it was its abuse which had imprinted itself most deeply in middle-class consciousness; in a work-oriented culture it represented an invitation to idleness and dissolution – the weakness of an ill-disciplined working class, the badge of an unduly privileged aristocracy. The prospect of leisure in abundance was therefore alarming, for it promised to extend a domain of free choice wherein the customary restraints of morality were more honoured in the breach than the observance, at a time when traditional primary and community controls were being atrophied by the strains of industrialisation and urban growth. The corruptions of leisure threatened to undo the painstakingly fashioned bonds of a new work discipline in the labour force, and its blandishments seriously unsettled the internal disciplines of the middle-class world.

Rational recreation was an attempt to forge more effective behavioural constraints in leisure. Popular recreations were to be improved, not through repression, but through the operation of superior counter-attractions. Within the new controlled environments, reformers would instruct workingmen in the elementary accomplishments of social economy – time-budgeting and money management – and introduce them to the satisfactions of mental recreation, thus immunising them against the contagion of the pub and the publican, and the animal regression of 'sensuality'. Building the new play discipline depended upon motivating the resources of self-help, but reformers recognised the need to provide some collective reinforcement for individual initiative in the fluid and open milieu of leisure. From the mid-1860s occasional voices could be heard canvassing for State direction and subsidy for certain popular pastimes,[2] but in general reformers put their faith in the voluntary and fraternal association of the classes as a more appropriate and effective instrument of rational recreation. The middle classes were to be the superintendents of the reformation, taking the lead in providing new amenities, and ensuring by their presence the display and projection of approved standards of leisure conduct to their inferiors; in the enaction of the superior example, the middle classes would be reminded of their own moral responsibilities. The taking of recreation in common would, it was claimed, assuage the hostilities of capital and labour, and restore a sense of community between the classes.

Conceived as a measure of humanitarian relief and an antidote to political subversion in the Chartist era, rational recreation became more than an exercise in repair or pacification: it became part of the ongoing and fundamental re-socialisation of the working classes. For Henry Solly, it was one of the three vital fronts upon which working-class improvement had to proceed. Recreation, Temperance and Education, he claimed, were like a three-legged stool – remove one and the whole project collapsed. To the reformer, Francis Fuller, the question of popular recreations went 'to the root of the social tree – to the deepest foundation of the political fabric'.[3]

Implementing the new regimen of rational recreation was a difficult business. The reformer's counter-attractions had to supersede those of a powerful rival. With his manoeuvrability along the margins of the class line, his commercial expertise and his historical capital of social skills, the publican still enjoyed the strategic advantage in the expanding world of popular leisure. The history of the music hall shows how well some men in the trade seized the new market opportunities, transforming the recreational function of the publican from obliging pedlar of popular merry-making to large-scale manager and entrepreneur. The reformers were unable to attract capable management for schemes like the coffee taverns and palaces, which anticipated later successful enterprises by commercial interests, but which could not survive as essentially amateur ventures in the competitive retail sector which formed a growing adjunct to the leisure market.[4] It was difficult too, to supplant the public house in the affections and habits of the workingman. Despite legislative curtailment and the loss of some of its functions to more specialised institutions, the pub continued to offer the irreducible attractions of drink and good fellowship which still qualified it, in Brian Harrison's phrase, as 'the working man's voluntary association'. Some club promoters tried to encourage new loyalties by urging members to regard their club 'as a schoolboy regards his school, or the university man his college', but even with the allowance of beer, the Club movement found it hard to approximate the comforting rituals and ambience of the public house and the traditional mediations of its steward.[5] Because many institutions of rational recreation duplicated the material apparatus of the pub with considerable authenticity, the shortcomings in social warmth were all the more obvious.

A major impediment to the achievement of sociability in rational recreation was the heavy prescriptive burden that the reform experiments were obliged to bear. Although the formula of the Club movement represented a tactical modification of the didactic design, much of CIU literature, in general with that of other reform sources, is like an admonitory finger held under the reader's nose. Coffee taverns which provided refreshment and entertainment put across their fundamental raison d'être in the friezes of improving tracts which covered their walls. Striking a balance between easy congeniality and earnest improvement – 'How to steer between weak tea and good behaviour and a rollicking free and easy' – was a social exercise for which the bourgeois philanthropist was ill equipped.[6]

A further problem in achieving a fruitful modus vivendi in a reform setting sprang from the reformer's impatience with the culture he sought to reform. The working classes were credited with the fundamental potential which allowed of their ultimate perfectibility, but this acknowledgement was often compounded by an insistent note of moral censure at their current delinquency. Henry Solly could discern the angel in marble, the new Greeks among the roughs and toughs of Victorian London, but realisation of the ideal was slow and frustrating. Thus Samuel Greg could talk in one breath of 'gently leading' his work-men, in the next of 'breaking them into my system'. In promoting reform through voluntary association, the reformers settled for a norma-tive authority which provided few effective sanctions, certainly nothing like the statutory power of temperance and education legislation or the coercive power implicit in the semi-custodial institutions of factory villages or board schools. In their concern to expedite improvement, reformers frequently rejected the osmosis of example-setting and adopted an autocratic manner which alienated workingmen. Obtrusive patronage evidenced the best intentions perhaps, but it was also sympto-matic of a social distance between the classes which disallowed of any easy informality of address. Autocracy was the mode which sat most comfortably with an upper bourgeoisie that saw itself as a new urban gentry, but manifestly lacked the traditional common touch. As Canon Barnett remarked of a later generation of reform endeavour, what was offered was 'machine hospitality'.[7]

The middle classes in general failed to answer the reformers' call to community. A good deal of the debate on recreation in middle-class family periodicals was concerned only to legitimise bourgeois leisure, and while the middle classes acknowledged the need for improved and expanded amenities for working people, they refused the role of super-intendent. Whatever assurance reformers gave to the contrary, popular recreation seemed unlikely ground whereon to preserve one's own respectability, let alone impress it successfully upon the strident mob that was Matthew Arnold's populace:

that vast portion ... of the working class which, raw and half-developed, has long lain half-hidden amidst its poverty and squalor, and is now issuing from its hiding-place to assert an Englishman's heaven-born privilege of doing as he likes, and is beginning to perplex us by marching where it likes, meeting where it likes, bawling what it likes, breaking what it likes.

Popular recreations were viewed by middle-class opinion as a series of nuisances. If the commonest bourgeois experience was that of being jostled by rowdies on the promenade or offered contumely by the loafers in the street, one can understand the distaste for joining in what Matthew Browne described – accurately enough, but to the detriment of his case – as 'monstrous symposia of the people'. Indeed one recurrent argument on this question relieved respectable citizens of any responsibility for reforming popular assemblies by their presence by suggesting that such places were better left unreformed. The delinquencies of popular recreation could never be completely extinguished, so it was claimed, but they could none the less be contained and isolated if some natural law of quarantine was left to operate – 'Let the vices that cannot be suppressed by law collect in their own haunts, and thus relieve other places of their loathsome presence.'[8]

It was no recommendation that recreational improvement promised to remake the workingman in the image of his master. Encouraging working people to 'ape their betters', as Stanley Jevons proposed, was acceptable where it fostered moral rectitude, but not where it produced the 'sham gentility' that *Tinsley's Magazine* noted among the music hall crowds. Here, emulation parodied the status insignia of the superior classes, threatening class and status differentials that the latter were trying anxiously to reinforce. Defending social frontiers became increasingly important as the economic and political primacy of the middle classes seemed jeopardised by business uncertainties and the extension of the franchise – 'The destruction of a political privilege', said the *Saturday Review*, 'is tacitly compensated by an increase of social exclusiveness.' Leisure in particular represented an area where social distinctions were vulnerable. It was here, in 1860, that *The Times* had discerned the makings of 'a great revolution . . . great displacement of masses, momentous changes of level'.[9] The defence of the reformed athletic sports against infiltration from below is a good example of middle-class determination to maintain existing levels. Thus the bourgeoisie refused to indulge in 'workingman worship', and withheld their active support from a reform programme which appeared as much a social solvent as a social anodyne.

Despite the many difficulties which dogged reformers, popular recreations had much improved by the mid-1880s, and afforded one of the major proofs of national progress in the Jubilee year.[10] The irregular and spasmodic flux of pre-industrial leisure was now contained in the standardised instalments that came with the routine of the modern working week and year. With certain gross exceptions drink was becoming more of an incidental social lubricant and less of a total experience. Though it was true that, as Chesterton later remarked, the Englishman was more interested in the inequality of horses than the equality of man, some areas of popular sport had been purged of gambling under the new reformed codes. Bolton's butcher boys no longer undertook bizarre eating contests, and no latter-day Ben Hart emptied the mills in working hours; if there were still loungers in the street, passers-by were no longer 'slutched and stoned by wild natives', as one of the town's chroniclers had recorded in the 1830s. In Bolton, as in England, popular recreations had undergone a considerable transformation – 'From the Roaring Boys to the Boys' Brigade', as the social anthropologist Geoffrey Gorer has neatly put it.[11]

What had the various campaigns for rational recreation contributed to this? The Club movement and innumerable individual and municipal benefices were owed to reforming zeal, and in their conception, if not always their propagation, the new sporting codes can be credited to rational recreation. It would, however, be impossible to arrive at a precise balance sheet, for reformers were only one element in a broader process of social change. The continued tightening of discipline that came with increasing mechanisation, the further sub-division of labour and the spread of scientific management in the workplace; the development of major institutionalised agencies of social control in state education and modern policing; the more pervasive and effective jurisdiction of local government; improvements in working-class purchasing power and the increasing availability and more forceful marketing of cheap consumer goods; perhaps too the habits that came with the routine use of trains and trams – all contributed to the house-training of the English proletariat in this period, and the rationing and rationalisation of its leisure. As we have seen, there were many times when the prescriptions of rational recreation seemed counter-productive; certainly, reformers did not achieve the moral monopoly of working-class recreation that they had hoped for and, on the face of it, they had little success in effecting a fraternal association of the classes in play. Yet, if rational recreation failed to achieve regular occasions of social community, it was likely to have played an important part in the dissemination of those middle-class values of discipline and conformity which allegedly linked the upper sections of the working classes to the bourgeoisie in a common vertical allegiance to the tenets of respectability. Thus if the practice of leisure was still compartmentalised according to class, it may none the less have answered to the authority of a shared ideology which cut across class lines.

In seeking to explain what it was that gave mid-Victorian England its relative cohesion and stability, a number of recent students of the period have identified respectability as a key factor. Drawing upon one of the commonplaces of contemporary social observation, they have confirmed to their own satisfaction a basic division in society between respectables and non-respectables. Essentially a secular distillation of evangelical disciplines enjoining moral rectitude and economic self-sufficiency, respectability is represented as a pervasive value system that exerted, in Geoffrey Best's words, 'a socially-soothing tendency, by assimilating the most widely separated groups (separated socially or geographically) to a common cult'. 'Here', he maintains, 'was the sharpest of all lines of social division, between those who were and those who were not respectable: a sharper line by far than that between rich and poor, employer and employee, or capitalist and proletarian.' The spread of respectability, it is argued, secured social compliance of the upper strata of the working classes, and opened up a gulf between them – the respectable poor – and their inferior brethren – the roughs. The gulf was particularly noticeable, according to Brian Harrison, in the public conduct of recreation. Harrison argues that the temperance movement, with its strong presence in rational recreation, consolidated bonds between middle and working-class respectables, who then worked in concert to improve the remainder.[12] Other researchers have identified distinct temperance communities in working-class areas which preserved a complete sub-culture of respectability over several decades.[13]

Schemes of rational recreation outside the sphere of the major temperance organisations recruited from the 'respectable' working class. Henry Solly, though not always discriminatory on this count, appealed to 'the more prudent, worthier members of the working class' to seek refuge in the clubs, away from 'their reckless, drinking, cowardly or dishonest neighbours', and a guest MP at the CIU's first annual meeting distinguished between 'Thinkers and Drinkers' among the Union's prospective clientèle.[14] The enforcement of standards of dress, cleanliness and previous good conduct as conditions of membership in certain schemes, while perhaps designed to encourage a wholesale improvement in manners, seems aimed at recruiting those workingmen who had made some important elementary accommodations to respectability. The specific social and occupational membership of the institutions of rational recreation requires further research, but we may assume that except in the case of casual or itinerant working-class custom, such as that drawn to the coffee taverns, the clientèle was self-selective, comprising the superior workingmen who actively sought improvement. The fragmentary evidence of the composition of committees and teams in workingmen's social and sports clubs suggests the dominance of the artisanat or labour aristocracy, the element in the working classes supposedly most susceptible to the embraces of respectability.

Thus far, we may allow that rational recreation assisted in extending and reinforcing the constituency of respectables: what is much less certain is the degree to which the respectability of workingmen represented a stable and consistent pattern of behaviour and belief denoting real attachment to bourgeois values. The new scholarly emphasis on the normative power of respectability carries with it some acknowledgement of the variations and ambiguities that attended its operation. Significantly here, those historians who have tested the embourgeoisement thesis against detailed reconstructions of the social and material culture of the labour aristocracy in specific localities have suggested that workingmen generated their own kind of respectability; in important respects they reformulated its conventional values and preserved a distinctive working-class identity in its practice.[15] In demonstrating the complex nature of respectability in working-class sub-cultures, these studies also emphasise that its ideals were expressed in terms of style and appearance as much as in a set of beliefs and attitudes. A fuller study of respectability as a behavioural mode may enable historians to understand more clearly the nature and implications of its operation, particularly in inter-class relationships. To do this properly, however, we need a more realistic and conceptually apposite appreciation of the urban context. Certainly we need to guard ourselves against the tendency to represent working-class respectability, whether primarily emulative or indigenous, as a cultural absolute in the lives of its practitioners – once a respectable, always a respectable – for this is to adopt Victorian presumptions of behavioural consistency that ignore the changes wrought in personal behaviour patterns by the new circumstances of modern city life. It may be more fruitful if for the moment we disregard respectability as the manifestation of a generalised social code or ideology, and consider its incidence in the more limited and situational sense as the performance of a particular role.

The combination of elementary role analysis and a simple ecological model of the urban process suggests a further modification of the respectability thesis. The expansion of the urban population and the development of a society ordered by the priorities of industrial growth fragmented social interaction, and the coherent and readily comprehensible pattern of social life shared within the small-scale traditional community was increasingly supplanted by a pattern of life notable for its discontinuities of experience in terms of time, space and personnel. In the city, residential segregation and the establishment of new work routines compartmentalised social classes and the basic activities of work, leisure and home life to such a degree that man the social actor was obliged to play out his encounters in an ever greater number of discrete situational settings. As personal behaviour became increasingly segmentalised, so did those units of responsive conduct that sociology identifies as roles become more insulated from the continuous observation of others.[16] Insulation was most pronounced in inter-class relationships, for here physical discontinuities were compounded by the bourgeois concern to maintain social distance. However, although middle-class commentators frequently acknowledged how little they really knew of the world of working people – it was, in a much used phrase, *terra incognita* – they had a rudimentary map of the territory; this they peopled with stereotypes constructed from the imaginary projections of the role-specific behaviour met with in the intermittent social exchanges of real life. Only rarely were they confronted with evidence which revealed their mistake in presuming upon a consistency in role progression that duplicated the conventional uniformity of their own lives. The Birmingham manufacturer, William Sargant, who is quoted in chapter 2, realised as much when he discovered by accident that one of his steadiest and, as he had thought, most temperate workmen was a heavy drinker away from the workshop. Sargant's bewilderment on being met with the evidence of this aberration suggests how little cognisant of role discontinuities contemporaries could be, particularly in inter-class relationships. The role progression of Bill Banks on his day off is germane here too, for it suggests how readily a workingman could move in and out of respectability as a succession of situations dictated. In his social classification of *The Nether World*, George Gissing offered that the broad distinction lay between two great sections of workingmen: 'those who do, and those who do not, wear collars'.[17] It is plausible that respectability was assumed or discarded, like a collar, as the situation demanded.

If we approach respectability as a role rather than as an ideology or a uniform life-style the nature of class relationships in leisure takes on a new light. Thus working-class membership of church football teams can be seen as a purely instrumental attachment, calculated to extract certain benefits often unobtainable from the resources of working-class life. In this case, working-class behaviour which might have appeared as deferential mimesis from above, functioned as a kind of exploitation in reverse for its actors, who assumed respectability to meet the role demands of their class superiors.[18] Given the episodic and otherwise limited nature of most class exchanges, respectability was an undemanding role to play for workingmen who possessed the minimal apparatus of dress, speech and demeanour required to match its standardised public image. It may be too, that the middle class were particularly susceptible to calculative or instrumental adoptions of respectability by working-class men, because of the bourgeois need to believe in the existence of a regiment of working-class respectables recruited from the denizens of Victorian England's terra incognita. To the middle-class outsider, the myth of substantial working-class respectability was a necessary prop to the self-esteem of his own class, proof of the middle-class capacity to remake society in its own image, a preservative of the flattering fiction of an open society and, not least, a source of reassurance in a period whose conventional appellation as an age of equipoise obscures the extent to which the bourgeoisie were still mindful of the social and political combustibility of the urban masses.[19] At the same time, it is possible that the unease of the bourgeois patron in the company of workingmen derived in part from his vague perception of the latter's capacity for dissembling; in CIU official reports, the emphasis placed on the well-mannered behaviour of club audiences at lectures and the respect accorded visiting middle-class speakers suggests a need for reassurance that all was truly what it seemed, and indicates a certain apprehension at the tenuous hold of the normative sanctions of respectability in the relatively unstructured territory of modern leisure.

Obviously not all respectable behaviour was superficial and calculative, but the degree to which some or other variant of respectability operated as a consistent or exclusive imperative in working-class life must not be exaggerated. The elevation of respectability as a key concept in the ordering of our understanding of mid-nineteenth century England reflects the current scholarly concern to acknowledge and explain major determinants of group behaviour other than simply class. But in the more sophisticated social map of Victorian society that is emerging, class will not go away, and in the world of recreation its differentials are more striking than those of other significant social categories that have recently been explored.

Popular recreations in the latter years of the period under consideration were marked by a strong class character; though they conformed to certain features of the reform design, the marks of rationalisation and respectability which they bore were no proof of cultural embourgeoisement.

In part, the rationalisation which overtook working-class recreation – the regular programming of sport, for example, and the stabilising of the weekend break – represented an internal adjustment to the irreversible pressures on time, space and energy brought by a modern industrial society. In part, rationalisation was an extension of existing disciplines in working-class life, an amplification of the rules and regulations that had long ordered the good fellowship of the friendly societies. Within these constraints the working classes maintained a considerable autonomy of style and jurisdiction. Thus the early clubmen secured important modifications of Solly's original prescription, and in the 1880s a later generation won democratic control of the CIU administration. In the same decade working-class enthusiasm brought professionalism to association football, and infused the game with an atavistic tribalism which put it beyond the reach of middle-class tolerance or understanding. At the same time the beleaguered music halls continued to nourish a vigorous popular sub-culture that celebrated life with such unabashed vulgarity that the halls were accused of practising inverted class discrimination. In his investigation of the remaking of working-class culture in London in the last thirty years of the century, Stedman Jones suggests that an increasing addiction to the consolations of a new leisure world contributed significantly to the dilution of any widespread class combativity among workers. Here, so we are told, was a distinctive new way of life (in essence duplicated among the English working class as a whole) which remained impervious to middle-class attempts to determine its character or direction, yet in the manner of its resistance was 'no longer threatening or subversive, but conservative and defensive'. Much of the evidence from recreational life that I have drawn upon reinforces this impression of the impermeability of working-class culture, yet there seems to be more here than simply the refusal to comply. The cultural politics of the 1880s indicate a capacity for collective assertiveness among working people that goes beyond the simply conservative and defensive. Moreover, as I have suggested, there is a case to be made that in various leisure time transactions with their class superiors workers were capable of manipulating the social order to their own advantage; this can be seen as a form of class-based combativity, albeit more piecemeal and less demonstrative than a formally organised and overtly political mode of opposition.[20]

There is obviously a great deal more to be learned of the place and function of leisure in working-class culture in this period. Its significance for the understanding of the dialectic of social class is clearly considerable, but there are other questions to be asked. What, for example, were the nature and extent of its satisfactions? Leisure is more than the simple conjunction of time and activity in whatever areas of life we conventionally designate as 'free'. In today's world leisure, to be authentic, must be felt to be free, and in many people's minds it is closely associated with a positive sense of enjoyment and the opportunity for self-expression and growth. Though the historian can by several criteria identify a phenomenon called modern leisure in Victorian society he cannot therefore assume that it was fully perceived as such by any but a small and socially sensitive minority. Yet working people throughout this period did articulate a high regard for leisure as freedom. This regard was most commonly expressed in what Robert Baker, the factory inspector, called 'Labour's great motto' – 'The master's right in the master's time, and the workman's right in his own time', a sentiment echoed from the floor at more than one annual conference of the CIU.[21] It may be objected that any freedom that is bought by a surrender in the workplace must be fatally flawed, and there is considerable evidence of the contamination of modern leisure by the long shadow of alienated labour; in this respect free leisure may have been as dubious a gain as the free labour market. This consideration cannot be ignored, but there is more to understanding leisure than locking it into some work-leisure dichotomy and there is an affirmative quality to popular recreation in these years which disallowed the reduction of its gratifications to those of simple compensation for the frustrations of work.

Yet if we are to understand the satisfactions of popular leisure we must take into account the frustrations that impinged upon them, and these were undoubtedly considerable. Leisure could rarely have been a constant in the lives of working people. In the course of industrialisation the ample resources of time and space that were the sureties of much traditional recreation were expropriated, and the modern worker was in large part obliged to pay for their retrieval, as well as for much else that made leisure palatable. Though there was an overall improvement in working-class income in the second half of the century, this relative affluence was acutely vulnerable to short-term fluctuations in trade, changes in family size and the vagaries of money management in the working-class home. There were, it was true, always some pleasures to be had very cheaply or for free, but as the cycle of poverty turned so the good things of modern leisure must have continually advanced then receded, moving within then beyond the reach of individual men and women for whom such a pattern was now likely to be perceived less as part of some eternal order of things, than as one of the major and demoralising inequities of relative deprivation. Bites at the cherry were in any case fewer for the women in working-class life; many of its leisure institutions were predominantly masculine and what evidence there is suggests that married men often persisted in funding their own pleasures at the expense of their dependants.[22] These were some of the problems of leisure for working people that their betters ignored; but they were none the less real, and the advent of leisure for the masses may have intensified rather than ameliorated the endemic social and psychological anxieties of life in a modern urban industrial society in a way that reduces the much advertised agonies of the bourgeois conscience and the conventional 'problem of leisure' to the level of a moral charade.

Yet amid its contradictions, leisure served as an important milieu for preserving the identity of a working class which offered substantial resistance to the cultural hegemony of its superiors. Contemplating the question 'How to win our workers?', the *Saturday Review*, 5 July 1862 recognised the stubborn reality that confronted all campaigns to change their social life:

> As classes rise in social importance (as our working classes un-
> doubtedly do), as they acquire a position and make a law and society
> for themselves, they almost necessarily become more inaccessible to
> external influence. They grow in a sense more sufficient for them-
> selves, and the sympathy implied by mixing of classes becomes more
> difficult. We suspect the great working classes as a body become every
> day a firmer phalanx, not really impressible or subject to change – or
> rather, only to be changed through causes which go deeper than their
> 'betters' can easily get at.

In the last two decades of the century the broadening impact of tech-nology and the quickening of commercialisation constituted the forces that were to impress themselves more deeply on leisure and popular culture than any social reform campaign. Though the debate on leisure was far from extinguished, society was coming to terms with its modern role. Leisure was now less to be explained than exploited, and the eventual success of the reformed music halls in turning its customers into disciplined consumers adumbrated a new formula for capitalist growth that was to make the mass leisure industries of the present century more formidable agents of social control than anything experi-enced in Victorian society. In this sense, the contest for the hearts, minds and pockets of the new leisure class had only just begun.

Abbreviations

BC	*Bolton Chronicle*
BM	British Museum (now British Library)
BRL	Bolton Reference Library
Bull.SSLH	*Bulletin of the Society for the Study of Labour History*
CIJ	*Club and Institute Journal*
PP(HC)	*Parliamentary Papers* (House of Commons)
PP(HL)	*Parliamentary Papers* (House of Lords)
RC	Royal Commission
SC	Select Committee
SR	*Saturday Review*
Trans.NAPSS	*Transactions of the National Association for the Promotion of Social Science*

Notes

Introduction

1 For the dark age, see 'Working-class culture: conference report', *Bull.SSLH*, 9 (1964), 6; 'Work and leisure in industrial society: conference report', *Past and Present*, 30 (1965), 96–103. Cf. J. L. and B. Hammond, *The Age of the Chartists, 1832–1854: A Study of Discontent* (1930). For the emergence of the new 'traditional' culture, see E. J. Hobsbawm, *Industry and Empire* (1968), 135–7; *idem, Worlds of Labour* (1984), 194–213. For the final stage see A. Briggs, *Mass Entertainment: The Origins of a Modern Industry* (Adelaide, 1960).

2 R. W. Malcolmson, *Popular Recreations in English Society, 1700–1850* (1973). See, however, H. Cunningham's critique of his idea of a climacteric or vacuum in 1830s and 1840s, *Leisure in the Industrial Revolution: c. 1780–1880* (1980), 9–10, in which see also chs 1–2. Also useful for reconstructing the world of pre-industrial recreations are K. Thomas, 'Work and leisure in pre-industrial society', *Past and Present*, 29 (1964), 50–62; E. P. Thompson, *The Making of the English Working Class* (1963), *passim*, esp. 402–12; *idem*, 'Time, work-discipline, and industrial capitalism', *Past and Present*, 38 (1967), 56–97; *idem*, 'Patrician society, plebeian culture', *Journal of Social History*, vii (1974), 382–405; B. Bushaway, *By Rite: Custom, Ceremony and Community in England, 1700–1880* (1982).

3 For the general structural transformation of leisure in the period, see S. de Grazia, *Of Time, Work and Leisure* (1964), 181–95; J. Dumazedier, *Toward a Society of Leisure* (1967), 33–41; T. Burns, 'Leisure in industrial society', in M. A. Smith, S. Parker and C. S. Smith (eds), *Leisure and Society in Britain* (1973), 40–55. For the historian's appreciation, see M. R. Marrus, *The Rise of Leisure in Industrial Society* (1974); J. Myerscough, 'The recent history of the use of leisure time', in I. Appleton (ed.), *Leisure Research and Policy* (1974), 3–16. For the new history of leisure published since the mid-1970s, see the Introduction to the paperback edition, below.

4 W. C. Lake, 'Leisure time', in J. E. Kempe (ed.), *The Use and Abuse of the World*, 3 vols (1873–5), i, 39–56.

5 For the problems of definition see J. Dumazedier, *Sociology of Leisure* (1974), 67–76; B. M. Berger, 'The sociology of leisure; some suggestions', *Industrial*

Relations, i (1962), 31–45. For the neo-classicists, see de Grazia, op. cit., and
W. R. Torbert and M. P. Rogers, *Being for the Most Part Puppets: Interactions among Men's Labor, Leisure and Politics* (1973). For more recent
sociology, see S. Parker, *Leisure and Work* (1983); N. C. A. Parry, 'Sociologi-
cal contributions to the study of leisure', *Leisure Studies*, ii (1983), 57–81;
J. Clarke and C. Critcher, *The Devil Makes Work: Leisure in Capitalist
Britain* (1985); C. Rojek, *Capitalism and Leisure Theory* (1985).
6 For other contextual studies of leisure in sizable towns and cities, see H. E.
Meller, *Leisure and the Changing City 1870–1914* (1976) on Bristol; S. Yeo,
Religion and Voluntary Organisations in Crisis (1976) on Reading; A. Delves,
'Popular recreation and social conflict in Derby, 1800–1850', in E. and
S. Yeo (eds), *Popular Culture and Class Conflict* (1981), 89–127; R. Poole,
Popular Leisure and the Music Hall in Nineteenth Century Bolton (1982);
A. Redfern, 'Crewe: leisure in a railway town', in J. K. Walton and J. Walvin
(eds), *Leisure in Britain, 1780–1939* (1983), 117–136; J. Crump, 'Amuse-
ments of the People: Recreational Provision in Leicester, 1850–1914',
University of Warwick Ph.D thesis (1985). See also the several articles by
D. Reid on aspects of leisure in Birmingham, noted below. For further com-
parison, see R. Rosenzweig, *Eight Hours for What We Will: Workers and
Leisure in an Industrial Society, 1850–1920* (1983) on Worcester, Mass., and
F. G. Couvares, *The Remaking of Pittsburgh: Class and Culture in an
Industrialising City, 1877–1919* (1984).

Introduction to the paperback edition

For various forms of assistance with this piece I have to thank Chris Waters, Alan
Tomlinson, Bob O'Kell, Carol Adam and Bonnie Bailey.

1 G. Stedman Jones, 'Class expression versus social control? a critique of
recent trends in the social history of "leisure"', reprinted in his *Languages of
Class* (1983), pp. 76–89. The 1975 conference papers and discussions are
reported in *Bull.SSLH*, 32 (1976), 5–18.
2 F. M. L. Thompson, 'Social control in Victorian Britain', *Economic History
Review* (May 1981), 189–208. See also A. Tomlinson (ed.), *Leisure and Social
Control* (1981).
3 S. Cohen and A. Scull (eds), *Social Control and the State: Historical and
Comparative Essays* (1983). See also A. P. Donajgrodzki (ed.), *Social Control
in Nineteenth Century Britain* (1977), though only the editor engages fully
with the theory.
4 On Gramsci, see the readings in T. Bennett, G. Martin, C. Mercer and
J. Woollacott (eds), *Culture, Ideology and Social Process* (1981), section 4;
Bennett, 'Popular culture and "the turn to Gramsci"' in Bennett, Mercer
and Woollacott (eds), *Popular Culture and Social Relations* (1986), xi–xix;
E. Laclau and C. Mouffe, *Hegemony and Social Strategy* (1985). The Open

University course U203, *Popular Culture*, makes considerable use of hegemony in its published teaching materials; for a dissenting voice in the course team, see J. Golby, 'Bourgeois hegemony? the popular culture of mid-nineteenth century Britain', *Social History Society Newsletter* (Autumn 1981), 7–8, whose liberal populist perspective is further developed in Golby and A. W. Purdue, *The Civilisation of the Crowd: Popular Culture in England, 1750–1900* (1984). Historians who have made particularly effective use of the concept of hegemony are R. Q. Gray, *The Labour Aristocracy in Victorian Edinburgh* (1976) and P. Joyce, *Work, Society and Politics: The Culture of the Factory in later Victorian England* (1980) though their interpretations differ. For a useful review of the general engagement with theory in nineteenth-century studies, see C. Kent, 'Presence and absence: history, theory and the working class', *Victorian Studies*, xxix (1986), 437–62.

5 On appropriation in history, see the essays by R. Chartier and D. Hall in S. Kaplan (ed.), *Understanding Popular Culture: Europe from the Middle Ages to the Nineteenth Century* (Berlin, 1984), and its extensive employment in P. Bourdieu, *Distinction: A Social Critique of the Judgment of Taste* (1984).

6 Jones, 'Working-class culture and working-class politics in London, 1870–1900: notes on the remaking of a working class', *Journal of Social History*, vii (1974), 460–508, reprinted in Jones, *Languages of Class*, 179–238.

7 See also S. Hall, 'Popular culture and the state', in Bennett *et al.*, *Popular Culture*, 22–49 and P. Corrigan and D. Sayer, *The Great Arch: English State Formation as Cultural Revolution* (1985).

8 For other useful general treatments, see J. Lowerson and J. Myerscough, *Time to Spare in Victorian England* (1977); J. Walvin, *Leisure and Society, 1830–1950* (1978); Golby and Purdue, op. cit.

9 For a similar emphasis on vitality and renewal in the 1830s and 1840s, see this book, chapter 1 above. See also P. N. Stearns, 'The effort at continuity in working-class culture', *Journal of Modern History*, lii (1980), 626–55.

10 Waters, ' "All sorts of outlandish recreations": history, sociology and the study of leisure in England, 1820–70', *Historical Papers of the Canadian Historical Association* (1981), 8–33. His important Ph.D thesis, 'Socialism and the Politics of Popular Culture in Britain, 1884–1914' (Harvard, 1985), is shortly due for publication.

11 Storch (ed.), *Popular Culture and Custom in Nineteenth Century England* (1982), in which see D. Reid, 'Interpreting the festival character', 125–153.

12 M. Bakhtin, *Rabelais and his World* (1968). For modern projections of carnival in a still relatively compact holiday form, see G. Thompson, 'Carnival and the calculable', and Bennett, 'Blackpool pleasure beach', in *Formations of Pleasure* (1983), 124–37, 138–55; Bennett, 'Hegemony, ideology, pleasure: Blackpool', in Bennett *et al.*, *Popular Culture*, 135–54. See also V. Turner, 'Comments and conclusions', in B. A. Babcock, *The Reversible World: Symbolic Inversion in Art and Society* (1978), 276–96.

13 The Open University course booklets for U203, 'Popular Culture', provide a sophisticated primer in Cultural Studies theory and method. For a report

from its other institutional stronghold in the Centre for Contemporary Cultural Studies at the University of Birmingham, see Hall, 'Cultural Studies and the Centre: some problematics and problems', in S. Hall, D. Hobson, A. Lowe and P. Willis (eds), *Culture, Media, Language* (1980), 15–47. See also J. Clarke, C. Critcher, C. and R. Johnson (eds), *Working Class Culture: Studies in History and Theory* (1979), and Johnson, 'The story so far: and further transformations?', in D. Punter (ed.), *Introduction to Contemporary Cultural Studies* (1986), 277–313. For the culturalist/structuralist debate at its most theatrical see 'Culturalism' in R. Samuel (ed.), *People's History and Socialist Theory* (1981), 375–408 and the editor's admirable 'History and theory', xiv–lvi. See also Bennett, 'Popular culture: divided territory', *Social History Society Newsletter* (Autumn 1981), 5–6.

14 For example, D. Hebdige, *Subculture: The Meaning of Style* (1979); D. Laing, *One Chord Wonders: Power and Meaning in Punk Rock* (1985). For a suggestive study of a modern leisure institution that makes meanings as well as money, see S. Frith, *Sound Effects: Youth, Leisure and the Politics of Rock 'n' Roll* (1983).

15 On particular problems of definition, see Hall, 'Notes on deconstructing "the popular"', in Samuel, op. cit., 227–40; Bennett, 'The politics of the "popular" and popular culture', in Bennett *et al., Popular Culture*, 6–21.

16 J. K. Walton and J. Walvin (eds), *Leisure in Britain, 1780–1939* (1983) in which see J. Richards, 'The cinema and cinema-going in Birmingham in the 1930s', 31–52. (For an introduction to the underworked inter-war period, see A. Howkins and J. Lowerson, *Trends in Leisure, 1919–1939* (1979).) For another useful regional study, see A. Metcalfe, 'Organised sport in the mining communities of South Northumberland, 1800–89', *Victorian Studies*, xxv (1982), 469–95.

17 Walton, *The English Seaside Resort: A Social History, 1750–1914* (1983), 210. See also his *The Blackpool Landlady: A Social History* (1978).

18 A. Mason, *Association Football and English Society, 1863–1915* (1980). See also S. Tischler, *Footballers and Businessmen: The Origins of Professional Soccer in England* (1981). The history of sport is a rapidly expanding field and the newest research can be sampled in the *British Journal of Sports History* (1984–). An important new work from the perspective of radical historical sociology is John Hargreaves, *Sport, Power and Culture: A Social and Historical Analysis of Popular Sports in Britain* (1986). See also 'Sport, Labour and Society', Conference Report, *Bulletin of the Society for the Study of Labour History*, 50 (Spring 1985), 4–12.

19 P. Bailey (ed.), *Music Hall: The Business of Pleasure* (1986); J. S. Bratton (ed.), *Music Hall: Performance and Style* (1986). There is some attempt here to wed the methods of social history and cultural studies. See also R. Poole, *Popular Leisure and the Music Hall in Nineteenth Century Bolton* (1982); P. Summerfield, 'The Effingham Arms and the Empire: the evolution of music hall in London', in E. and S. Yeo (eds), *Popular Culture and Class Conflict* (1981), 209–40, and 'Patriotism and empire: music hall entertainment,

1870–1914', in J. M. Mackenzie (ed.), *Imperialism and Popular Culture* (1986), 17–48.

20 H. Cunningham, 'Leisure', in J. Benson (ed.), *The Working Class in England 1875–1914* (1985), 133–64.

21 R. McKibbin, 'Work and hobbies in Britain, 1880–1950', in J. M. Winter (ed.), *The Working Class in Modern British History: Essays in Honour of Henry Pelling* (1983), 127–46.

22 McKibbin, 'Why was there no Marxism in Great Britain?', *English Historical Review*, xcix (1984), 329. For other readings of late Victorian and Edwardian popular or working-class culture in addition to those referred to above, see J. H. S. Kent, 'The role of religion in the cultural structure of the late Victorian city', *Transactions of the Royal Historical Society*, xxiii (1973), 163; S. Yeo, *Religion and Voluntary Organisations in Crisis* (1976), 185–210; S. Meacham, *A Life Apart: The English Working Class, 1890–1914* (1977); B. Waites, 'Popular culture in late nineteenth and early twentieth century Lancashire', in Open University, *Popular Culture* (1981), block 2, unit 6; E. J. Hobsbawm, *Worlds of Labour* (1984), 194–213; Golby and Purdue, op. cit., 164–202.

23 Johnson, 'Culture and the historians', in Clarke *et al*, op. cit., 61–2; Hall, 'Notes on "the popular"', 229–31.

24 For the new freedoms of working-class youth on the first upswing of the poverty cycle, see M. J. Childs, 'Working-class youth in late Victorian and Edwardian England', McGill University Ph.D thesis, 1986.

25 For a critique of liberal representations of pluralism, and a review of the new indigenous sociology of leisure in Britain, see J. Clarke and C. Critcher, *The Devil Makes Work: Leisure in Capitalist Britain* (1985).

26 P. L. Berger, B. Berger and H. Kellner, *The Homeless Mind: Modernisation and Consciousness* (1974), 62–77. For the selective rehabilitation of American sociology in cultural studies, see Hall, 'Cultural Studies and the Centre', 23–4. On 'the subject', see R. Coward and J. Ellis, *Language and Materialism* (1977).

27 P. Bailey, '*Ally Sloper's Half-Holiday:* comic art in the 1880s', *History Workshop*, 16 (1983), 4–31.

28 See however, A. J. Kidd and K. W. Roberts (eds), *City, Class and Culture: Studies of Social Policy and Cultural Production in Victorian Manchester* (1985). John Lowerson is preparing a book on sport and the English middle classes, see his various articles, e.g. '"Scottish croquet": the English golf boom, 1880–1914', *History Today* (May 1983), 25–30. Note too Golby and Purdue, op. cit., 144–63; Cunningham, *Leisure in the Industrial Revolution, passim*; Walton, *English Seaside Resort*, 165–6.

29 P. N. Furbank, *Unholy Pleasure: The Idea of Social Class* (1985), 100–6 and, on reading the hierarchies of cultural taste, Bourdieu, op. cit. See also R. Bowlby, *Just Looking: Consumer Culture in Dreisser, Gissing and Zola* (1985); Samuel, 'A nice class of people: the middle class between the wars', *New Socialist* (January–March 1983). On the upper classes, see D. Cannadine, 'The theory

and practice of the English leisure classes', *Historical Journal* (1978), 445–67.

30 G. Crossick (ed.), *The Lower Middle-Class in Britain, 1870–1914* (1980).

31 See Bailey, '*Ally Sloper's Half-Holiday*' and cf. C. Mercer, 'Complicit pleasures', in Bennett *et al*, *Popular Culture*, 50–68.

32 See however, D. Vincent, 'Reading in the working-class home', and J. Walvin, 'Children's pleasures', in Walton and Walvin, op. cit., 207–26, 227–41, and S. Constantine, 'Amateur gardening and popular recreation in the nineteenth and twentieth centuries', *Journal of Social History*, xiv (1981), 387–406.

33 See V. Hey, *Patriarchy and Pub Culture* (1986); the essays by J. S. Bratton and J. Traies in Bratton (ed.), *Music Hall*; T. C. Davis, '"Does the theatre make for good?" actresses' purity and temptation in the Victorian era', *Queen's Quarterly* (Spring 1986), 33–49. See also Walvin, *Leisure and Society*, 41–6; Cunningham, *Leisure in the Industrial Revolution*, 129–32; C. Griffin *et al*, 'Women in leisure', in Jennifer Hargreaves (ed.), *Sport, Culture and Ideology* (1982), 88–116; E. Ross, 'Survival networks: women's neighbourhood sharing in London', *History Workshop*, 15 (1983), 10–11.

34 Johnson, 'Culture and the historians', 61.

35 The theme is expanded in Bailey, '"Will the real Bill Banks please stand up?" a role analysis of mid-Victorian working-class respectability', *Journal of Social History*, xii (1979), 336–53.

1 Popular recreation in the early Victorian town

1 J. L. and B. Hammond, *The Skilled Labourer* (1920), 7. The pessimistic view finds contemporary support in P. Gaskell, *The Manufacturing Population of England* (1833), 24, and F. Engels, *The Condition of the Working Class in England* (1969), 56, 128, 156–8.

2 M. Shearman, *Athletics and Football* (1889), 269; L. Faucher, *Manchester in 1844: Its Present Condition and Future Prospects* (1844), 83–4; F. Place, *The Improvement of the People* (1834), 12–15; J. M. Ludlow and Lloyd Jones, *The Progress of the Working Class, 1832–67* (1867), 18.

3 J. Lawson, *Letters to the Young on Progress in Pudsey* (1887), 58.

4 Bolton's history in the nineteenth century can be studied from C. H. Saxelby, *Bolton Survey* (1953); H. Hamer, *Bolton, 1838–1938* (1938); J. C. Scholes, *History of Bolton* (1892); W. Brimelow, *Political and Parliamentary History of Bolton* (1888). J. Clegg, *Annals of Bolton* (1888), is useful for chronology. The course of urban development is covered in A. Dingsdale, 'Bolton: A Study in Urban Geography, 1793–1910', University of Durham BA Hons thesis, 1967. For a very useful bibliography, see A. Sparke, *Bibliographia Boltoniensis* (1913). Of Bolton's press I have most frequently used the *Bolton Chronicle*, the longest surviving newspaper in continuous existence in the period 1830–85. See also, more recently, R. Poole, *Popular Leisure and the Music Hall in Nineteenth Century Bolton* (1982); P. Joyce, *Work, Society and Politics: The Culture of the Factory in Later Victorian England* (1980) for Lancashire mill towns, including Bolton.

5 SC further report on the licensing of places of public entertainment, *PP*(HC) 1854, xii, qq. 195–6, 3175. Sources for the study of the public house are many and diverse. Brian Harrison offers a selection in 'Drink and sobriety in England, 1815–1872', *International Review of Social History*, xii (1967), 204–76, and provides an admirable review of the pub and the role of strong drink in society in the 1820s in *Drink and the Victorians: The Temperance Question in England, 1815–1872* (1971), 37–63. See also Harrison, 'Pubs', in H. J. Dyos and M. Wolff, *The Victorian City*, 2 vols (1973), i, 161–90; B. Spiller, *Victorian Public Houses* (1972). M. Girouard, *Victorian Pubs* (1975), is a social as well as an architectural history, and very good on both counts, though mainly confined to London. See also P. Clark, *The English Ale-house: A Social History, 1200–1830* (1983); M. A. Smith, 'Social usages of the public drinking house', *British Journal of Sociology*, xxxiv (1983), 367–85.

6 For the general prominence of the societies in working-class life, particularly in Lancashire, see J. H. Clapham, *An Economic History of Modern Britain*, 3 vols (1932), ii, 471–3; P. H. J. H. Gosden, *The Friendly Societies in England, 1815–1875* (1961), 62–6, 115–27. For Bolton's societies, see BRL, *Grand Lodge Circular*, 115 vols (1831–1959), and B. T. Barton, *Historical Gleanings of Bolton and District* (1881), 11–13 for the women's societies which also flourished in the 1840s. *BC*, 17 August 1850, has a useful list of club anniversaries.

7 W. L. Sargant, *Economy of the Labouring Classes* (1857), 352.

8 J. W. Hudson, *The History of Adult Education* (1851), 148, 211; *BC*, 7 March 1857; Faucher, op. cit., 49–53. For pub debates in Birmingham, see Harrison, *Drink and the Victorians*, 337–8; for working-class music-making in industrial Staffordshire, see R. Nettel, *Music in the Five Towns, 1840–1914: A Study in the Social Influence of Music in an Industrial District* (1944), 7–9. See also R. Elbourne, *Music and Tradition in Early Industrial Lancashire, 1780–1840* (1980).

9 V. E. Chancellor (ed.), *Master and Artisan in Victorian England: The Diary of William Andrews and the Autobiography of Joseph Gutteridge* (1969), 84–7; C. M. Smith, *The Working Man's Way in the World* (1853), 259–60. For the recreations of other self-improvers see D. Vincent, *Bread, Knowledge and Freedom: A Study of Nineteenth Century Working Class Autobiography* (1981), 172–3, 182–5.

10 S. Bamford, *Walks in South Lancashire* (1844), 13–14. See also E. P. Thompson's claim in *The Making of the English Working Class* (1963), 831, that 'This was, perhaps, the most distinguished popular culture England has known.'

11 E. P. Thompson, 'Time, work-discipline, and industrial capitalism', *Past and Present*, 38 (1967), 56–97. For the general question of working hours, see M. A. Bienefeld, *Working Hours in British Industry: An Economic History* (1972). See also H. Cunningham, *Leisure in the Industrial Revolution* (1980), ch. 2.

12 SC on the operation of the Factory Act, *PP*(HC) 1840, x, qq. 1602–6; J. Fielden, *The Curse of the Factory System* (1836), 30.

13 SC on public institutions, *PP*(HC) 1860, xvi, qq. 444, 1484. John Ruskin defended the Sunday lie-in before the same committee, q. 1693.

14 W. R. Smee, *National Holidays* (1871), 2–4; J. A. R. Pimlott, *The English-man's Holiday: A Social History* (1947), 81. For early examples of employers' restrictions on traditional holidays, see S. Pollard, *The Genesis of Modern Management* (1968), 214–15.

15 B. Disraeli, *Sybil, or the Two Nations* (1904), 217. But St Monday was not always spent on, or recovering from, the bottle: Douglas Reid shows that many Birmingham workers took the opportunity to attend exhibitions, visit the local botanical gardens and organise rail excursions, 'The decline of Saint Monday, 1766–1876', *Past and Present*, 71 (1976), 76–101.

16 SC on the operation of the Factory Act, qq. 370–85; *BC*, 4 October, 15 November 1834, 22 May, 18 September 1841; RC Children's Employment, *PP* 1842, xv, 134–7.

17 *Morning Chronicle*, 12 April 1828, in Place collection of newspaper cuttings, xli, Manners and morals, p. 43, BM; E. P. Thompson quotes *The Times* in *The Making of the English Working Class* (Penguin edn, 1968), 935–6. (All other references to this work are to the American edition.)

18 SC further report on licensing, qq. 259–61. Evidence of Revd J. J. Baylee, secretary of the Lord's Day Observance Society.

19 R. Rooney, *The Story of My Life* (1947), 28–9.

20 K. Allan, 'Recreations of the Industrial Working Class in Lancashire, *c.* 1825–50', University of Manchester MA thesis, 1947, 22–5; J. Lilwall, *The Half-Holiday Question Considered* (1856), 25; Bienefeld, op. cit., 47, 79.

21 Reports of the assistant hand-loom weavers commissioners, *PP*(HC) 1840, xxiv, 315–16; *BC*, 2 October 1852.

22 W. Wroth, *Cremorne and the Later London Gardens* (1907), 11, 44–5. See also R. D. Altick, *The Shows of London* (1978).

23 *BC*, 22 June 1850. On footpaths, see W. Cooke Taylor, *Notes of a Tour in the Manufacturing Districts of Lancashire* (1842), 136; E. Chadwick, *Report on the Sanitary Condition of the Labouring Population of Great Britain* (1842, ed. M. W. Flinn, 1965), 337.

24 C. Dickens, *Sketches by Boz*, 2 vols (1836), i, 314–30. There is a particularly good account of Bolton's New Year Fair in *BC*, 13 January 1872. Representative reports on Halshaw Moor Wakes, Deane Church Wakes and the historic Turton Fair are to be found in *BC*, 5 October 1833, 13 September 1834, 13 and 27 September 1851, respectively. See also S. Alexander, *St. Giles' Fair, 1830–1914: Popular Culture and the Industrial Revolution in Nineteenth Century Oxford* (1970) and, for recollections of boisterous times at Lansdown Fair in Bath, 'Lord' George Sanger, *Seventy Years a Showman* (1910), 86–7. For fairs and wakes in general, see Thompson, *English Working Class*, 403–7; Malcolmson, op. cit., 16–33. More recently, see Cunningham, 'The Metropolitan Fairs', in A. P. Donajgrodzki (ed.), *Social Control in Nineteenth Century Britain* (1977), 163–184; D. Reid, 'Interpreting the festival calendar: wakes and fairs as carnivals', in R. Storch (ed.), *Popular Culture and Custom in Nineteenth Century England* (1982), 125–153; M. Judd, '"The oddest combination of town and country": popular culture and the London

fairs, 1800–60', in J. K. Walton and J. Walvin (eds), *Leisure in Britain, 1780–1939* (1983), 11–30.

25 Henry Mayhew records the exodus of London's street children to the Derby; some appeared at other race meetings as far afield as Wolverhampton. *London Labour and the London Poor*, 4 vols (Frank Cass edn, 1967), i, 166, 265, 478. For Manchester, see C. Aspin, *Lancashire, The First Industrial Society* (1969), 165–9.

26 SC on the observation of the sabbath, *PP*(HC) 1831–2, vii, 247; *Era*, 28 July 1850; H. Shimmin, *Town Life* (1858), 163–70; SC on the operation of the Factory Act, qq. 4047–54.

27 Mayhew, op. cit., is the most obvious source for the study of street life. See also, for the young, J. Gillis, *Youth and History* (1974), 62.

28 SC on drunkenness, *PP*(HC) 1834, viii, qq. 3327–33.

29 For contemporary descriptions of the gin palace, see Dickens, op. cit., i, 276–87; Faucher, op. cit., 49. For the new-style publican and the barmaid as glamour object, see SC on drunkenness, q. 3270; *Town*, 22 July 1837; J. C. Coyne, 'The barmaid', in A. Smith (ed.), *Sketches of London Life and Character* (1859), 142–8. For changes in the operation and logistics of the pub, see M. Gorham and H. McG. Dunnett, *Inside the Pub* (1950), 26, 64–5, 94–113; Girouard, op. cit., 23–53.

30 'Public amusements', *Colburn's Monthly Magazine*, lvi (1938), 300; 'The age before the music halls', *All The Year Round*, xi (December 1873), 175–80. Note should be made too, of the proliferation of penny theatres or 'gaffs' which provided cheap entertainment, mainly for youths and children. Here again, any available space was pressed into service – empty shop premises, stables, etc. Mayhew, op. cit., i, 18, 40–2, stumbled upon scores of these dens in his perambulations. See also J. Springhall, 'Leisure and Victorian youth: the penny theatre in London, 1830–1890', *History of Education Society Proceedings* (1980), 101–24.

31 *The Times*, 18 October 1834.

32 S. Pollard, 'Factory discipline in the industrial revolution', *Economic History Review*, xvi (1963), 254–91. For the fullest treatment on the general assault on popular recreations, see R. W. Malcolmson, *Popular Recreations in English Society* (1973), 89–107. See also, R. D. Storch, 'The problem of working-class leisure: some roots of middle-class moral reform in the industrial North', in Donajgrodzki, op. cit., 138–62.

33 'Public amusements: the pretensions of the Evangelical class', *Edinburgh Review*, liv (1831), 100–14. For the Methodists, see RC on children's employment, *PP* 1843, xiii, 527.

34 For Bishop Blomfield and the new regime, see R. A. Solloway, *Prelates and People: Ecclesiastical Social Thought in England, 1783–1852* (1969), 150, 219, 240, 319–30. The old-style sporting parson was however far from extinct: clergymen were noted among the crowd at the famous Sayers–Heenan prize fight in 1860, and there was consternation in church circles in 1874 when it was discovered that the winner of the St Leger was owned by a vicar in Lincolnshire. See *The Times*, 12 October 1874.

35 For these various reform movements, see Harrison, 'Religion and recreation in nineteenth century England', *Past and Present*, 38 (1968), 98–125. For Stamford, see Malcolmson, op. cit., 130–3.

36 Representative debates can be found in *Hansard*, xxiii, 21 May 1835 (when the volume of petitions was remarked); xxxiii, 21 April 1836; lv, 14 July 1840.

37 The history and ramifications of the Temperance movement are examined at length in Harrison, *Drink and the Victorians*. The constructive role of the movement in recreation is considered below, ch. 2.

38 For the controversy over the Star, see *BC*, 14 August–9 October 1852, and *Era*, 29 August–9 October 1852. As a prominent local Tory (like most publicans) Sharples was obviously unlikely to attract the sympathies of a predominantly Liberal bench; significantly, the magistrates had refused his invitation to visit the Star, though JPs from other towns had accepted. See also Poole, op. cit., 51–61.

39 SC on public houses and places of public entertainment, *PP*(HC) 1844, vi, iii; SC on the observance of the sabbath, 176.

40 T. Frost, *The Old Showman and the Old London Fairs* (1874), 337–56. See also Judd, op. cit.

41 *Hansard*, lvii, 22 March 1841.

42 W. Howitt, *The Country Year Book* (1850), 263; W. E. Adams, *Memoirs of a Social Atom*, 2 vols (1903), i, 54; reports of James Fogg, *BC*, 30 November 1850, 17 May 1851.

43 Sanger, op. cit., 37–41, 178; F. Place, *Autobiography* (ed. M. Thale, 1972), 65–7, 77; 'A working man', *Scenes from My Life* (1858), 30–1; Storch, 'The plague of blue locusts: police reform and popular resistance in northern England, 1840–57', *International Review of Social history*, xx (1975), 61–90. On Derby, see A. Delves, 'Popular recreation and social conflict in Derby, 1800–1850', in E. and S. Yeo, *Popular Culture and Class Conflict* (1981), 88–127.

44 E.g. *BC*, 24 April, 1 May 1841; 7 May 1842; 29 September 1849.

45 G. Godwin, *Town Swamps and Social Bridges* (1859), 94–5, also records a police campaign against the penny gaffs.

46 S. Dyson, 'Local Notes and Reminiscences of Farnworth' (Farnworth, Lancs, 1894), 39–42, typescript in Farnworth Central Library; and his 'Recollections of rural Congregationalism', *BC*, 29 April 1882.

47 As Max Gluckman observes in his study of the licence in ritual in certain African societies, rituals which allow people to behave in normally prohibited ways can only be tolerated where all parties agree to the normal rightness of a particular kind of social order: once the social order is questioned (as was clearly the case in the 1830s and 1840s) such rituals become inappropriate, *Customs and Conflict in Africa* (1956), 109–37.

48 Diary of Henry Richard, 22 March 1853, National Library of Wales, MS 10199B. I owe this reference to Dr Eric Sager. In previous times householders had been glad to invite the pace-eggers into their houses; by the 1850s the term had become synonymous with disturber of the peace in local reports of

of any kind of disorder. For Ashton, see W. E. Axon, *The Black Knight of Ashton* (Manchester, 1870).

49 SC on the laws governing gaming, *PP*(HL) 1844, xii, v–vii, 78; H. Custance, *Riding Recollections and Turf Stories* (1894), 23, 40–1; R. Mortimer, *The Jockey Club* (1958), 69. See also W. Vamplew, *The Turf: A Social and Economic History of Horse Racing* (1976).

50 'Doncaster races', *Bentley's Miscellany*, xxxi (1851), 116–22; SC on the laws governing gaming, 95; J. Ashton, *History of Gambling in England* (1898).

51 Pam's part in the 1853 bill is described in *Era*, 1 January 1854. For the rest, see SC on the suppression of betting houses, *PP*(HC) 1852–3, i; *Hansard*, cxxix, 11 July 1853.

52 C. Dickens, *The Uncommercial Traveller* (1861), 139; Mayhew, op. cit., i, 11–16; Shimmin, op. cit., 59–71. Modern accounts include J. C. Reid, *Bucks and Bruisers: Pierce Egan and Regency England* (1971), and J. Ford, *Prizefighting* (1971).

53 'The decline of the Ring', *Tinsley's Magazine*, iv (1869), 552–8; H. Hawkins, *Reminiscences*, 2 vols (1904), 58.

54 H. D. Miles (ed.), *Tom Sayers, His Life and Pugilistic Career* (1866). The fight ended in a draw; among other things, Sayers was rewarded with a public subscription and a reception at the Stock Exchange. The Queensberry Rules were introduced in the same year.

55 SC on the observation of the sabbath, 24; *Era*, 8 September 1850.

56 Storch, 'Plague of blue locusts', p. 79; SC on the education of the poorer classes, *PP*(HC) 1838, vii, 96; Malcolmson, op. cit., 126–33. The Stamford bull-running was however still being celebrated at an annual dinner in 1850, see *Era*, 17 November 1850.

57 W. Andrews, *Bygone England* (1892), 179–80; P. H. Ditchfield and W. Page (eds), *The Victoria History of Berkshire*, 3 vols (1907), ii, 296. One bull could provide up to six days' sport.

58 Dyson, op. cit., 39–42. BRL, T. Hampson, *Horwich: Its History, Legends and Church* (1883), 229–35. S. Rothwell, *Local Reminiscences* (1899), 6.

59 BRL, R. S. Hilton, T. Grimshaw and W. Witherington, *Sunday Closing* (1853); *BC*, 4, 11 June 1853; Harrison, 'The Sunday trading riots of 1855', *Historical Journal*, viii (1965), 219–45.

60 The story appears in A. L. Crauford, *Sam and Sallie: A Romance of the Stage* (1933), 145–55, a respectable piece of theatre history recording the careers of the Lane family who ran the Britannia in Hoxton, and there are allusions to such an incident in other sources. See also C. Barker, 'A theatre for the people', in K. Richards and P. Thomson (eds), *Essays on Nineteenth Century British Theatre* (1971), 1–17.

61 BM, 'A Fellow Workman', *The Races Defended as an Amusement* (Newcastle, 1853). The writer was careful to dissociate himself from the drink interest.

62 G. J. Holyoake, *The Rich Man's Six and the Poor Man's One Day: A Letter to Lord Palmerston* (1856). See also the observations of the old Chartist, R. J. Richardson, before SC further report on licensing, 1854, q. 3589.

63 *Bolton Free Press*, 16 September 1843. (The *Press* provided – intermittently – a Liberal voice to counter the Tory and Anglican bias of the *Chronicle*.)

64 *Era*, 28 July 1850, 12 September 1852. A national trade paper of the licensed victuallers, the *Era* is an excellent source for the study of popular recreation throughout most of the nineteenth century, with particular attention to the theatre and music hall.

65 The early history of licensing, in Report on the supply of beer, Monopolies Commission, *Sessional Papers* (HC) 1969, ccxvi, app. 8, 153–8; Harrison, *Drink and the Victorians*, 73–4.

66 SC on the observation of the sabbath, 254–5; *Town*, 21 July 1838. In Birmingham, the publican and later music hall impresario, James Day, was organising canal and railway excursions in 1841. For the obituary of this unsung Thomas Cook, see *Era*, 27 February 1876.

67 Dickens, *The Uncommercial Traveller*, 63–6.

68 J. Macmillan, 'Description of the Checks issued by Birmingham Concert Halls, 1850–1920', MS 1924 in Birmingham Central Reference Library. The young patrons of penny gaffs bought entrance with an empty bottle or a scrap of food.

69 SC further report on licensing, qq. 3175–6; SC on public houses and places of public entertainment, q. 3964.

70 J. Adams, *A Letter to the Justices of the Peace of the County of Middlesex, on the subject of Licences for Public Music and Dancing* (1850); *Town*, 18 August 1838.

71 SC on drunkenness, qq. 571, 4297–9; Hudson, op. cit., 157; W. Dodd, *The Factory System Illustrated in a Series of Letters to Lord Ashley* (1842), 182–3. See also Disraeli's entertaining description of a singing saloon in the factory town of Mowbray (perhaps based on Dodd), op. cit., 105–16.

72 *BC*, 17 July 1852 provided a history and description of the Star on the famous occasion of its destruction by fire. See also BRL, Star Music Hall account book, 1847–50, xerox copy from the original in the possession of Mrs D. Scholefield, St Mary's Cray, Kent. For Gray's evidence, see SC report on licensing, qq. 7715–16, 7653, 7789, where there is further material on the number and composition of northern audiences. Bolton's population was then about 60,000. See also Poole, loc. cit; M. B. Smith, 'Victorian Entertainment in the Lancashire cotton towns', in S. P. Bell (ed.), *Victorian Lancashire* (1974), 169–85.

73 There is an interesting analysis of theatre and saloon entertainments in Manchester, 1837–54, by R. J. Richardson in SC further report on licensing, qq. 3621–3. A major limitation on saloon repertoire followed from the 1843 Theatre Act which virtually prohibited the staging of legitimate drama where there was smoking or the sale of intoxicants in the auditorium; this ruling did much to determine the unique character of saloon, and later, music hall entertainment, though opposed by music hall interests throughout the century. The main quotation is from 'The amusements of the mob', *Chambers's Edinburgh Journal*, xxvi (1856), 225, 281.

74 Taylor, op. cit., 136; SC on public houses and places of public entertain-
    ment, qq. 3927–31.
75 *Bowtun Luminary*, 13 January 1855; *BC*, 18 September 1852.
76 (J. Clay) *Chaplain's Report on the Preston House of Correction* (1841), 6.
77 Hudson, op. cit., 140; J. Hole, *An Essay on the History and Management of
    Literary, Scientific, and Mechanics Institutes* (1853), pp. 74–5.

2 Rational recreation: voices of improvement

1 For the state of society and the idea of improvement in this period, see
    A. Briggs, *The Age of Improvement, 1783–1867* (1959); J. F. C. Harrison, *The
    Early Victorians, 1832–51* (1973), 162–73. For rational recreation see also
    R. D. Storch, 'The problem of working-class leisure: the roots of middle
    class reform in the industrial North: 1825–50', in A. P. Donajgrodzki (ed.),
    Social Control in Nineteenth Century Britain (1977), 138–62; H. Cunning-
    ham, *Leisure in the Industrial Revolution* (1980), chs 3, 4.
2 E. Bulwer Lytton, *England and the English*, 2 vols (1833), i, 35–8. See also
    T. Arnold, *Thirteen Letters on our Social Condition* (1832), 29–31.
3 *Hansard*, xv (1833), cols 1049–59; R. A. Slaney, *A Plea for the Working
    Classes* (1847), 134–43.
4 E. Chadwick, *Report on the Sanitary Condition of the Labouring Population of
    Great Britain* (1842, ed. M. W. Flinn, 1965), 337–8; B. Heywood, *Addresses
    delivered at the Manchester Mechanics Institute* (1843), 120; J. C. Symons,
    Tactics for the Times (1849).
5 Report of the commission on the state of the population in mining districts,
    PP 1850, xxiii, 578–87. For recent investigations of miners at play, see
    J. Benson, *British Coalminers in the Nineteenth Century: A Social History*
    (1980), ch. 6; R. Colls, *The Collier's Rant: Song and Culture in the Industrial
    Village* (1977).
6 W. Cooke Taylor, *Notes of a Tour in the Manufacturing Districts of Lancashire*
    (1842), 132–6.
7 J. P. Kay-Shuttleworth, *The Moral and Physical Condition of the Working
    Classes* (1832), 61–3, quoted in R. Johnson, 'Educational policy and social
    control in early Victorian England', *Past and Present*, 49 (1970), 101–2.
8 W. Howitt, *The Rural Life of England*, 2 vols (1838), ii, 142–3, 272–3.
9 SC on drunkenness, viii.
10 *Hansard*, xxxvii, 9 March 1837, 23 April 1839; SC on public walks, *PP*(HC)
    1833, xv, 54–5, 57; Second report of the commission for enquiring into the
    state of large towns and populous districts, *PP* 1845, xviii, 73–4; *The Times*,
    26 March 1845. The C in C of the Army, Lord Hill, issued an order in 1841
    providing for cricket grounds to be made near every barrack station in the
    kingdom.
11 Quoted in W. A. Munford, *Penny Rate: Aspects of British Public Library
    History, 1850–1950* (1951), 14–15.
12 *Hansard*, xxvii, 2 May 1835; xxxv, 11, 12 July 1836; lxxi, 15 August 1843;

SC on public houses and places of public entertainment, *PP*(HC) 1852–3, xxxvii, q. 4486. The tag regarding opinions and manners is attributed to Bulwer-Lytton by C. S. Peel in G. M. Young (ed.), *Early Victorian England, 1830–65*, 2 vols (1934), i, 30.

13 *Hansard*, xxiii, 15 May 1834; *BC*, 25 September 1852.

14 SC on the observation of the sabbath, 242.

15 J. Manners, *A Plea for National Holydays* (1843). Cobden's concern is noted in J. A. Nicholls, *Collected Letters* (1862), 8.

16 B. H. Harrison, 'Two roads to social reform: Francis Place and the "Drunken Committee" of 1834', *Historical Journal*, xi (1968), 296; S. G. Green, *The Working Classes of Great Britain: Consideration of the Means for their Improvement and Elevation* (1850), 47–8.

17 W. Lovett, *The Life and Struggles of William Lovett* (1876), 287–8, 372–5; W. Blott, *A Chronicle of Blemundsbury* (1892), 204–6.

18 SC on public walks, 9.

19 S. Greg, *Two Letters to Leonard Horner on the Capabilities of the Factory System* (1840), 12; Report of inspectors of factories, *PP* 1856, xviii, 87.

20 Greg, op. cit., 21–3; *Dictionary of National Biography*.

21 J. F. C. Harrison, *Robert Owen and the Owenites in Britain and America* (1969), 223; R. Boyson, *The Ashworth Cotton Enterprise: The Rise and Fall of a Family Firm, 1818–80* (1970); App. to first report of the commission on children's employment, *PP* 1842, xiii, 201. For other examples of recreational provision by employers, see R. S. Fitton and A. P. Wadsworth, *The Strutts and Arkwrights, 1758–1830* (1958), 258–60; A. Raistrick, *Two Centuries of Industrial Welfare* (1938), 71.

22 *Spectator*, 22, 29 October 1842; A. Ure, *The Philosophy of Manufacturers* (1835), 349. See also W. Ashworth, 'British industrial villages in the nineteenth century', *Economic History Review*, iii (1950), 378; S. Pollard, 'Factory villages in the industrial revolution', ibid., lxxix (1964), 513–31.

23 Report of the commissioner on the population of mining districts, *PP* 1845, xxviii, 219–20; 1847, xvi, 425; 1849, xxii, 395. I am grateful to Tim Joss for alerting me to a possible confusion over which of the Greg family properties was struck in 1847.

24 App. to first report on children's employment, 381. See also Leonard Horner's remarks in Factory inspectors' reports, *PP* 1846, xx, 576.

25 See Horner again in Factory inspectors' reports, *PP* 1849, xxii, 148–55. Cf. J. Glyde, *The Moral, Social and Religious Condition of Ipswich* (1850), 64; P. A. Whittle, *Blackburn As It Is* (1852), 154, 159–60.

26 J. W. Hudson, *The History of Adult Education* (1851), p.v (his emphasis). Potter is quoted in Munford, op. cit., 60; cf. *Manchester and Manchester People . . . by a citizen of the World* (1843), 19. Factory inspectors' reports, *PP* 1849, xxii, 148–55.

27 There is a considerable literature on the Mechanics' Institutes. Hudson provides the best contemporary account and notes the various expedients to which some institutes resorted in 'straining for popularity' in the 1840s. Their

manipulation by the middle class and the difficulties of attracting a working-class membership are dealt with in M. Tylecote, *Mechanics' Institutes of Lancashire and Yorkshire before 1851* (1957); J. F. C. Harrison, *Learning and Living, 1790–1960: A Study in the History of the English Adult Education Movement* (1961); B. Simon, *Studies in the History of Education, 1780–1870* (1960).

28　T. Heywood, *A Memoir of Sir Benjamin Heywood* (1863), 201; Hudson, op. cit., 137, 140.

29　BRL, J. Johnston, *Mawdsley Street Congregational Chapel, 1808–1908* (1908), 127. By 1837 the weekly attendance at Bolton's Sunday schools was estimated at close to 10,000, of which number the Anglican churches claimed a quarter, the Methodists a half, the balance being shared by other denominations. Later reports recorded continuing growth in attendance. J. Black, *A Medico-Topographical, Geological and Statistical Sketch of Bolton and its Neighbourhood* (1837), 70; P. A. Whittle, *A History of Bolton* (1855), 151. For the anti-singing saloon association, see *BC*, 28 August 1852.

30　SC on the education of the poorer classes, *PP*(HC) 1838, vii 19, 123–4.

31　Johnson, op. cit., 110; E. D. Mackerness, *A Social History of English Music* (1964), 154–65.

32　SC on drunkenness, p. viii, qq. 1067–73.

33　J. S. Pudney, *The Thomas Cook Story* (1953), 59; R. Marchant, 'Early excursion trains', *Railway Magazine*, c (1954), 426–9. Cf. above, ch. 1, n. 66.

34　L. L. Shiman, 'The Band of Hope movement: respectable recreation for working-class children', *Victorian Studies*, xviii (1973), 49–74; B. H. Harrison, 'Liberalism and the English Temperance press, 1830–72', ibid., xiii (1969), 126–58; *People's Journal*, 4 July 1846; W. Howitt, *The Country Year Book* (1850), 227. For digest histories of Bolton's Temperance movement by contemporaries, see *BC*, 15 March 1862, 11 March 1882.

35　J. G. Rule, 'The Labouring Miner in Cornwall, c. 1740–1870', University of Warwick Ph.D thesis, 1971, 316, and his 'Methodism, popular beliefs and village culture in Cornwall, 1800–1850', in R. D. Storch (ed.), *Popular Culture and Custom in Nineteenth Century England* (1982), 48–70; B. Harrison, 'Two roads to social reform'.

36　Lovett, op. cit., 311; *Address and Rules of the Workingmen's Association* (n.d.); W. Lovett and J. Collins, *Chartism: A New Organisation for the People* (1841), 33, 46, 60–1; SC on public libraries, *PP*(HC) 1849, xi, vii, qq. 2759–803. T. Cooper, *Letters to the Young Men of the Working Class* (1851), 9. See also, E. Yeo, 'Culture and constraint in working-class movements, 1830–1855', in E. and S. Yeo, *Popular Culture and Class Conflict* (1981), 155–86; J. Epstein, 'Some organisational and cultural aspects of the Chartist movement in Nottingham', in Epstein and D. Thompson (eds), *The Chartist Experience: Studies in Working-Class Radicalism and Culture* (1982), 221–68.

37　E. Yeo, 'Robert Owen and radical culture', in S. Pollard and J. Salt (eds), *Robert Owen, Prophet of the Poor* (1971), 84–114. See also the evidence of John Finch to SC on drunkenness, qq. 3814–30.

38　C. Thomson, *The Autobiography of an Artisan* (1847), 345–71.

39 *BC*, 20 September 1850.

40 For the 1840s, see *BC*, 7 December 1844; *Bolton Free Press*, 30 November, 14 December 1844; W. E. Brown, *Robert Heywood of Bolton* (1970). Then, *BC*, 18 November 1854, 31 October 1857.

41 App. to first report on children's employment, 201–2; Factory inspectors' reports, *PP* 1846, xx, 576; E. Waugh, *Sketches of Lancashire Life* (1855), 8; *The Times*, 22 April 1841; *Hansard*, lxxvii, 8 June 1846.

42 The printer was C. M. Smith, *The Working Man's Way in the World* (1853), 304. See also Report of the commissioner on the mining districts, *PP* 1850, xxiii, 520; *The Times*, 24 September 1844.

43 The history of the park scheme was reviewed in *BC*, 26 May 1866, on its opening. For the controversy over funding, see *BC*, February 1851 to September 1852.

44 *BC*, 4 June 1853.

45 *BC*, 17 March 1860.

46 W. L. Sargant, *Economy of the Labouring Classes* (1857), 390. For the rest, see E. P. Thompson, 'Patrician society, plebeian culture', *Journal of Social History*, vii (1974), 382–405; SC on public libraries, vii; SC on public walks, 66.

47 *BC*, 31 May 1851, 5 October 1850.

48 H. Mayhew, *London Labour and the London Poor*, 4 vols (Frank Cass edn, 1967), i, 42.

49 Report on mining districts, 1850, 578–87. Cf. G. R. Porter, *The Progress of the Nation* (1847), 680–8; Howitt, *The Rural Life of England*, ii, 257.

3 The new leisure world of the mid-Victorians: the expansion of middle-class recreation, its practice and problems

1 For a further discussion of the middle-class leisure experience, see Peter Bailey, '"A mingled mass of perfectly legitimate pleasures": the Victorian middle class and the problem of leisure', *Victorian Studies*, xxi (1977), 7–28. On the middle class in Bristol, see H. E. Meller, *Leisure and the Changing City, 1870–1914* (1976), 40–95. See also H. Cunningham, *Leisure in the Industrial Revolution* (1980), chs 3 and 4; J. Colby and A. W. Purdue, *The Civilisation of the Crowd: Popular Culture in England, 1750–1900* (1984), 144–63. There is a useful survey of leisure at all levels of society for this period in G. Best, *Mid-Victorian Britain, 1851–75* (1971), 197–227.

2 J. H. Plumb, 'The public, literature and the arts in the eighteenth century', in P. Fritz and D. Williams (eds), *The Triumph of Culture: Eighteenth Century Perspectives* (1972), 27–48; H. Perkin, *The Origins of Modern British Society, 1780–1880* (1969), 69–70; S. Bamford, *Walks in South Lancashire* (1844), 13; J. Clegg (ed.), *Autobiography of a Lancashire Lawyer* (1883), 23–125; W. Besant, 'The amusements of the people', *Contemporary Review*, xlv (1884), 342–53.

3 General improvements in the middle-class standard of living and the increasing range of satisfactions it allowed are charted in J. A. Banks, *Prosperity and Parenthood: A Study of Family Planning among the Victorian Middle Classes* (1954). For the economic background, see S. G. Checkland, *The Rise of an Industrial Society in England, 1815–1885* (1964), 35–60, 296–301. R. Boyson, *The Ashworth Cotton Enterprise* (1970), 39.

4 'Mind and muscle', *SR*, 21 April 1860. The *Saturday Review* was primarily a literary weekly, but it provides a valuable running commentary on bourgeois mores; its reputation for arrogance was due as much to the accuracy of its perceptions as to the abrasive nature of its style. See R. G. Cox, 'The reviews and magazines', in B. Ford (ed.), *Pelican Guide to English Literature: From Dickens to Hardy* (1964), 197–8.

5 (T. H. S. Escott), 'A Foreign Resident', *Society in London* (1886), 166–7; H. Mayhew, 'The Cockaynes in Paris', in *Shops and Companies of London, and the Trades and Manufactories of Great Britain* (1865), 81–4.

6 R. H. Mottram, *Portrait of an Unknown Victorian* (1936), 120–5; 'The rising generation', *SR*, 26 March 1864; E. Hodder, *Life of Samuel Morley* (1887), 430–43; *Daily Telegraph*, 8–21 January 1869. See also Banks, op. cit., 195–6.

7 T. H. S. Escott, *Social Transformations of the Victorian Age* (1897), 14; (P. W. Clayden), 'Off for the holidays: the rationale of recreation', *Cornhill Magazine*, xvi (1867), 315–22.

8 'Evening amusements', *SR*, 4 January 1862. For domestic games, see F. Bellew, *The Art of Amusing* (1866), the serial publication *Games for Quartets* (1857–63) and the monthly recreation supplement in *Gentleman's Journal and Youth's Miscellany* (November 1869–September 1872).

9 B. S. Frankle, 'The Genteel Family: High Victorian Conceptions of Domesticity and Good Behaviour', University of Wisconsin Ph.D thesis, 1969. For croquet, see E. L. Woodward, *The Age of Reform, 1815–70* (1938), 627; for tennis, J. M. Heathcote, *Tennis* (1890) and below.

10 W. F. Rae, *The Business of Travel* (1891); 'Mind and muscle', *SR*, 21 April 1860.

11 S. M. Ellis (ed.), *Letters and Memoirs of Sir William Hardman, A Mid-Victorian Pepys* (1923), 26.

12 Major foundations included the Football Association, 1863; Amateur Athletic Club, 1866; English Rugby Union, 1871. The county championship in cricket dates from 1873, by which time international matches between the home countries were a fairly common feature of most other organised games. For the Volunteers, see Cunningham, *The Volunteer Force: A Social and Political History, 1859–1908* (1975). The quotation is from A. Wynter, 'Our sports and pastimes', *Once a Week*, v (1861), 151–3. For women, see F. K. Prochaska, *Women and Philanthropy in Nineteenth Century England* (1980), 47–72.

13 S. Fiske, *English Photographs by an American* (1869), 127–8. For other reactions to the English Sunday, see E. Smith, *Foreign Visitors in England and What They Have Thought of Us* (1889), 151f. For the development of

respectable new places of resort, particularly for women, see R. Thorne, 'Places of refreshment in the nineteenth century city', in A. D. King (ed.), *Buildings and Society* (1980), 228–53.

14 C. Dickens, *Hard Times* (New York, Signet edn, 1961), 30–3 and his *The Uncommercial Traveller*, 170–85; 'An Australian's impression of England', *Cornhill Magazine*, xiii (1866), 110–20.

15 Cf. R. H. Mottram, 'Town life and London', and J. H. and M. H. Clapham, 'Life in the new towns', in G. M. Young (ed.), *Early Victorian England, 1830–65*, 2 vols (1934), i, 153–224, 225–44. See also, 'Provincial amusements', *SR*, 11 October 1862; K. Barker, 'The performing arts in Newcastle upon Tyne, 1840–70', in J. K. Walton and J. Walvin (eds), *Leisure in Britain, 1780–1939* (1983), 53–70.

16 T. Frost, *Forty Years' Recollections, Literary and Political* (1880), 349–61.

17 *BC*, 13 June, 31 October, 28 November 1857; 6 June 1868; 29 January 1875. Clegg, op. cit., 122–5; W. E. Brown, *Robert Heywood of Bolton* (1970), 12–13; J. Holden, *Autobiography of Joseph Holden of Bolton* (1872), 9, BRL.

18 A. Trollope, *The New Zealander* (1972), 150–70; M. Arnold, 'My countrymen', *Cornhill Magazine*, xiii (1866), 153–72.

19 *The Times*, 8 October 1861; 'Holiday plans', *SR*, 16 June 1866.

20 Clayden, loc. cit; *Daily Telegraph*, 12 January 1869.

21 G. J. Romanes, 'Recreation', *Nineteenth Century*, vi (1879), 401–24; (W. H. Miller), *The Culture of Pleasure* (1872), 64–5; J. Morley, *Studies in Conduct* (1867), 1–10.

22 Quoted in K. Inglis, *The Churches and the Working Classes in Victorian England* (1963), 74, concerning the middle class. See also 'Exeter Hall on popular amusements', *SR*, 21 March 1857.

23 H. R. Haweis, *Thoughts for the Times* (1872), 288.

24 J. B. Brown, *The Gregarious Follies of Fashion: An Address to the Younger Generation* (1876).

25 G. J. Chester, *The Young Man at Rest and at Play* (1860); S. Earnshaw, *The Tradition of the Elders* (1860). See also E. R. Wickham, *Church and People in an Industrial City* (1957), 153.

26 'What attitude should Christian churches take in relation to amusements?', *Congregationalist*, viii (1879), 543–56, 650–65.

27 'Popular recreations and their moral influence', *Dublin Review*, xlii (1857), 271–93; Miller, op. cit., 67–8; J. Kay, *The Church and Popular Recreations* (1883), 17.

28 W. Thomson, W. C. Lake in J. E. Kempe (ed.), *The Use and Abuse of the World*, 3 vols (1873–5), i, 57–74, 39–56. See also the report of an Anglican conference in 'Amusements', *All The Year Round*, xvi (1876), 133–6.

29 *BC*, 26 December 1868, 18 May 1872; R. Fitzsimmons, *The Baron of Piccadilly: The Travels and Entertainments of Albert Smith, 1816–60* (1967); J. Ella, *Musical Sketches* (1878), 149, quoted in E. D. Mackerness, *A Social History of English Music* (1964), 186.

30 F. E. Kingsley (ed.), *Charles Kingsley: His Letters and Memories of his Life*, 2 vols (1877), ii, 2; E. F. Johns (ed.), *Words of Advice to Schoolboys by Charles Kingsley* (1912), 6; C. Kingsley, *Health and Education* (1874), 2–17; H. Spencer, *Education, Intellectual, Moral and Physical* (1861), 146, 173. See also, B. Haley, *The Healthy Body and Victorian Culture* (1978).

31 'Mind and muscle', *SR*, 21 April 1860; *The Times*, 2 March 1869.

32 C. Box, *Musings for Athletes: Twelve Philosophical Essays* (1888); D. Newsome, *Godliness and Good Learning: Four Studies on a Victorian Ideal* (1961), 196–239.

33 E. C. Mack and W. H. G. Armytage, *Thomas Hughes* (1952); T. Hughes, *The Manliness of Christ* (1894), 232, 252.

34 *The Times*, 21 June 1871; Haweis, op. cit., 300. At the Hurlingham live birds were sprung from traps to provide relatively easy targets for sportsmen who wished to avoid the discomfiture and higher standards of marksmanship which prevailed in the field. The unusually high bag and the presence of fashionable ladies added to public disquiet; there was, however, considerably less condemnation of the pigeon-shooting organised by London publicans. There was a further outcry against the sport in 1883–4 though proscriptive legislation failed to pass a second reading in the Commons, see *Hansard*, cclxxvi (1883), 7 March 1883. For a contemporary debate on cruelty in field sports, see the exchanges between the historian E. A. Freeman and Anthony Trollope in *Fortnightly Review*, xii (1869), 353, 616; xiii (1869), 63; xiv (1870), 674. See also E. S. Turner, *All Heaven in a Rage* (1964), 174–87.

35 'Sports versus studies', *SR*, 30 August 1873; J. A. Hobson, *Confessions of an Economic Heretic* (1938), 31–2. See also R. Wilkinson, *The Prefects: British Leadership and the Public School Tradition* (1964), ch. 3; D. C. Coleman, 'Gentlemen and players', *Economic History Review*, xxvi (1973), 96–8; J. A. Mangan, *Athleticism in the Victorian and Edwardian Public School* (1981).

36 'Opinions of the press', in W. Wingfield, *The Game of Sphairistike* (1874). The Greek name that Wingfield coined for his brainchild understandably never caught on.

37 *Porcupine* (Liverpool), 10 February 1866.

38 Escott, 'A Foreign Resident', 163, and *Social Transformations*, 195. The progress of the briefly fashionable sport of indoor ice-skating can be studied in the periodical *Rink* (1876) and J. A. Harwood, *Rinks and Rollers* (1876). See also Bailey, 'Rinkomania', *Theatrephile*, i (1984), 3–8.

39 J. E. Ritchie, *The Night Side of London* (1857), 132–8.

40 A. Esquiros, *The English at Home*, 4 vols (1861–3), ii, 52–63. For the voluntary association as social fortress and quasi-kinship system, see also L. Davidoff, *The Best Circles: Women and Society in Victorian England* (1973), 24; H. McLeod, *Class and Religion in the Late Victorian City* (Hamden, Conn., 1974), 134–5; S. Yeo, *Religion and Voluntary Organisations in Crisis* (1976).

41 *BC*, 28 November 1857, 19 August 1865, 20 January 1872, 3 July 1875 and *passim*. See also R. Poole, *Popular Leisure and the Music Hall in Nineteenth Century Bolton* (1982), 16–37.

4 Dispensing recreation to the masses in the new leisure world

1 M. A. Bienefeld, *Working Hours in British Industry* (1972), ch. 4. The famous strike for the nine-hour day among Newcastle engineers in 1871 provided a rallying cry for several trade groups in Bolton, including miners, joiners, shop assistants and clerks. The comment on the half-holiday came from John Heap, secretary of the Sunday League, to SC on public institutions, *PP*(HC) 1860, xvi, qq. 1109–10, and his suspicions are confirmed by D. Reid, 'The decline of Saint Monday, 1766–1876', *Past and Present*, 71 (1976), 89.

2 *The Times*, 14 April 1873; SC on bank holidays, *PP*(HC) 1867–8, vii, qq. 825, 960; P. S. Bagwell, *Railwaymen* (1963), 66, cited in J. A. R. Pimlott, *Recreations* (1968), 68n. On wakes, see J. K. Walton and R. Poole, 'The Lancashire wakes in the nineteenth century', in R. D. Storch (ed.), *Popular Culture and Custom in Nineteenth Century England* (1982), 100–24; Poole, 'Oldham wakes', in Walton and J. Walvin (eds), *Leisure in Britain, 1780–1939* (1983), 71–98. See also Walton, 'The demand for working-class seaside holidays in Victorian England', *Economic History Review*, xxxiv (1981), 249–65; *idem, The English Seaside Resort: A Social History, 1750–1914* (1983); Walvin, *Beside the Seaside: A Social History of the Popular Seaside Holiday* (1978).

3 R. J. Morris, 'Leeds and the Crystal Palace', *Victorian Studies*, xiii (1970), 283–300; J. A. R. Pimlott, *The Englishman's Holiday* (1947), 96–115. For the Boltonians' trip to Paris, see J. T. Staton, *The Visit t' Paris Eggsibish* (1867), BRL, and for the venturesome Londoner (C. F. Blackburn) 'A Journeyman', *A Continental Tour of Eight Days for Forty Shillings* (1878).

4 Factory inspectors' reports, *PP* 1875, xvi, 135.

5 W. A. Abram, 'The social condition and political prospects of the Lancashire workmen', *Fortnightly Review*, iv (1868), 426–41. For some figures on the proportions of open space to population size, see M. J. Vernon, 'Public parks and gardens', *Trans. NAPSS* (1867), 471; (1877), 498. See also H. E. Meller, 'Cultural provisions for the working classes in urban Britain in the second half of the nineteenth century', *Bull.SSLH*, 17 (1968), 18–19.

6 B. H. Harrison, 'Religion and recreation in nineteenth century England', *Past and Present*, 38 (1968), 111; *BC*, 8, 13 June 1867, 15 May 1869. *BC*, 31 August 1867 remarked on the continued aversion of the bench to granting new licences in the face of organised opposition. The licence for the Museum Music Hall was granted only after a public protest meeting, at which there were many references to previous wranglings over the Star, *BC*, 18 January–22 February 1873.

7 *BC*, 17 March 1866. Will Thorne records how the police in Birmingham in the 1870s interfered with his athletic training, carried out perforce in the streets, *My Life's Battles* (1925), 26–7.

8 See the letter to the *BC*, 18 March 1871, on the morality of the streets, and R. D. Storch, 'The policeman as domestic missionary: urban discipline and popular culture in northern England, 1850–1880', *Journal of Social History*, ix (1976), 481–509.

9 A. E. Dingle, 'Drink and working-class living standards in Britain, 1870–1914', *Economic History Review*, xxv (1972), 608–22.

10 J. Spencer Curwen, 'The progress of popular music', *Contemporary Review*, lii (1887), 236–48; D. Russell, 'Popular musical culture and popular politics in the Yorkshire textile districts, 1880–1914', in Walton and Walvin, op. cit., 99–116. H. Cunningham, *The Volunteer Force* (1975), 18–32, 154.

11 (T. Wright), *Some Habits and Customs of the Working Classes by a Journeyman Engineer* (1867), 184–248.

12 T. Barclay, *Memoirs and Medleys: The Autobiography of a Bottle Washer* (1934). Baker appears in F. Rogers, *Labour, Life and Literature: Some Movements of Sixty Years* (1913), 27. The Leeds report is in *Beehive*, 27 August 1870 – I owe this and most subsequent references from the paper to Eric Sager. See also A. Esquiros, *The English at Home*, 4 vols (1861–3), i, 344–7.

13 'Racing and counter attractions', *SR*, 31 July 1869; S. Alexander, *St. Giles Fair, 1830–1914* (1970); Cunningham, 'The metropolitan fairs', in A. P. Donajgrodzki (ed.), *Social Control in Nineteenth Century Britain* (1977), 163–184; Reid, 'Interpreting the festival calendar', in Storch (ed.), *Popular Culture*, 125–53. See also in Storch, his own account of the career of Guy Fawkes night as a popular festival in the South of England, 'Please to remember the Fifth of November', 72–99. *BC*, 11 January 1872 offers a lengthy report on the New Year's Fair by a clergyman investigating the condition of Bolton's masses.

14 A. Wynter, 'Our sports and pastimes', *Once a Week*, v (1861), 151–3; 'The suburban race nuisance', *SR*, 17 May 1879. W. Vamplew, *The Turf: A Social and Economic History of Horse Racing* (1976) details the modernisation of the sport. For a vignette of the bookmaker and his cronies, see H. Shimmin, *Liverpool Life, its Pleasures, Practices and Pastimes* (1856), 96–123. The earliest cheap daily racing sheet I have found is the *Bradford Chronicle and Mail Sporting Echo*, first published in 1877.

15 See, for example, G. S. R. Kitson Clark, *The Making of Victorian England* (1962), 62; G. Best, *Mid-Victorian Britain, 1851–75* (1971), 203.

16 R. H. Dana, *Hospitable England in the Eighteen Seventies: The Diary of a Young American, 1875–6* (1921), 294–9, is the Anglophile. The comment is from Paul Blouet, French master at a London boys' school in the 1870s, see 'Max O'Rell', *John Bull and his Island* (1883), 114. See also T. Wright, *Our New Masters* (1873), 70; H. Taine, *Notes on England* (1872), 37–44.

17 Dingle, op. cit.; B. H. Harrison, 'Pubs', in H. J. Dyos and M. Wolff (eds), *The Victorian City*, 2 vols (1973), i, 170–1; M. Girouard, *Victorian Pubs* (1975), 34, 54–73, 93. Cf. M. R. Marrus, 'Social drinking in the belle époque', *Journal of Social History*, vii (1974), 115–41.

18 The quote is from Esquiros, op. cit., i, 269. See also T. Coleman, *The Railway Navvies* (1965).

19 *BC*, 14 July 1866; 26 May 1877. A contemporary estimate suggests that over half of Bolton's male labour force were members of friendly societies, *BC*, 8 November 1877. For the weekly routine of club life in the 1860s and 1870s,

see A. Bennett, *Clayhanger* (Methuen edn, 1947), 76–86, and (a more critical treatment) (Wright T.), *Some Habits and Customs* (1867), 67–82.

20 Wright, in A. Halliday (ed.), *The Savage Club Papers* (1968), 214–30.

21 S. W. Jevons, 'Methods of social reform: amusements of the people', *Contemporary Review*, xxxiii (1878), 499–513; *Working Men's College Magazine*, 1 March, 1 November 1859. See also Cunningham, *Leisure in the Industrial Revolution* (1980), ch. 4, and the important work of Meller, *Leisure and the Changing City, 1870–1914* (1976), on the complementary ideology of 'social citizenship' and the attempt to implant a common culture by Bristol's middle class – there is however too little acknowledgement of the illiberal face of liberal culture.

22 T. Cooper, *The Life of Thomas Cooper* (1872), 393 and *Thoughts at Fourscore* (1885), 31–2.

23 K. Inglis, *The Churches and the Working Classes in Victorian England* (1963), 267; B. H. Harrison, *Drink and the Victorians* (1971) 267–89.

24 J. L. Clifford-Smith, *The National Association and its Twenty Fifth Anniversary: A Manual and a Narrative* (1882); O. R. McGregor, 'Social research and social policy in the nineteenth century', *British Journal of Sociology*, viii (1957), 146–57.

25 C. Kingsley, *Sanitary and Social Essays* (1880), 207–10; B. G. Orchard, *The Clerks of Liverpool* (1871), 3–4; H. Shimmin, *Town Life* (1858), 139. See also now, G. Anderson, *Victorian Clerks* (1976); G. Crossick (ed.), *The Lower Middle Class in Britain 1870–1914* (1977).

26 'The genesis of the cad', *Tinsley's Magazine*, iv (1869), 178–81.

27 Quote from Revd E. Corderoy, 'Popular amusements', *Lectures to the YMCA* (1857), 45–6. See also C. Binfield, *George Williams and the YMCA: A Study in Victorian Social Attitudes* (1973), 296–315, and for a similar though secular rescue operation, C. Kent, 'The Whittington Club: a bohemian experiment in middle-class social reform', *Victorian Studies*, xviii (1974), 31–55.

28 Revd J. E. Clarke, *Plain Papers on the Social Economy of the People* (1858), 7; 'The philosophy of amusement', *Meliora: A Quarterly Review of Social Science*, vi (1864), 193–210; Revd H. S. Brown, *Lectures to Working Men* (1870), 11. Unless otherwise stated the emphasis is in the original.

29 *Working Men's College Magazine*, 1 January 1861.

30 *The Times*, 11 October 1872.

31 J. Belford, *The Saturday Half-Holiday: Its Bearing on the Due Observance of the Sabbath* (1867); *Quarterly Messenger of the YMCA*, October 1864; Corderoy, op. cit.

32 M. Browne, *Views and Opinions* (1866), 253; Spottiswoode to Horner, Factory inspectors' reports, *PP* 1857, xvi, 37; (W. R. Greg), 'The proletariat on a false scent', *Quarterly Review*, cxxiii (1872), 251–94.

33 G. Smith, 'The labour movement', *Contemporary Review*, xxi (1873), 226–51; W. Rathbone, *The Increased Earnings of the Working Classes and their Effect on Themselves and on the Future of England* (1877).

34 'Labour and recreation: a plea for a mens sana', *Tinsley's Magazine*, xiv (1874), 424–31.

35 R. B. Litchfield, 'The social economy of a working men's college', *Trans.NAPSS* (1862), 787–93. For the fear of social disintegration as a motive for reform, see G. Stedman Jones, *Outcast London: A Study in the Relationship between Classes in Victorian Society* (1971), 241–61, and his 'Working-class culture and working-class politics in London, 1870–1900', in *Languages of Class* (1983), ch. 4, for an account of the 'middle-class onslaught' on proletarian culture in London.

36 *BC*, 3 June 1882.

37 R. K. Dewhurst, 'Saltaire', *Town Planning Review*, xxxi (1960), 135–44; J. Reynolds, *The Great Paternalist: Titus Salt and the Growth of Nineteenth Century Bradford* (1983). Cf. J. N. Tarn, 'The model village at Bromborough Pool', *Town Planning Review*, xxxv (1965), 329–36.

38 The claims of home life were a recurrent theme in the evangelical paper *After Work: A Magazine for Workmen's Homes*, published 1874–87. See also W. G. Blaikie, *Better Days for Working People* (1863), 243–5.

39 W. T. Marriott, *Some Real Wants of the Working Classes* (1860), 12–13; Shimmin, *Liverpool Life*, 2–3.

40 *Licensed Victuallers' Gazette*, 24 February 1866, and the proposals of Liverpool philanthropist William Rathbone, in M. B. Simey, *Charitable Effort in Liverpool in the Nineteenth Century* (1951), 55.

41 See E. H. Currie, *Appeal for a People's Palace* (1886) and Thomas Brassey's enthusiasm for the 'social palace' of the French industrialist and philanthropist Godin in *Lectures on the Labour Question* (1878), 150–2. See also P. J. Keating, *The Working Classes in Victorian Fiction* (1979), *passim*, on Walter Besant and the East End palace.

42 For a convert from sabbatarianism who became vice-president of the National Sunday League which campaigned for the opening of museums and galleries, see M. L. Bruce, *Anna Swanwick: Memoir and Recollections* (1903), 32–3. For a counterpart working-class movement, see the evidence of R. M. Morrell of the Recreative Religionists to SC on the sale of liquors on Sunday, *PP*(HC) 1867–8, xiv, qq. 6318–26. For the People's Garden Company, see *Beehive*, 3 September 1870, and for correspondence on the squares, see *The Times*, 14, 17 July 1871.

43 Report of Dr Lyon Playfair on the London Mechanics' Institution, *PP* 1857–8, xlviii, 327.

44 *Working Men's College Magazine*, 1 February 1861; *Quarterly Messenger of the YMCA*, July 1864. Charles Coborn recalled that Temperance societies recruited music hall acts on the understanding that any reference to drink must be deprecatory, *The Man Who Broke The Bank: Memories of the Stage and Music Halls* (1928), 139–40.

45 E. H. Hall, *Coffee Taverns, Cocoa Houses and Coffee Palaces: Their Rise, Progress and Prospects* (1878) is the best source for these related movements, together with the files of the *Coffee Public House News*, and the later

Refreshment News. There are reports on the dry pubs in *Trans.NAPSS* (1871), 591–2, and the other societies are noted in *Time*, July 1879 and *Work and Leisure*, June 1880.

46 J. Macmillan, 'Description of Checks issued by Birmingham Concert Halls, 1850–1920', MS in Birmingham Central Reference Library. See also The Coffee Tavern Company, *Practical Hints for the Management of Coffee Taverns* (1878).

47 J. Hole, *The History and Management of Literary, Scientific and Mechanics Institutes* (1853), 74–6.

48 Shimmin, *Liverpool Life*, 2–3.

49 *Trans.NAPSS* (1865), 7; ibid. (1866), 792.

50 W. Besant, 'Amusements of the people', *Contemporary Review*, xlv (1884), 342.

51 Reports on Church Congresses at Sheffield, *The Times*, 4 October 1878, and Wakefield, ibid., 8 October 1886. A progressive figure in the Church's approach to social reform, Fraser was speaking in Bolton on recreation for workers, *BC* 4 September 1875. See also P.d'A. Jones, *The Christian Socialist Revival, 1877–1914: Religion, Class and Social Conscience in Late-Victorian England* (1968); Revd T. Hancock, 'The church and the pub', *Church Reformer*, May 1888.

52 *BC*, 29 January 1876, 29 May 1875.

53 *Trans.NAPSS* (1865), 7.

54 *BC*, 26 May 1866; *The Times*, 14 November 1865.

55 *BC*, 29 January, 4 September 1875. See also the dialect letter from an artisan, 'Dicky Drawfoile', ibid., 21 August 1875.

56 Cf. P. Joyce, *Work, Society and Politics: The Culture of the Factory in Later Victorian England* (1980), who argues for the persistence of employer paternalism in the Lancashire factory towns (including Bolton), in this period. For the co-existence of harmony *and* conflict, see R. Poole, *Popular Leisure and the Music Hall in Nineteenth Century Bolton* (1982), 5 n.18.

57 E. Hopkins, *Work Amongst Working Men* (1879), 131.

58 *The Times*, 14 April 1873; 'The workingman', *SR*, 22 February 1873. See also, 'On strike and on spree', *Meliora*, ix (1866), 323–33.

59 'Behind the scenes', *Daily News*, 18 December 1868; J. E. Ritchie, *Days and Nights in London* (1880), 49–50. For middle-class finances, see J. A. Banks, *Prosperity and Parenthood: A Study of Family Planning among the Victorian Middle Classes* (1954), 129–38; S. G. Checkland, *The Rise of an Industrial Society in England, 1815–1885* (1964), 35–60.

60 Reproduced in J. F. Sullivan, *The British Workingman by One Who Does Not Believe in Him* (1878), 86. Ritchie, op. cit., 182–95; Ouida (M. de la Ramée), *Views and Opinions* (1895), 333–4, 340. The image of vomiting was common to the latter kind of commentary. See also George Gissing's account of an August Bank Holiday outing in *The Nether World* (John Murray edn, 1903), 104–13.

61 M. Browne, op. cit., 280; J. K. Cook, 'The labourer's leisure', *Dublin University Magazine*, xc (1877), 174–92; W. Besant, 'The People's Palace' (1887), in *As We Are and As We May Be* (1903), 55.

5 Rational recreation in operation: the Working Men's Club movement

1 Materials for the study of the club movement are to be found in the seventeen volumes of the Solly Collection of cuttings and manuscripts, assembled by Henry Solly, founder of the CIU, British Library of Political and Economic Science, London School of Economics, Misc. MSS 154. There is a typescript index but the collection is often difficult to use and generally disappointing in content. The first official history, *Our Fifty Years: The Story of the Working Men's Club and Institute Union* (1912), by B. T. Hall, secretary of the union in the early years of this century, is still useful, as is his edited collection of Solly's pamphlets, *Working Men's Social Clubs and Educational Institutes* (1904). Solly's autobiography, *These Eighty Years*, 2 vols (1893) is also helpful. A centenary history of the movement, G. Tremlett, *The First Century* (1962), adds little of substance for the Victorian period. Several periodicals which served intermittently as the house organ of the CIU and provide an entrée to club life itself are referred to below. I know of only three surviving examples of individual club minutes books from the period and these are also referred to more precisely below. Other scholars have been luckier, but I was refused access to such papers as the present Union possesses, though this may be no great disadvantage since Hall mentions that many early minute books were lost by the time he was writing.

   For scholarly work on the clubs see R. Price, 'The working men's club movement and Victorian social reform ideology', *Victorian Studies*, xv (1971), 117–47 and *An Imperial War and the British Working Class* (1972), 47–67; S. Shipley, *Club Life and Socialism in Mid-Victorian London* (1971); J. Taylor, *From Self-Help to Glamour: The Working Man's Club, 1860–1972* (1972); T. G. Ashplant, 'London Working Men's Clubs, 1875–1914', in E. and S. Yeo (eds), *Popular Culture and Class Conflict 1590–1914* (1981), 241–70.

2 C. Knight, *Passages of a Working Life*, 3 vols (1873), iii, 84–6; S. A. Brooke, *Life and Letters of F. W. Robertson* (1865), 131–51. The designation is Price's, 'The club movement', 119.

3 S. G. Osborne, 'The beer shop evil', in C. J. C. Talbot (ed.), *Meliora, or Better Times to Come* (1852), 1–11; T. H. Bastard, 'The Charlton club for labourers', *Trans. NAPSS* (1863), 685–6; Revd J. E. Clarke, 'Labourers' clubs and working men's refreshment rooms', *Church of England Monthly Review*, January 1859; (C. Dickens), 'The poor man and his beer', *All the Year Round*, i (1859), 126–31; J. E. Clarke, *Plain Papers on the Social Economy of the People* (1858), 14–27. See also the list of early clubs in *Occasional Papers of the Working Men's Club and Institute Union*, 1 (March 1863). G. D. H. Cole and R. Postgate, *The Common People* (1961), 378–9.

4 M. Bayly, *Ragged Homes and How to Mend Them* (1860); F. M. Gladstone, *Notting Hill in Bygone Days* (1924), 146–7.

5 Solly to Brougham, 9, 24 August 1861, Brougham MSS, University College Library, London; Solly, *These Eighty Years*, ii, 159–60. See also the exchange of letters on the difficulties of running Adeline Cooper's club in Duck Lane, Westminster, *The Times*, 9, 11 January 1862.

6 Solly, *Social Clubs and Institutes* (1904), 28–9; *These Eighty Years*, ii, 189–93; Solly to Brougham, 13 December 1862, Brougham MSS.

7 H. Solly, *James Sandford, Carpenter and Chartist*, 2 vols (1883). See also R. V. Holt, *The Unitarian Contribution to Human Progress* (1948).

8 Solly, draft for pamphlet, *The Rich and the Poor*, n.d. Solly Coll. xii, probably from the mid-1860s; 'Working men's clubs and institutes in relation to the upper classes and to national progress', *Trans.NAPSS* (1866), 791, in which Solly declares the aristocracy 'with a few notable exceptions' enfeebled; *How to Deal with the Unemployed Poor of London and with its Roughs and Criminal Classes?* (1868). For the background of insecurity in the capital, see G. Stedman Jones, *Outcast London* (1971), 241–3.

9 Address to TUC in 1871, recorded in *Occasional Papers*, 20 (January 1872); Solly, *Social Clubs and Institutes* (1904), 57; Knight, op. cit., iii, 220–1.

10 Solly, *Social Clubs and Institutes* (1904), 57; E. V. Neale, *True Refinement: Address to the Rochdale WMC* (1876). See also Taylor, op. cit., 10–11.

11 B. T. Hall, op. cit., 20–1; Lyttelton to Brougham, 30 August 1864, 22 February 1865, Brougham MSS; Lyttelton to Solly, 29 July 1871, Solly Coll. xvi. A list of vice-presidents for 1874–5 is given in Taylor, op. cit., 3–5. At one time or another almost every member of the familiar cast of mid-Victorian friends of the working classes appeared on the list – F. D. Maurice, Thomas Hughes, Samuel Smiles, Samuel Morley *et al.*

12 The dispute centred on Solly's refusal to co-operate with other officers of the Union, particularly Paterson, whom he accused of leading intrigues against him. See, inter alia, Solly to Lichfield, 27 June 1868; Solly to Pratt, 3 July 1870; Lyttelton to Solly, 10 November 1871; Hole to Solly, 5 July 1872, Solly Coll. xvi. For Paterson, see the introduction by his wife in his *New Method of Mental Science* (1886), i–viii. He was a cabinetmaker, secretary of the Clerkenwell WMC and active in the Workmen's Peace Association, but his obvious credentials as a self-improving artisan failed to recommend him to Solly – perhaps he lacked the deference of James Sandford, alias Bainbridge.

13 Adam Weiler, prominent in London working-class associations in the 1870s, quoted in Price, 'The club movement', 131n. Solly's claims for travelling expenses was one of the points at issue in the office politics of the Union.

14 H. Solly, *Hints and Suggestions for the Formation and Management of Working Men's Clubs and Institutes* (1862).

15 Pratt to *The Times*, 5 January 1872. A prematurely retired civil servant, Pratt became a member of the Union council in 1864, secretary in 1874 and president in 1883. His interest in the condition of the working classes derived

from boyhood memories of the Chartist movement in Bristol and he was active in several reform causes. Less assertive in manner than Solly, and decidedly secularist in intention, Pratt helped turn away the charge of 'parsondom' which had dogged the Union under his predecessor. *Dictionary of National Biography*; J. J. Dent, *Hodgson Pratt, Reformer: An Outline of his Work* (1932).

16 Lyttelton to *The Times*, 13 July 1863.

17 *The Times*, 11 May 1864; *Occasional Papers*, 10 (1867), 20 (1869). For a later round of discussions, see *Workmen's Club Journal*, 29 April, 20 May 1876.

18 Pratt to *The Times*, 13 January 1872; Solly, 'The growing importance of working men's clubs', *Trans.NAPSS* (1871), 592; SC on intemperance, *PP*(HL) 1877, xi, 171; Shaen to Solly, 23 July 1869, Solly Coll. xiv.

19 *The Times*, 20 July 1875. His son later recalled how Rosebery's gift of £180 on debenture had seen the Union through a sticky patch.

20 B. T. Hall, op. cit., 24–5; *The Times*, 9 January 1872; Solly, *Social Clubs and Institutes* (1904), 7, 56–7.

21 'Working men's clubs', *Meliora*, v (1863), 259–66.

22 *BC*, 2 April 1864. The Bolton club was one of the casualties of the difficult early years of the Union; its demise was attributed to bad management and restrictive supervision which forbade, among other things, all political discussion. The club was wound up in 1869 though a fresh start was made in the 1870s.

23 B. T. Hall, op. cit., 35.

24 Censorship had its farcical side – a music hall artist performing at a Sunday concert in a club in Burnley discovered that members were forbidden to applaud on the sabbath, but were allowed to show their appreciation by raising their hands. W. H. Boardman, *Vaudeville Days* (1935), 201.

25 *The Times*, 15 April 1863; R. Harrison, *Before the Socialists: Studies in Labour and Politics, 1861–81* (1965), 226–8; Solly, quoted in *Wisbech Advertiser*, 2 February 1887, cutting in Solly Coll. xv.

26 *CIJ*, 7 December 1883; *Common Good*, 15 January 1881. There are few reliable figures for the growth of the Club movement in these years, but there were over 800 clubs known to the Union by the early 1880s. It is difficult to know what passed as a 'political' club, but we may allow that it was the independent Radical clubs that offended Solly and the Union oligarchy rather than those formed under the auspices of the two political parties (whose history remains to be written).

27 *List of Clubs Known to the Union*, November 1869, May 1871, CIU pamphlets; H. Pratt, *Notes of a Tour among Workmen's Clubs* (1870); F. J. Gardiner, *The Fiftieth Birthday of a Model Institution: An Account of the Origin and Development of Wisbech WMC and Institute* (1914). The only big city club to win an honourable mention in Pratt's tour was one in Liverpool.

28 *Occasional Papers*, 5 (May 1864); *The Times*, 11 July 1866.

29 *The Times*, 29 February 1864; copy of the 11th Annual Report in Solly Coll. xvi; *BC*, 24 April 1869.

30 J. Hollingshead, *Today: Essays and Miscellanies*, 2 vols (1865), i, 171–7. See also Taylor, op. cit., 18–20.

31 *Workman's Magazine*, 6 (June 1873). See also the history of the Cobden Club in Westbourne Park, London, recalled in *CIJ*, 4 July 1884, and the report of a club conference in Manchester, *BC*, 20 January 1872.

32 There is an interesting commentary on the course of this campaign in London in the *Beehive*, 24 June–22 July 1871; for later developments see Marriott in *CIJ*, 6 July 1883.

33 E. T. Hall, *Coffee Taverns, Cocoa Houses and Coffee Palaces* (1878); Pratt in *CIJ*, 6 July 1883. See also evidence of Solly and Pratt in Fourth report of commissioners inquiring into friendly and benefit building societies, *PP* 1874, xxiii, 614–6.

34 The official view of the defection of the London clubs can be found in *House and Home*, 11 December 1880, and Solly's report in *Trans.NAPSS* (1880), 504–5. For the conference itself see *CIJ*, 16, 23 November 1883; for subsequent deliberations in committee, *CIJ*, 18 January 1884 and Price, *An Imperial War*, 56–8.

35 *CIJ*, 21 November 1884; *The Times*, 26 May 1884.

36 H. Mayhew, *Report of the Trade and Hours of Closing at Working Men's Clubs* (1871) – a piece of detective work for the licensed victuallers; *The Times*, 8, 9 January 1872, 18 April 1873; unidentified cutting re Leeds WMC, August 1873, Solly Coll. xv. The surviving minute books of the Newcastle WMC for 1865–6, 1870–3 are bound in two volumes in the Newcastle Central Reference Library. The club seems to have been self-managed and the committee in 1865–6 comprised joiners, cabinetmakers, whitesmiths and a tailor. The only other extant material of this kind relates to village clubs, namely Horringer and Ickworth Village Club minute books, mostly intact from 1877 onwards, together with the club accounts, held by Mrs Z. Ward of Horringer, Suffolk, the granddaughter of one of the founder members; the minute book of the Romsley WMC in Worcestershire for 1879, deposited with the Marcy Hemingway papers, bundle 486, in the County Record Office. The Horringer club was started by Lord John Hervey for his estate workers; Romsley was similarly a proprietary club, patronised by Lord Lyttelton, president of the CIU. I have not consulted the Romsley material.

37 *Occasional Papers*, 7 (December 1865); *Workmen's Club Journal*, 10 July 1875, 29 July 1876.

38 *The Common Good*, 15 January 1881; *CIJ*, 5 December 1884; F. Rogers, *Labour, Life and Literature: Some Movements of Sixty Years* (1913), 73, 96–7.

39 *CIJ*, 1 August 1884; RC on the companies of the City of London, PP 1884, xxxix, 115–17.

40 See the comments of Shaw and William Morris on lecturing engagements in the clubs, quoted in Taylor, op. cit., 59. For the increasing emphasis on professional entertainment in the clubs from the 1890s, see also Taylor, and Ashplant, op. cit.

41 Newcastle WMC minute book, 1866; R. Harrison, op. cit., 227; *Beehive*, 14 April 1875. The Kingsland Club in Stoke Newington, London, had a political council of twelve elected annually 'to watch over social and political events, and to give their support to measures calculated to advance the interest of the masses. It shall report to the club before it pledges the club to any policy in any election contest.' From club by-laws for 1876, copy in Solly Coll. xv, item 27.

42 Club members at Tower Hamlets Radical Club and Institute recalled how they were hounded from tavern to tavern by the police until the opening of their club in 1874, *CIJ*, 26 September 1884.

43 W. Besant, *All Sorts and Conditions of Men*, 2 vols (1882), ii, 206–36; Solly, *Social Clubs and Institutes* (1904), 71.

44 Rogers, op. cit., 68. Brian Jackson has an interesting account of modern club life in his *Working Class Community* (1968), 39–68, which shows how these qualities still mark the character of club leadership.

45 B. T. Hall, op. cit., 176.

6 Rational recreation and the new athleticism

1 W. E. Gladstone, 'Locksley Hall and the Jubilee', *Nineteenth Century*, xxi (1887), 1–18.

2 R. C. K. Ensor, *England, 1870–1914* (1936), 164. Salvador de Madariaga's epigram is at once less congratulatory and ominously more specific: 'One Englishman, a fool; two Englishmen, a football match; three Englishmen, the British Empire'. Quoted in J. L. and B. Hammond, *The Growth of Common Enjoyment* (1933), 9.

3 E. G. Magnane, *Sociologie du sport* (1947), 43: 'Sport is the chief pole of attraction toward approved activities: licit, consciously social and, in the broadest sense of the term, docile.' Quoted in E. Weber, 'Gymnastics and sports in *fin de siècle* France: opium of the classes?', *American Historical Review*, lxxvi (1971), 91. See also *Sport and the Community: Report of the Wolfenden Committee on Sport for the Central Council of Physical Recreation* (1960), 6: 'Sportsmanship . . . in its deeper (and usually inarticulate) significance . . . still provides something like the foundations of an ethical standard . . . in hard practice it is no bad elementary guide to decent living together in society.' For a discussion of this orthodoxy, see E. Dunning (ed.), *Sport: Readings from a Sociological Perspective* (1972), 233–78 and, from a more critical position, Jennifer Hargreaves (ed.), *Sport, Culture and Ideology* (1982), and John Hargreaves, *Sport, Power and Culture: A Social and Historical Analysis of Popular Sports in Britain* (1986). See also K. A. P. Sandiford, 'The Victorians at play: problems in historiographical methodology', *Journal of Social History*, xv (1981), 271–88. For other work in the new social history of sport see below and *British Journal of Sports History* (1984–).

4 W. Collins, *Man and Wife*, 3 vols (1870), i, viii–xi; B. E. Haley, 'Sports and the Victorian World', *Western Humanities Review*, xii (1968), 115–25 and his *The Healthy Body and Victorian Culture* (1978).

5 M. Shearman, *Athletics and Football* (1889), 241. This is one of the Badminton series of handbooks which provides a useful introduction to Victorian sport.

6 J. S. Smith, *Social Aspects* (1850), 1, 43; 'Physical puritanism', *Westminster Review*, i, new series (1852), 405–42.

7 'Physical strength', *SR*, 10 December 1859; J. Hulley's address to the Athletic Society of Great Britain, *Athletic Review and Journal of Physical Education*, 2 July 1867.

8 L. Stephen, 'Athletic sports and university studies', *Fraser's Magazine*, ii, new series (1870), 691–704; J. Morley, *Studies in Conduct* (1867), 256–65.

9 *The Times*, 5 August 1858, and a debate by correspondence during the Crimean War, recalled by L. Blanc, *Letters on England*, 4 vols (1866–7), i, 32–5; F. Gale, *Modern English Sports: Their Use and Abuse* (1885), 60.

10 W. Hardwicke, 'Recreation for the working classes?', *Trans.NAPSS* (1867), 471–7, 552–7; Lord Brabazon, 'The decay of bodily strength in towns', *Nineteenth Century*, xxi (1887), 673–6 and his *Social Arrows* (1886). Lord Elcho had tried, unsuccessfully, to pass a bill through the Commons in 1862 to organise a national programme of gymnastic training. The big railway companies instituted physical tests for job applicants in the mid-1870s and reported a large number of rejects.

11 C. Kingsley, *Health and Education* (1874), 2–17; H. Spencer, *Education, Intellectual, Moral and Physical* (1861), 146, 173. For Darwinism in medical terms, see H. W. Acland, *National Health: Health, Work and Play* (1871); for popular Darwinism, G. J. Romanes, 'Recreation', *Nineteenth Century*, vi (1879), 401–24.

12 C. Dukes, *Health at School* (third edn, 1894), 284.

13 J. Kay, *The Church and Popular Recreations* (1883), 10.

14 W. H. G. Armytage, 'Thomas Arnold's views on physical education', *Journal of Physical Education*, xlvii (1955), 27–44; Dunning, 'Development of modern football', in *idem*, op. cit., 133–51.

15 E. Lyttelton, 'Athletics in public school', *Nineteenth Century*, vii (1880), 43–57. Educators also recommended games as a counter to 'unnatural lusts' prevalent in public schools. See (Thomas Markby), 'Athletics', *Contemporary Review*, iii (1866), 374–91; *The Science of Life: A Pamphlet Addressed to All Members of the Universities of Oxford and Cambridge and to All Who Are, or Who Will Be Teachers, Clergymen, or Fathers* (1877).

16 N. L. Jackson, *Sporting Days and Sporting Ways* (1932), 9–10; C. Box, *Musings for Athletes* (1888), 167. See also T. Cook, *Character and Sportsmanship* (1927); Dunning, *Sport* (1972). See now also, J. A. Mangan, *Athleticism in the Victorian and Edwardian Public School* (1981).

17 H. B. Philpott, *London at School: The Story of the School Board* (1904), 127. I owe this reference to Raphael Samuel.

18 G. J. Cayley, *The Working Classes: Their Interest in Reform* (1858). Cricket had in fact been criticised in its early years for mixing inferiors and superiors, see J. Strutt, *The Sports and Pastimes of the People of England* (1903), 102. For

its mythical qualities, see, for example, T. Sparks (C. Dickens), *Sunday Under Three Heads* (1836), 39–44. For recent scholarly attention to the history of cricket see the several articles of Sandiford, e.g. 'Cricket and the Victorians: an historiographical essay', *Historical Reflexions*, ix (1982), 421–36.

19 J. Lawson, *Letters to the Young on Progress in Pudsey* (1887), 63. The claims made for cricket were many and remarkable, but one in particular I find irresistible; it comes from Thomas Hughes, reporting a letter from an officer in the engineers before Sebastopol: 'The round shot which were ever coming at him were very much like cricket balls from a moderately swift bowler; he could judge them quite as accurately, and by just turning round when the gun which bore on him was fired, and marking the first pitch of the shot, he could tell whether to move or not, and so got on with his work very comfortably.' 'Physical education', *Working Men's College Magazine*, May 1859.

20 *Hansard*, ccxxv, 1 July 1875; Shearman, op. cit., 226–7.

21 *The Times*, 13 September 1861; T. Okey, *A Basketful of Memories* (1930), 22–3; Philpott, op. cit., 115–33. Official obstacles were not removed until the introduction of a new elementary school code in 1890.

22 P. C. McIntosh, *Physical Education in England since 1800* (second edn, 1968), 11–14, 50; Copy of papers submitted to the education committee by Mr Chadwick, *PP* 1862, xlii, 1–88; J. Hurt, 'Drill, discipline and the elementary school ethos', in P. McCann (ed.), *Popular Education and Socialisation in the Nineteenth Century* (1977), 167–92. The quotations are from F. H. Spencer, *An Inspector's Testament* (1938), 63–5; W. McLaren in the preface to A. McLaren, *Physical Education* (1895), vi, quoted in McIntosh, op. cit., 120.

23 H. F. Wilkinson (ed.), *The Athletic Almanack* (1868); Shearman, op. cit., 48–53. The *Almanack* for 1872 provides a useful list of clubs registered with AAC.

24 Rye Collection of press cuttings, Guildhall Library, London, 189–90.

25 The contemporary press provides the major source for the study of pedestrianism. For its leading performers, see P. Lovesey, *Kings of Distance* (1968), 15–40, and for Scotland, D. A. Jamieson, *Powderhall and Pedestrianism: The History of a Famous Sports Enclosure, 1870–1943* (1943). A brief biography of Richard Manks, the 'Warwickshire Antelope', in *Era*, 2 March 1862 provides a picture of pedestrianism among its lesser luminaries, and A. R. Downer, *Running Recollections and How to Train* (1908) reveals the sharp practices which attended it.

26 C. Hole, *English Sports and Pastimes* (1949), 24–5.

27 A. Wynter, 'Our sports and pastimes', *Once a Week*, v (1861), 151–3. See also Dickens's amiable dissection of the sporting press in 'The roughs' guide', *All the Year Round*, 16 December 1865. For an interesting account of traditional working-class sports and the role of the innkeeper in a distinctive regional and occupational culture, see A. Metcalfe, 'Organized sport in the mining communities of south Northumberland, 1800–1889', *Victorian Studies*, xxv (1982), 469–95.

28 H. Ellington, 'Athletes of the present and past', *Nineteenth Century*, xxi (1887), 517–29.

29 H. Jones, 'Recreation', *Good Words*, xxii (1881), 43–9.

30 'Questionable amusements', *Young Men of Great Britain*, 25 August 1868.

31 Gale, op. cit., 43–6. A good account of contemporary gambling is provided in A. Esquiros, *The English at Home*, 4 vols (1861–3), ii, 388–413.

32 *All-England Cricket and Football Journal* (Sheffield), March 1879.

33 W. Rye, *An Autobiography of an Ancient Athlete and Antiquarian* (1916), 31–2. A young solicitor in the City in the 1860s, and a member of the London Athletic Club, Rye, left a useful collection of materials to the Guildhall Library. A. Trollope, *British Sports and Pastimes* (1868), 1–7.

34 Such a case, involving 'the second rate professionals' of the Prince of Wales and White Star Clubs (obviously pub-based) in London, is reported in the *Athletic Record and Monthly Journal of Amateur Amusements*, September 1876.

35 Rye Coll.; 'The athletic sports at Beaufort House', *SR*, 20 April 1867.

36 Letter to *Athletic Record and Monthly Journal*, June 1876, emphasis in original.

37 S. Smiles, *Self-Help* (1859), 241–6; W. Lovett, *Elementary Anatomy and Physiology* (1851), 129–52. See also B. H. Harrison's comments in 'Work and leisure in industrial society: conference report', *Past and Present*, 30 (1965), 96–103 and W. H. G. Armytage, 'Care of the shape: changing views in the nineteenth century', *Journal of Physical Education*, xlvii (1955), 71–4.

38 C. E. Maurice (ed.), *Life and Letters of Octavia Hill* (1913), 317–8; J. Johnston, *Parks and Playgrounds for the People* (1885); C. L. Lewes, 'How to ensure breathing space', *Nineteenth Century*, xxi (1887), 677–82; Haley, *The Healthy Body* (1978).

39 For sports propaganda in the Anglican Church, see Canon Money at the Croydon Church Congress, *The Times*, 11 October 1877 and Revd H. C. Shuttleworth at the *Leicester Congress*, ibid., 2 October 1880. See also Dickens's parody of Canon Septimus Crisparkle in *Edwin Drood* (1870), 9, 62–3; (W. L. Collins), 'Our amusements', '*Blackwood's Magazine*', c (1866), 698–712.

40 M. H. Elsworth, 'The Provision for Physical Recreation in Bolton in the Nineteenth Century', Dissertation for the Diploma in the Advanced Study in Education, University of Manchester, 1972, 48; P. Scott, 'Cricket and the religious world in the Victorian period', *Church Quarterly*, iii (1970), 134–44.

41 Quote from P. M. Young, *A History of British Football* (1968), 111; D. D. Molyneux, 'The Development of Physical Recreation in the Birmingham District', University of Birmingham MA thesis, 1957, 39–42. The most authoritative and wide-ranging of the new scholarly works on the growth of soccer is A. Mason, *Association Football and English Society, 1863–1915* (1980). From a different perspective is S. Tischler, *Footballers and Businessmen: The Origins of Professional Soccer in England* (1981); see also J. Walvin, *The People's Game* (1975) and R. Q. Gray, *The Labour Aristocracy in Victorian Edinburgh* (1976) for the cultural context, 116–18.

42 *BC*, 24 July 1875. Bolton's Peel Park charged a rent for pitches, which discouraged workingmen's teams.

43 W. T. Marriott, *Some Real Wants of the Working Classes* (1860), 29; Dean of York speaking to Church Congress at Derby, *The Times*, 6 October 1882 and the Dean of Buxton to the same body at Wakefield, ibid., 7 October 1886.

44 Jackson, op. cit., 21–3; Elsworth, op. cit., 48; E. L. Levy, *History of the Birmingham Athletic Club, 1866–98* (1898), 25.

45 See the recollections of working-class boyhood in F. H. Spencer, op. cit., 31, 85; H. Snell, *Men, Movements and Myself* (1936), 15; and R. Roberts, *The Classic Slum* (1971), 127, who describes his bewilderment at the conflicting claims of the moral codes of Greyfriars and Salford.

46 'The rise and progress of the Aston Villa Club', *Birmingham Mail*, 24 October 1883, in the Osborne collection of cuttings, Birmingham Central Reference Library; P. M. Young, *The Wolves* (1959), 23–31; *idem, Bolton Wanderers* (1961), 19; G. W. Simmons, *Tottenham Hotspur Football Club* (1947), 15–16.

47 W. Thorne, *My Life's Battles* (1925), 25.

48 *Athlete*, March 1871.

49 The controversy can best be followed in *Athletic News*, a Manchester paper which emerged from the ruck of lesser rivals as the most influential provincial sports weekly, see ibid., 11 June, 9 July, 1 October, 3 December 1879. See also Shearman, op. cit., 216–21. The Bicycle Union dropped the mechanics clause two years previously, *Wheel World*, May–September 1878.

50 Professional pedestrianism survived longer in Scotland, see Jamieson, op. cit., who also gives examples of the scandals and riots which accelerated its decline in England, 46, 63–5.

51 G. Green, J. R. Witty and H. V. Usill, *The History of the Football Association* (1953), 19–33.

52 McIntosh, op. cit., 25; P. M. Young, *Football in Sheffield* (1962), 16, 43; F. Wall, *Fifty Years of Football* (1935), 2.

53 Mason, op. cit., provides the best account of the onset of professionalism. See also W. F. Mandle, 'Games people played: cricket and football in England and Victoria in the late nineteenth century', *Historical Studies*, xv (1973), 511–35.

54 *BC*, 11, 18, 25 October 1884. The first protest meeting was held in Bolton.

55 Ibid., 22 November 1884.

56 *Athletic News*, 29 November, 6 December 1884.

57 Green *et al.*, op. cit., 95–109.

58 C. E. Sutcliffe and F. Hargreaves, *History of the Lancashire Football Association, 1878–1928* (1928), 147–51.

59 'Villa Incorporated', *Birmingham Gazette*, 9 January 1888, Osborne Coll.

60 J. A. H. Catton, *Wickets and Goals* (1943), 135; Young, *A History of British Football*, 123–6; *idem, Manchester United* (1960), 41–4.

61 E. Ensor, 'The football madness', *Contemporary Review*, lxxiv (1898), 751–60; 'Creston', 'Football', *Fortnightly Review*, lv (1894), 24–38; C. Edwardes,

'The new football mania', *Nineteenth Century*, xxxii (1892), 622–31. Cf.
W. Vamplew, 'Ungentlemanly conduct: the control of soccer-crowd behaviour in England, 1885–1914', in T. C. Smout (ed.), *The Search for Wealth and Stability* (1979), 139–54. On rugger, see Dunning and K. Sheard, *Barbarians, Gentlemen and Players: A Sociological Study of the Development of Rugby Football* (1979).

62 H. Spencer, *Facts and Comments* (1902), 128–9.

63 For soccer as a subculture which preserved a significant continuity in working-class life, see I. R. Taylor, 'Soccer consciousness and soccer hooliganism', in S. Cohen (ed.), *Images of Deviance* (1971), 134–64. See also C. Critcher, 'Football since the war', in J. Clarke, C. Critcher and R. Johnson (eds), *Working Class Culture: Studies in History and Theory* (1979) and A. Tomlinson (ed.), *Explorations in Football Culture* (1983).

64 W. F. Mandle, 'The professional cricketer in England in the nineteenth century', *Labour History*, xxiii (1972), 1–16; R. Bowen, *Cricket: A History of its Growth and Development* (1970), 116, 144–5. Sandiford, 'Amateurs and professionals in Victorian county cricket', *Albion* (1983), 32–51.

65 'Professionals', *SR*, 14 July 1883; R. G. Barlow, *Forty Seasons of First Class Cricket* (1908), 2; O. F. Christie, *The Transition from Aristocracy, 1832–1867* (1927), 115.

7 Rational recreation and the entertainment industry: the case of the Victorian music halls

1 For the most recent scholarly work on a wide range of aspects of music hall operation and performance, see P. Bailey (ed.), *Music Hall: The Business of Pleasure* (1986) and J. S. Bratton (ed.), *Music Hall: Performance and Style* (1986). See also G. Stedman Jones, 'Working-class culture and working-class politics in London, 1870–1900: notes on the remaking of a working class' (1974), reprinted in his *Languages of Class* (1983), 204–7, 224–35; Bailey, 'Custom, capital and culture', in R. D. Storch (ed.), *Popular Culture and Custom in Nineteenth Century England* (1982), 180–208; P. Summerfield, 'The Effingham Arms and the Empire: deliberate selection in the evolution of music hall in London', in E. and S. Yeo (eds), *Popular Culture and Class Conflict 1590–1914* (1981), 209–40; B. Waites, 'The music hall', in *The Historical Development of Popular Culture in Britain*, 1 (1981), 43–76, Open University's *Popular Culture* course booklet. There is now too a first class bibliography: L. Senelick, D. F. Cheshire and U. Schneider, *British Music Hall 1840–1923: A Bibliography and Guide to Sources* (1981), while D. Howard, *London Theatres and Music Halls, 1850–1950* (1970) retains its considerable utility as bibliography and reference work. Cheshire, *Music Hall in Britain* (1974) is a handy source book and, among general histories, the following remain useful: C. D. Stuart and A. J. Park, *The Variety Stage* (1895); H. Scott, *The Early Doors: Origins of Music Hall* (2nd edn, 1977), R. Mander and J. Mitchenson, *The British Music Hall* (2nd edn, 1974). Other new work is noted below.

2 SC on public houses and places of public entertainment, *PP*(HC) 1852–3, xxxvii, q. 4198.
3 C. M. Smith, *Curiosities of London Life* (1853), 166–7; J. Rivière, *My Musical Life* (1893), 133; Renton 'Baron' Nicholson, *Autobiography of a Fast Man* (1863), 284–7. For development in the north east, see D. Harker, 'The making of the Tyneside concert hall', *Popular Music*, i (1981), 27–56.
4 Though important, Morton was not the solitary pioneer that music hall mythology has made him out to be. He acceded to the title of Father of the Halls in the 1890s by the happy contrivance of outliving his rivals; apotheosis was completed in W. H. Morton and H. C. Newton, *Sixty Years' Stage Service: The Life of Charles Morton* (1905). Scott, op. cit., 131–41 gives a more realistic appreciation. For the Canterbury, see J. Earl and J. Stanton, *The Canterbury Hall and Theatre of Varieties* (1982) and for a history of the architectural development of the halls in London, see Earl, 'Building the halls', in Bailey (ed.), *Business of Pleasure* 33–52. On another important London hall, see Bratton, *Wilton's Music Hall* (1980), and P. Honri, *John Wilton's Music Hall: The Handsomest Room in Town* (1985).
5 W. White, *Illustrated Handbook of the Royal Alhambra Palace* (1869).
6 Stuart and Park, op. cit., 86–92; SC on theatrical licences and regulations. *PP*(HC) 1866, xvi, app. 3, 313.
7 S. Fiske, *English Photographs by an American* (1968), 130; Dion Boucicault to the *Era*, 5 October, 21 December 1862; Bailey, 'A community of friends: business and good fellowship in London music hall management, 1860–85', in Bailey (ed.), *Business of Pleasure*, 33–52. Music halls outnumbered theatres of all descriptions by eight to one in London by the 1880s, but the popular theatre often interspersed music hall acts with the straight drama, and retained considerable working-class support.
8 Stuart and Park, op. cit., 86–92; 'The cost of amusing the public', *London Society*, i (1862), 193–8; *Era Almanack* (1868). G. J. Mellor, *The Northern Music Hall: A Century of Popular Entertainment* (1971) makes a start on the history of the provincial halls. M. Vicinus, *The Industrial Muse: A Study of Nineteenth Century British Working-Class Literature* (1974), 238–85 is good on the north east (for which see also Harker, op. cit.) as well as general developments. See also R. Poole, *Popular Leisure and the Music Hall in Nineteenth Century Bolton* (1982); K. Barker, 'The Performing Arts in Five Provincial Towns, 1840–70', University of Leicester Ph.D thesis, 1982; J. Crump, 'Provincial music hall: promoters and public in Leicester, 1863–1929', and C. Waters, 'Manchester morality and London capital: the battle over the Palace of Varieties', in Bailey (ed.), *Business of Pleasure*, 33–52, 141–61.
9 *Era*, 7 September 1856; SC on theatrical licences, 1866, q. 1006; SC on theatres and places of entertainment, *PP*(HC), xviii 1892, qq. 2079–80, 2320, 3773.
10 *Financial News*, 15 February 1887; Stuart and Park, op. cit., 190–201; Cheshire, op. cit., 98–105; Summerfield, op. cit.

11 Cheshire, op. cit., 87 quotes some salary figures, and G. H. McDermott, who introduced the notorious 'By Jingo' hit of the 1870s, provides some further details on the occasion of his bankruptcy, *Era*, 8, 29 August 1885.

12 The brief careers of these unions are recorded in *Magnet* (Leeds), 17 August–28 December 1872; *Era*, 7 September–21 December 1872. For militancy in the 1880s, see *Music Hall Artists' Association Gazette*, 30 August–3 November 1886. For a full account, including the famous strike of 1907, see L. Rutherford, 'Managers in a small way: the professionalisation of variety artists, 1860–1914', in Bailey (ed.), *Business of Pleasure*, 93–117.

13 L. Blanc, *Letters on England*, 4 vols (1866–7), i, 61–2.

14 D. Cook, 'Coffee and comic songs', *Time*, May 1881; J. Hollingshead, 'Music hall history', *Entr'acte Annual* (1886).

15 For individual performers see essays by Bailey on Leybourne, Bratton on Jenny Hill, and Harker on a regional favourite Joe Wilson, in Bratton (ed.), *Performance and Style* (1986). See also, Honri, *Working the Halls* (1973).

16 For cases brought by the society, formed in 1875, see *The Times*, 10 June 1882.

17 A. Roberts, *Fifty Years of Spoof* (1927), 28–9.

18 J. Burnley, *Phases of Bradford Life* (1871), 59; D. J. Kirwan, *Palace and Hovel, or Phases of London Life* (1963 reprint of 1870 US edn). The Victoria is a good example of a popular theatre which played music hall entertainment.

19 E. Jepson, *Memories of a Victorian* (1933), 230–3. Perhaps this was the formidable Bessie Bellwood – ex-rabbit skinner turned star, see Vicinus, op. cit., 252–3.

20 C. Coborn, *The Man Who Broke the Bank: Memories of the Stage and Music Halls* (1928), 111, 159; *The Times*, 29 December 1879. On the 'moral economy' of the audience, see Bailey, 'Custom, capital and culture', and see also G. Pearson, *Hooligan: A History of Respectable Fears* (1983), 86. On popular theatre, see C. Barker, 'The audiences of the Britannia, Hoxton', *Theatre Quarterly*, ix (1979), 27–41; D. Reid, 'Popular theatre in Victorian Birmingham', in D. Bradby, L. James and B. Sharratt (eds), *Performance and Politics in Popular Drama* (1980), 65–89.

21 Fiske, op. cit., 133–4. For music hall patriotism see Jones, op. cit., and Summerfield, 'Patriotism and empire: music hall entertainment, 1870–1914', in J. M. Mackenzie (ed.), *Imperialism and Popular Culture* (1986), 17–48.

22 W. R. Titterton, *From Theatre to Music Hall* (1912), 121–3, L. Senelick, 'Politics as entertainment: Victorian music hall songs', *Victorian Studies*, xix (1975), 149–80 is the modern skeptic, and see also Jones, op. cit. on 'the culture of consolation'. On songs and their performance, see the essays by Bailey and J. Traies in Bratton (ed.), *Performance and Style* (1986) and, on other entertainment types, in the same collection, M. Pickering on negro minstrelsy, L. Rutherford on the sketch and A. Bennett on the music.

23 W. Besant and J. Rice, *Ready-Money Mortiboy: A Matter of Fact Story*, 3 vols (1872), iii, 19. I owe this reference to Anna Davin. Cf. for Birmingham and Bradford, SC on theatrical licences, 1866, q. 7436, Burnley, op. cit., 55–63. See now D. Höher, 'The composition of music hall audiences, 1850–1900', in Bailey (ed.), *Business of Pleasure*, 73–92.

24 *The Times*, 5 January 1865; *Music Halls' Gazette*, 8 August 1868.

25 (T. Wright), *Some Habits and Customs of the Working Classes by a Journeyman Engineer* (1867), 198–9.

26 *Music Halls' Gazette*, 23 May 1868. See also *Musician and Music Hall Times*, 28 May 1862, and *Glowworm*, 6 September 1865. These were some of the short-lived music hall papers of the 1860s; the staple professional papers were the *Era*, the licensed victuallers' paper, which overcame its initial distaste for the halls by the late 1850s, and the Leeds *Magnet*, which first appeared in 1866, but outlived the other newcomers.

27 J. Greenwood, 'Music hall morality', *London Society*, xiv (1868), 486–91.

28 *The Times*, 15 October 1883; *Judy*, 2 September 1885.

29 Greenwood, op. cit.; Morton and Newton, op. cit., 12–14. See also Hollingshead's evidence on the Alhambra, SC on theatrical licences, 1866, q. 5263.

30 Coborn, op. cit., 102–4, 129–30; G. Chirgwin, *Chirgwin's Chirrups* (1912), 25.

31 *Era*, 19 September 1885. Bill Holland granted free use of his North Woolwich Pleasure Gardens to engineers and their families who held a benefit for striking Newcastle engineers, *The Times*, 4 October 1871.

32 J. Hole, *The Working Classes of Leeds* (1863), 116.

33 E.g. 'The drama in danger', *SR*, 7 January 1865; M. Browne, 'Theatres and music halls', *Argosy*, ii (1866), 117–28; 'Music halls and their effects', *Meliora*, x (1867), 246–56; J. Valentine, 'A plea for music in common life', *Good Words*, vii (1866), 473–6.

34 *Era*, 26 October 1856; W. Lovett, *The Life and Struggles of William Lovett* (1876), 288, 372–5.

35 SC on public houses and places of public entertainment, 1852–3, q. 870; SC on theatrical licences, 1866, q. 956, and qq. 969, 1124–5 for Sir Richard Mayne's assessment of London halls. Bolton's chief constable supported the Museum Music Hall against its critics, see *BC*, 1 February 1873.

36 M. Browne, 'Theatres and music halls', and *Views and Opinions* (1866), 266–8, and Boucicault to SC on theatrical licences, 1866, qq. 4237–8.

37 S. Headlam, 'The social work of the Church', *Church Reformer*, February 1882, and *The Function of the Stage* (1889). See also F. G. Bettany, *Stewart Headlam: A Biography* (1926), 43–4; P. d'A. Jones, *The Christian Socialist Revival* (1968), 102. For Headlam among the Fabians and their views on music hall, see I. Britain, *Fabianism and Culture* (1982), 235–40.

38 Headlam, report of speech at Newcastle, *Church Reformer*, 15 September 1884.

39 *House and Home*, from the 1880s, exact reference mislaid. See also 'Social characteristics of London life', *Beehive*, 25 October 1865.

40 Besant and Rice, op. cit., ii, 159–66, 260–74. A number of London caterers and a leading agent, H. J. Didcott, were Jewish. Morton's biographers were rather coy on this matter: he was, said Chance Newton, 'not altogether un-Hebraic', *idem, Cues and Curtain Calls* (1927), 270.

41 H. Shimmin, *Liverpool Life* (1856), 28–9; J. E. Ritchie, *Days and Nights in London* (1880), 61–3; 'Our popular amusements', *Dublin University Magazine*, lxxxiv (1874), 233–44.

42 H. Mayhew, *London Labour and the London Poor*, 4 vols (Frank Cass edn, 1967), i, 40–2.

43 SC on theatrical licences, 1866, q. 3607.

44 'Music hall lyrics', *SR*, 20 September 1862. See also C. Mackay, 'Music hall literature', *Social Notes*, 1 June 1878. For working-class writers, see G. J. Holyoake, *The Social Means of Promoting Temperance* (1860), 18–19; J. M. Ludlow and L. Jones, *The Progress of the Working Class, 1832–67* (1867), 256; J. D. Burn, *Autobiography of a Beggar Boy* (1882), 605.

45 Ritchie, op. cit., 49–50.

46 'Our music halls', *Tinsley's Magazine*, iv (1869), 216–33. See also H. Manton, *Letters on the Theatres and Music Halls* (1888), Birmingham Central Reference Library.

47 H. Shimmin, *Town Life* (1858), 152–4. Prostitutes visited the halls in considerable numbers, whether for business, recreation, or both, though the metropolitan police gave the London halls a clean bill of health before the 1866 SC on theatrical licences, qq. 916, 1215. This is an obscure and contentious area that needs research.

48 SC on public houses and places of public entertainment, 1852–3, qq. 4013–30; Revd E. Corderoy, *Popular amusements: Lectures to the YMCA* (1857), 37–8; SC on theatrical licences, 1866, q. 583; M. Browne, 'Theatres and music halls'.

49 *BC*, 18 January–22 February 1873, 29 January 1876.

50 For other campaigns against provincial halls and singing saloons, see respective reports from Gosport, Manchester, West Hartlepool and Bristol in *Era*, 5 October 1862; ibid., 12 September 1885; *The Times*, 14 November 1871; SC on intemperance, *PP*(HL) 1877, xi, qq. 5301–20; Waters, op. cit.

51 The contest can be studied in G. Thorne, *The Great Acceptance: The Life of F. N. Charrington* (1912), 104–34; 'The music halls and their enemies', *SR*, 7 March 1885; several reports and articles in *Church Reformer*, notably Headlam, 'The battle of the music halls', November 1889. For the role of the *Methodist Times* and the Social Purity movement, see D. P. Hughes, *The Life of Hugh Price Hughes* (1904), 338–42. See now also E. J. Bristow, *Vice and Vigilance: Purity Movements in Britain since 1700* (1977), 209–14; Summerfield, 'Effingham Arms to the Empire', op. cit.; S. Pennybacker, 'The London County Council and the music halls', in Bailey (ed.), *Business of Pleasure*, 118–40.

52 Among the supporters of the company were Frederic Harrison, Tom Hughes, Samuel Morley and Dean Stanley; its history is recorded in C. Hamilton and L. Bayliss, *The Old Vic* (1926) 176–88.

53 *Social Notes and Club News*, 16 July 1881; J. Hollingshead, *My Lifetime*, 2 vols (1895), ii, 151–2; *Coffee Public House News*, 1 February 1881. The charge of a trade boycott was made by William Poel, the Victoria's manager, *Church Reformer*, October 1884. See also R. Morton, *The Adventures of Arthur Roberts* (1895), 17–18.

54 *Coffee Public House News*, 1 May 1884; *Church Reformer*, October 1884.

55 J. Humphreys to *The Times*, 16 October 1883 and *idem*, 'Up in the gallery', *All The Year Round*, 29 July 1882.

56 *Era*, 29 August, 12 September 1852.

57 'A Journalist' (W. Mackay), *Bohemian Days in Fleet Street* (1913), 23. There is a picture in Cheshire, op. cit., 22.

58 The proprietors' case is put in a pamphlet published by their association, *Regulation of Music Halls* (1883), copy in the British Library of Political and Economic Science.

59 House rules of the early 1880s are reproduced in SC on theatres and places of entertainment, 1892, app. 3 and 4, 437–44.

60 Coburn, op. cit., 232; W. Thorne, *My Life's Battles* (1925), 28–9; G. Foster, *The Spice of Life: Sixty Five Years in the Glamour World* (1939), 135.

61 *Church Reformer*, November 1889. Estimates of the relative revenues of refreshments and admissions are given in SC on theatrical licences, 1866, qq. 1349–1758. See also Hollingshead to *The Times*, 17 October 1883.

62 SC on theatres and places of entertainment, 1892, qq. 1551–87.

63 Signs of status gratification show in several careers: Henry Holden, erstwhile Brummagem butcher, retired to a country estate at Malvern; Sam Lane of the Britannia in Hoxton became president of the Royal Thames Yacht Club; several London caterers – Morton, William Purkiss and Frederick Strange – took commissions in the Volunteers.

64 The sale of intoxicants was not, it should be noted, dispensed with – it was removed to the relative quarantine of ante-room bars. Proprietors of new purpose-built halls in London circumvented some of the hazards of the licensing procedure by taking out a theatre licence from the Lord Chamberlain's office, and obtaining permits for as many bars as they needed under a simple Excise licence; they were then covered for music and liquor but could not serve drink or allow smoking in the auditorium, thus destroying one of the characteristic features of the classic music hall. *Entr'acte Annual* (1897), 11–13.

65 The apostle of the new conformity was Oswald (later Sir Oswald) Stoll who was soon to be found outside Charing Cross Station with a notebook, calculating the common denominator of a reformed popular taste, F. Barker, *The House That Stoll Built: The Story of the Coliseum Theatre* (1957), 11.

66 *Entr'acte Annual* (1900), 13.

67 D. Farson, *Marie Lloyd and Music Hall* (1972).

68 Stuart and Park, op. cit., 190–201; H. G. Hibbert, *Fifty Years of a Londoner's Life* (1916), 40–2; Titterton, op. cit., 120–3.

69 National Social Purity Crusade, *The Nation's Morals: Proceedings of the Public Morals Conference* (1910), 194–9.

Conclusions

1 J. Strutt, *The Sports and Pastimes of the People of England* (Methuen reprint edn, 1903), 15.

2 E.g. W. Hardwicke, 'Recreation of the working class', *Trans.NAPSS* (1867), 471–7, 552–7; G. Turner, 'Amusements of the English people', *Nineteenth Century*, ii (1877), 820–30. See also Lord Brabazon, 'Great cities and social reform', *Nineteenth Century*, xiv (1883), 798–803.

3 H. Solly, *These Eighty Years*, 2 vols (1893), ii, 160. The title of Fuller's address is instructive – 'On our paramount duty to provide wholesome and pure recreations and amusements for the people, and the dire results and dangers which attend our neglect of it', *Trans.NAPSS* (1874), 745–8.

4 C. Wilson, 'Economy and society in late-Victorian Britain', *Economic History Review*, xviii (1965), 183–98.

5 The speaker is Viscount Cranbrook, at the opening of his Bradford WMC, *CIJ*, 3 August 1883.

6 J. K. Cook, 'The labourer's leisure', *Dublin University Magazine*, xc (1877), 174–92.

7 S. A. Barnett, 'Hospitality', in J. M. Knapp (ed.), *The Universities and the Social Problem* (1895), 51–66. Cf., however, the considerable social skills of the industrial grandees in P. Joyce, *Work, Society and Politics: The Culture of the Factory in Later Victorian England* (1980). For the later phase, see H. E. Meller, *Leisure and the Changing City, 1870–1914* (1976).

8 M. Arnold, *Culture and Anarchy* (1966 reprint of 1869 edn), 105; M. Browne, *Views and Opinions* (1866), 280; F. Freeman, 'Publicans and sinners', *Weekly Dispatch*, 11 February 1883.

9 S. W. Jevons, 'Methods of social reform: amusements of the people', *Contemporary Review*, xxxiii (1878), 499–513; 'Our music halls', *Tinsley's Magazine*, iv (1869), 216–33; 'Social barriers', *SR*, 26 April 1873; *The Times*, 30 August 1860.

10 E.g. J. Lawson, *Letters to the Young on Progress in Pudsey* (1887); W. E. Gladstone, 'Locksley Hall and the Jubilee', *Nineteenth Century*, xxi (1887), 1–18.

11 G. Gorer, *Exploring English Character* (1955), 13. On gambling see R. McKibbin, 'Working-class gambling in Britain, 1880–1939', *Past and Present*, 82 (1979), 147–78.

12 G. Best, *Mid-Victorian Britain, 1815–75* (1971), 256–63; B. H. Harrison, *Drink and the Victorians* (1971), 23–7. See also J. Lowerson and J. Myerscough, *Time to Spare in Victorian England* (1977).

13 R. J. Morris, 'The history of self-help', *New Society*, 3 December 1970, on the Woodhouse Temperance community in Leeds; L. L. Shiman, 'The Band of Hope movement', *Victorian Studies*, viii (1973), 65; *idem*, 'The Birstall Temperance Society', *Yorkshire Archaeological Journal*, xlvi (1974), 128–39.

14 Solly's address to the TUC in 1871 recorded in *Occasional Papers of the Working Men's Club and Institute Union*, 20 (January 1872); W. Cowper, MP, in *The Times*, 13 July 1863.

15 R. Q. Gray, *The Labour Aristocracy in Victorian Edinburgh* (1976); G. Crossick, 'The labour aristocracy and its values', *Victorian Studies*, xix (1976), 301–28; T. R. Tholfsen, *Working-Class Radicalism in Mid-Victorian England* (1976). For a critical review of the extended debate on the labour aristocracy, see Gray, *The Aristocracy of Labour in Nineteenth Century Britain, 1850–1914* (1981).

16 H. H. Gerth and C. Wright Mills, *Character and Social Structure* (1964), 10–11, 120–4; R. Frankenberg, *Communities in Britain: Social Life in Town and Country* (1966), 240–2. On observability, see R. K. Merton, 'The role-set: problems in sociological theory', *British Journal of Sociology*, viii (1957), 112–20.

17 G. Gissing, *The Nether World* (John Murray reprint edn, 1903), 69.

18 These themes are examined more fully in P. Bailey ' "Will the real Bill Banks please stand up?": A role analysis of mid-Victorian working-class respectability', *Journal of Social History*, xii (1979), 336–53. See also E. Goffman, 'Role distance', in *Encounters: Two Studies in the Sociology of Interaction* (Penguin University edn, 1972), 75–134 and his 'The nature of deference and demeanour', in *Interaction Ritual* (Penguin University edn, 1972), 58; H. Newby, 'The deferential dialectic', *Comparative Studies in Society and History*, xvii (1975), 139–64.

19 G. Stedman Jones, *Outcast London: A Study in the Relationship Between Classes in Victorian Society* (1971).

20 Jones, 'Working-class culture and working-class politics in London, 1870–1900: notes on the remaking of a working class', *Journal of Social History*, vii (1974), 460–508, reprinted in his *Languages of Class* (1983), 179–238. For other readings of late century popular or working-class culture see the discussion and references above in the introduction: 'Leisure, culture and the historian'.

21 Report of factory inspectors, *PP* 1867, xvi, 376.

22 P. N. Stearns, *Lives of Labour: Work in a Maturing Industrial Society* (1975), 269–99 and his 'Working-class women in Britain, 1890–1914', in M. Vicinus (ed.), *Suffer and Be Still: Women in the Victorian Age* (1972), 100–20. See also S. Meacham, ' "The sense of an impending clash": English working-class unrest before the First World War', *American Historical Review*, lxxvii (1972), 1343–64.

Bibliography

Primary sources

Manuscript and other unpublished materials

Solly Collection, 17 vols, London, British Library of Political and Economic Science (Misc. MSS 154).

Osborne Collection of newspaper cuttings, 1874–1907, Birmingham, Central Public Library.

Place Collection of newspaper cuttings, BM.

Rye Collection of newspaper cuttings, London, Guildhall Library.

Horringer and Ickworth Village Club minute and account books, 1877–1902, in the possession of Mrs Z. Ward, Horringer, Suffolk.

Newcastle upon Tyne Working Men's Club minute books, 1865–6, 1870–3, Newcastle, Central Public Library.

Star Music Hall account book, 1847–50, xerox copy from the original in the possession of Mrs D. Scholefield, Orpington, Kent BRL.

Dyson, S., 'Local Notes and Reminiscences of Farnworth', typescript 1894, Farnworth, Lancs, Central Public Library.

Greenhalgh, R., 'Sixty Years: Local Records and Reminiscences', MS 1908 BRL.

MacMillan, J., 'Description of Checks issued by Birmingham Concert Halls, 1850–1920', MS 1924, Birmingham, Central Public Library.

Parliamentary materials

Hansard's Parliamentary Debates.

Annual reports of the factory inspectors.

Parliamentary Papers (Commons and Lords):

Select committee (SC) on the observation of the sabbath (HC), 1831–2, vii.

SC on public walks (HC), 1833, xv.

SC on drunkenness (HC), 1834, viii.

SC on the education of the poorer classes (HC), 1838, vii.

Report of the commission on constabulary, 1839, xix.

SC on the operation of the Factory Act (HC), 1840, x.

First report of the commission on children's employment, 1842, xv.

Second report of the commission on children's employment, 1843, xiii, xiv.

SC on gaming (HC), 1844, vi.

SC on the laws governing gaming (HL), 1844, xii.

Report of the commission on the state of large towns, 1844, xvii.

Report of the commissioner on the state of mining districts, 1844, xvi.

SC on the observation of the sabbath (HC), 1847, ix.

SC on public libraries (HC), 1849, xi.

Report of the commission on the state of the population in mining districts, 1850, xxiii.

SC on the suppression of betting houses (HC), 1852–3, i.

SC on public houses and places of public entertainment (HC), 1852–3, xxxvii.

SC further report on the licensing of places of public entertainment (HC), 1854, xiv.

Lyon Playfair, Report on the London Mechanics Institution, 1857–8, xlviii.

SC on public institutions (HC), 1860, xvi.

Report of the commission on popular education in England, 1861, xxi.

SC on theatrical licences and regulations (HC), 1866, xvi.

SC on bank holidays (HC), 1867–8, vii.

SC on the sale of liquors on Sunday (HC), 1867–8, xiv.

SC on intemperance (HL), 1877, xi.

SC on theatres and places of entertainment (HC), 1892, xviii.

Third report of the commission on liquor licensing laws, 1898, xxxvi.

Contemporary press, limited to those most extensively sampled (place of publication is London, unless otherwise stated)

(a) NEWSPAPERS

Beehive; *Bell's Life in London*; *Bolton Chronicle*; *Bolton Evening News*; *Bolton Free Press*; *Bolton Weekly Journal*; *Bowtun Luminary* (Bolton); *Daily News*; *Daily Telegraph*; *Era*; *Porcupine* (Liverpool); *The Times*; *Weekly Dispatch*.

(b) PERIODICALS

All The Year Round; *Argosy*; *Bentley's Miscellany*; *Blackwood's Magazine*; *Chambers's Edinburgh Journal*; *Colburn's Monthly Magazine*; *Congregationalist*; *Contemporary Review*; *Cornhill Magazine*; *Dublin Review*; *Dublin University Magazine*; *Edinburgh Review*; *Fortnightly Review*; *Fraser's Magazine*; *Fun*; *Good Words* (Edinburgh); *Journal of the Society of Arts*; *London Society*; *Nineteenth Century*; *Punch*; *Quarterly Review*; *St James Gazette*; *Saturday Review*; *Time*; *Tinsley's Magazine*.

(c) SPECIALIST, INSTITUTIONAL AND REFORMING PRESS

After Work: A Magazine for Workmen's Homes; *The All-England Cricket and Football Journal and Athletic Review* (Sheffield); *Amateurs' Guide and Stage and Concert Hall Reporter* (Birmingham); *Athlete*; *Athletic News* (Manchester); *Athletic Record and Monthly Journal of Physical Education*; *Baily's Magazine of Sports and Pastimes*; *Church Reformer*; *Club and Institute Union Journal*; *Coffee Public House News*; *Coffee Tavern Gazette and Journal of Food Thrift*; *Common Good*; *Dramatic and Musical Circular: An Epitome of Music Hall Requirements*; *Drury Lane Workmen's Hall Messenger*; *House and Home*; *Illustrated Sporting and Dramatic News*; *Illustrated Sporting News*; *Leisure Hour: A Family Journal of Instruction and Recreation*; *Licensed Victuallers Gazette*; *Magnet* (Leeds); *Manager's Guide and Artistes Advertiser* (Manchester); *Midland Sporting News* (Birmingham); *Music Hall Artists Association Gazette*; *Music Halls' Gazette*; *Musical Gazette*; *Musician and Music Hall Times*; *People's Journal*; *Quarterly Messenger of the Young Men's Christian Association*; *Referee*; *Refreshment News*; *Rink*; *Social Notes and Club News*; *Sporting Gazette*; *Timethrift: Or All Hours Turned to Good Account*; *Tonic Sol-fa Reporter*; *Town*; *Wheel World*; *Working Men's College Magazine*; *Workmen's Club Journal*; *Workman's Magazine*

(d) ANNUAL PUBLICATIONS

Athletic Almanack; *Dramatic, Equestrian and Musical Sick Fund Almanack*; *Dramatic, and Musical Directory of the United Kingdom*; *Entr'acte Annual*; *Era Almanack*; *Musical Artists, Lecturers and Entertainers Guide, and Entrepreneurs Directory*; *Walters Theatrical and Sporting Directory*.

Contemporary books, pamphlets, tracts and sermons (place of publication is London, unless otherwise stated)

Adams, J. (1850) *A Letter to the Justices of the Peace of the County of Middlesex, on the Subject of Licences for Public Music and Dancing*.

Adams, W. E. (1903) *Memoirs of a Social Atom*, 2 vols.

Anstey, F. (1892) *Mr. Punch's Model Music Hall Songs*.

Arnold, M. (1966) *Culture and Anarchy* (Cambridge, reprint of 1869 edn).

Arnold, T. (1832) *Thirteen Letters on our Social Condition* (Sheffield).

Axon, W. E. (1870) *The Black Knight of Ashton* (Manchester).

Bamford, S. (1844) *Walks in South Lancashire* (Blackley).

Barclay, T. (1934) *Memoirs and Medleys: The Autobiography of a Bottle Washer* (Leicester).

Barlow, R. G. (1908) *Forty Seasons of First Class Cricket* (Manchester).

Bayly, M. (1860) *Ragged Homes and How to Mend Them*.

Belford, J. (1867) *The Saturday Half-Holiday: Its Bearing on the Due Observance of the Sabbath* (Glasgow).

Bennett, A. (1947) *Clayhanger* (Methuen reprint edn).

Bennett, A. R. (1924) *London and Londoners in the Eighteen Fifties and Sixties*.

Besant, W. (1903) *As We Are and As We May Be.*
—— and Rice, J. (1872) *Ready-Money Mortiboy: A Matter of Fact Story*, 3 vols.
Best, T. (1862) *The Love of Pleasure* (Sheffield).
(Blackburn, C. F.) (1878) 'A Journeyman', *A Continental Tour of Eight Days for Forty Shillings.*
Blaikie, W. G. (1863) *Better Days for Working People.*
Blanc, L. (1866–7) *Letters on England*, 4 vols.
(Blouet, P.) (1883) 'Max O'Rell', *John Bull and His Island.*
Boardman, W. H. (1935) *Vaudeville Days.*
Box, C. (1877) *The English Game of Cricket.*
—— (1888) *Musings for Athletes: Twelve Philosophical Essays.*
Brassey, T. (1878) *Lectures on the Labour Question.*
Brown, H. S. (1870) *Lectures to Working Men.*
Brown, J. B. (1871) *First Principles of Ecclesiastical Truth.*
——(1876) *The Gregarious Follies of Fashion: An Address to the Younger Generation.*
Browne, M. (1866) *Views and Opinions.*
Buckingham, J. S. (1849) *National Evils and Practical Remedies.*
Bulwer-Lytton, E. (1833) *England and the English*, 2 vols.
Burn, J. D. (1882) *The Autobiography of a Beggar Boy.*
Burnley, J. (1871) *Phases of Bradford Life* (Bradford).
Chadwick, E. (1842) *Report on the Sanitary Condition of the Labouring Population of Great Britain* (new edn ed. M. W. Flinn, 1965).
Chancellor, V. E. (ed.) (1969) *Master and Artisan in Victorian England: The Diary of William Andrews and the Autobiography of Joseph Gutteridge.*
Chester, G. J. (1860) *The Young Man at Rest and at Play* (Sheffield).
—— (1862) *The Temptations of Young Men in Towns* (Sheffield).
Clarke, J. E. (1858) *Plain Papers on the Social Economy of the People.*
(Clay, J.) (1841) *Chaplain's Report on the Preston House of Correction* (Preston).
Clifford-Smith, J. L. (1882) *The National Association and its Twenty Fifth Anniversary: A Manual and a Narrative.*
Coborn, C. (1928) *The Man Who Broke The Bank: Memories of the Stage and Music Halls.*
Collins, W. (1870) *Man and Wife*, 3 vols.
Cooper, T. (1872) *The Life of Thomas Cooper.*
—— (1885) *Thoughts at Fourscore.*
Corderoy, E. (1857) 'Popular Amusements', *Lectures to the Young Men's Christian Association.*
Coyne, J. S. (1859) 'The Barmaid', in A. Smith (ed.), *Sketches of London Life and Character.*
Cumming, J. (1855) *Labour, Rest and Recreation: Lectures to the YMCA.*
Currie, E. H. (1886) *Appeal for a People's Palace.*
Dana, R. H. (1921) *Hospitable England in the Eighteen Seventies: The Diary of a Young American, 1875–6.*
Dickens, C. (1836) *Sketches by Boz*, 2 vols.
—— (1861) *The Uncommercial Traveller.*

Disraeli, B. (1904) *Sybil, or the Two Nations* (Brimley Johnson reprint edn).

Dodd, W. (1842) *The Factory System Illustrated in a Series of Letters to Lord Ashley.*

Downer, A. R. (1908) *Running Recollections and How to Train.*

Doyle, R. (1854) *The Foreign Tour of Messrs. Brown, Jones, and Robinson.*

Earnshaw, S. (1857) *Upon the State of Education and the Working Classes of Sheffield* (Sheffield).

—— (1860) *The Tradition of the Elders* (Sheffield).

Ellis, S. M. (ed.) (1923) *Letters and Memoirs of Sir William Hardman, A Mid-Victorian Pepys.*

Engels, F. (1969) *The Condition of the Working Class in England* (Pan paperback reprint).

Escott, T. H. S. (1885) *England: Its People, Polity and Pursuits.*

—— (1886) 'A Foreign Resident', *Society in London.*

—— (1897) *Social Transformations of the Victorian Age.*

Esquiros, A. (1861–3) *The English at Home,* 4 vols.

Faucher, L. (1844) *Manchester in 1844: Its Present Condition and Future Prospects* (Manchester).

'A Fellow Workman' (1853) *The Races Defended as an Amusement* (Newcastle upon Tyne).

Fiske, S. (1869) *English Photographs by an American.*

Fitzgerald, P. (1890) *Music Hall Land.*

Frost, T. (1874) *The Old Showmen and the Old London Fairs.*

—— (1880) *Forty Years' Recollections, Literary and Political.*

Gale, F. (1885) *Modern English Sports: Their Use and Abuse.*

—— (1888) *Sports and Recreations in Town and Country.*

Gardiner, F. J. (1914) *The Fiftieth Birthday of a Model Institution: An Account of the Origin and Development of Wisbech Workingmen's Club and Institute* (Wisbech).

Gibson, A. and Pickford, W. (1905) *Association Football and the Men Who Made It,* 4 vols.

Gissing, G. (1903) *The Nether World* (John Murray reprint edn).

Godwin, G. (1859) *Town Swamps and Social Bridges.*

Green, S. G. (1850) *The Working Classes of Great Britain: Consideration of the Means for their Improvement and Elevation* (Leeds).

Greg, S. (1840) *Two Letters to Leonard Horner on the Capabilities of the Factory System* (Manchester).

Guthrie, T. (1856) *Popular Innocent Entertainments* (Glasgow).

Hall, B. T. (1912) *Our Fifty Years: The Story of the Working Men's Club and Institute Union.*

Hall, E. H. (1878) *Coffee Taverns, Cocoa Houses and Coffee Palaces: Their Rise, Progress, and Prospects.*

Harrison, F. (1867) *Sundays and Festivals: A Lecture.*

Haweis, H. R. (1872) *Thoughts for the Times.*

Headlam, S. D. (1889) *The Function of the Stage.*

Heywood, B. (1843) *Addresses delivered at the Manchester Mechanics' Institute.*

Hodder, E. (1862) *The Junior Clerk: A Tale of City Life.*

—— (1887) *Life of Samuel Morley.*

Hole, J. (1853) *The History and Management of Literary, Scientific and Mechanics Institutes.*

Hollingshead, J. (1865) *Today: Essays and Miscellanies*, 2 vols.

—— (1895) *My Lifetime*, 2 vols.

Holyoake, G. J. (1856) *The Rich Man's Six, and the Poor Man's One Day: A Letter to Lord Palmerston.*

—— (1860) *The Social Means of Promoting Temperance.*

Hopkins, E. (1879) *Work Amongst Working Men.*

Howitt, W. (1838) *The Rural Life of England*, 2 vols.

—— (1850) *The Country Year Book* (New York).

Hudson, J. W. (1851) *The History of Adult Education.*

Hughes, D. P. (1904) *The Life of Hugh Price Hughes.*

Jackson, N. L. (1932) *Sporting Days and Sporting Ways.*

Jerrold, W. B. (1871) *The Cockaynes in Paris, or Gone Abroad.*

—— and Doré, G. (1872) *London: A Pilgrimage.*

Johns, E. F. (ed.) (1912) *Words of Advice to Schoolboys by Charles Kingsley.*

Johnston, J. (1885) *Parks and Playgrounds for the People.*

Jones, H. (1864) *Holiday Papers.*

Kay, J. (1883) *The Church and Popular Recreations.*

Kempe, J. E. (ed.) (1873–5) *The Use and Abuse of the World*, 3 vols.

Kingsley, C. (1874) *Health and Education.*

—— (1880) *Sanitary and Social Essays.*

Kingsley, F. E. (ed.) (1877) *Charles Kingsley: His Letters and Memories of his Life*, 2 vols.

Kirwan, D. J. (1963) *Palace and Hovel, or Phases of London Life* (reprint of 1870 US edn).

Knight, C. (1873) *Passages of a Working Life*, 3 vols.

Lawson, J. (1887) *Letters to the Young on Progress in Pudsey* (Stanninglen).

Levy, E. L. (1898) *History of the Birmingham Athletic Club, 1866–98* (Birmingham).

Lilwall, J. (1856) *The Half-Holiday Question Considered.*

Lovett, W. (1876) *The Life and Struggles of William Lovett.*

Ludlow, J. M. and Jones, L. (1867) *The Progress of the Working Class, 1832–1867.*

Manners, J. (1843) *A Plea for National Holydays.*

Manton, H. (1888) *Letters on the Theatres and Music Halls* (Birmingham, Birmingham Central Reference Library).

Marriott, W. T. (1860) *Some Real Wants of the Working Classes* (Manchester).

Mayhew, H. (1865) 'The Cockaynes in Paris', in *Shops and Companies of London, and the Trades and Manufactories of Great Britain.*

—— (1871) *Report of the Trade and Hours of Closing at Working Men's Clubs.*

—— (1967) *London Labour and the London Poor*, 4 vols (Frank Cass reprint edn).

Merion, C. (1884) *The Music Hall Stage and its Relationship with the Church.*

Miles, H. D. (ed.) (1866) *Tom Sayers, His Life and Pugilistic Career*.

Miller, D. P. (1849) *The Life of a Showman*.

(Miller, W. H.) (1872) *The Culture of Pleasure*.

Morley, J. (1867) *Studies in Conduct*.

Morton, R. (1895) *The Adventures of Arthur Roberts* (Bristol).

Morton, W. H. and Newton, H. C. (1905) *Sixty Years' Stage Service: The Life of Charles Morton*.

Neale, E. V. (1876) *True Refinement: Address to the Rochdale Working Men's Club* (Manchester).

Nicholson, R. (1863) *Autobiography of a Fast Man*.

Occasional Papers of the Working Men's Club and Institute Union (1863–72).

Okey, T. (1930) *A Basketful of Memories: An Autobiographical Sketch*.

Philpott, H. B. (1904) *London at School: The Story of the School Board*.

Place, F. (1834) *The Improvement of the People*.

—— (1972) *Autobiography* (ed. M. Thale, Cambridge).

Practical Hints for the Management of Coffee Taverns (1878).

Pratt, H. (1870) *Notes of a Tour among Workmen's Clubs*.

Primrose, A. (1848) *Address to the Middle Classes on Gymnastic Exercises*.

Rae, W. F. (1891) *The Business of Travel*.

Rathbone, W. (1877) *The Increased Earnings of the Working Classes and Their Effect on Themselves and on the Future of England* (Liverpool).

The Regulation of Music Halls: A Summary of the Attempts made by Music Hall Proprietors to obtain an Improvement of the Law (1883).

Ritchie, J. E. (1857) *The Night Side of London*.

—— (1880) *Days and Nights in London*.

Roberts, A. (1927) *Fifty Years of Spoof*.

Rogers, F. (1913) *Labour, Life and Literature: Some Memories of Sixty Years*.

Roth, M. (1870) *A Plea for the Compulsory Teaching of the Elements of Physical Education in our National Elementary Schools*.

Rye, W. (1916) *An Autobiography of an Ancient Athlete and Antiquarian* (Norwich).

Sala, G. A. (1859) *Gaslight and Daylight, With Some London Scenes They Shine Upon*.

Sanger, 'Lord' George (1910) *Seventy Years a Showman*.

Sargant, W. L. (1857) *Economy of the Labouring Classes*.

Shearman, M. (1889) *Athletics and Football*.

Shimmin, H. (1856) *Liverpool Life, its Pleasures, Practices and Pastimes* (Liverpool).

—— (1858) *Town Life* (Liverpool).

Slaney, R. A. (1847) *A Plea for the Working Classes*.

Smee, W. R. (1871) *National Holidays*.

Smith, C. M. (1853) *Curiosities of London Life*.

—— (1853) *The Working Man's Way in the World*.

Smith, J. S. (1850) *Social Aspects*.

Solly, H. (1868) *How to Deal with the Unemployed Poor of London and with its Roughs and Criminal Classes?*

Solly, H. (1883) *James Sandford, Carpenter and Chartist*, 2 vols.
—— (1893) *These Eighty Years*, 2 vols.
—— (1904) *Working Men's Social Clubs and Educational Institutes*.
Sparks, T. (C. Dickens) (1836) *Sunday Under Three Heads*.
Spencer, F. H. (1938) *An Inspector's Testament*.
Spencer, H. (1861) *Education, Intellectual, Moral and Physical*.
Strutt, J. (1903) *The Sports and Pastimes of the People of England* (Methuen reprint edn).
Stuart, C. D. and Park, A. J. (1895) *The Variety Stage: A History of the Music Halls from the Earliest Period to the Present Time*.
Sullivan, J. F. (1878) *The British Workingman by One Who Does Not Believe in Him*.
Taine, H. (1872) *Notes on England*.
Talbot, C. J. C. (ed.) (1852) *Meliora, Or Better Times to Come*.
Taylor, W. Cooke (1842) *Notes of a Tour in the Manufacturing Districts of Lancashire* (Manchester).
Thomson, C. (1847) *The Autobiography of an Artisan*.
Thorne, G. (1912) *The Great Acceptance: The Life Story of F. N. Charrington*.
Thorne, W. (1925) *My Life's Battles*.
Titterton, W. R. (1912) *From Theatre to Music Hall*.
Transactions of the National Association for the Promotion of Social Science, 1857–86.
Trollope, A. (1868) *British Sports and Pastimes*.
—— (1972) *The New Zealander* (Oxford).
Wall, F. (1935) *Fifty Years of Football*.
White, W. (1869) *Illustrated Handbook of the Royal Alhambra Palace*.
Whittle, P. A. (1852) *Blackburn As It Is* (Preston).
Wilkinson, H. F. (1868) *Modern Athletics*.
Williams, J. E. H. (1906) *Life of Sir George Williams*.
Wingfield, W. (1874) *The Game of Sphairistike*.
(Wright, T.) (1867) *Some Habits and Customs of the Working Classes by a Journeyman Engineer*.
—— (1868) *The Great Unwashed*.
—— (1873) *Our New Masters*.
—— (1868) 'Bill Banks's day out', in A. Halliday (ed.), *The Savage Club Papers*.

Contemporary books, etc. on Bolton and district (place of publication is Bolton, unless otherwise stated), BRL

Ancient Noble Order of United Oddfellows (Bolton Unity) Friendly Society, *Grand Lodge Circular*, 115 vols (1831–1959).
Baker, F. (1850) *The Moral Tone of the Factory System Defended*.
Barlow, W. (1933) *Some Recollections of Ridgway Gates Sunday School*.
Barton, B. H. (1881) *Historical Gleanings of Bolton and District*.
Black, J. (1837) *A Medico-Topographical, Geological and Statistical Sketch of Bolton and its Neighbourhood*.

Brimelow, W. (1888) *Political and Parliamentary History of Bolton.*

Chamberlain, W. (1882) *On the Causes that Public Worship is Neglected by the People.*

Clegg, J. (1879) *A Chronicle History of Bolton.*

—— (ed.) (1883) *Autobiography of a Lancashire Lawyer.*

—— (1888) *Annals of Bolton.*

Entwhistle, E. (1881) *Pastimes and Recreations,* Essay read before Bolton Parish Church Mutual Improvement Society.

Entwhistle, J. (1848) *Report on the Sanitary Condition of Bolton.*

—— (1884) *Light Upon Dark Places.*

Grimshaw, T. (1838) *The Cogitations of Thomas Grimshaw: Observations on the Customs, Manners, etc. of the People of Bolton.*

—— (1877) 'Autobiography', in *Bolton Weekly Journal,* 23 June–18 August.

Hampson, T. (1883) *Horwich: Its History, Legends and Church* (Wigan).

Hilton, J. D. (1898) *Memoir of J. H. Raper.*

Hilton, R. S., Grimshaw, T. and Witherington, W. (1853) *Sunday Closing.*

Holden, J. (1872) *Autobiography of Joseph Holden of Bolton.*

Johnston, J. (1908) *Mawdsley Street Congregational Chapel, Bolton le Moors, 1808–1908: A Notable Record* (London).

Musgrave, P. (ed.) (1911) *Annals of the Pleiades Society, 1871–1911.*

Peaples, F. W. (1910) *History of the Greater and Little Bolton Co-operative Society, 1859–1909.*

Richardson, H. M. (1884) *Reminiscences of Forty Years in Bolton.*

Rothwell, S. (1899) *Local Reminiscences.*

Scholes, J. C. (1892) *History of Bolton.*

Sparke, A. (1913) *Bibliography Boltoniensis* (Manchester).

Station, J. T. (1867) *The Visit t' Paris Eggsibish.*

Whittle, P. A. (1855) *A History of Bolton.*

Secondary sources

Books (place of publication is London, unless otherwise stated)

Addison, W. (1952) *English Fairs and Markets.*

Alexander, S. (1970) *St. Giles' Fair, 1830–1914: Popular Culture and the Industrial Revolution in Nineteenth Century Oxford* (Oxford).

Altham, H. S. (1962) *A History of Cricket,* 2 vols.

Altick, R. D. (1957) *The English Common Reader: A Social History of the Mass Reading Public, 1800–1900* (Chicago).

—— (1978) *The Shows of London* (Cambridge, Mass.).

Bailey, P. (ed.) (1986) *Music Hall: The Business of Pleasure* (Milton Keynes).

Baker, M. (1978) *The Rise of the Victorian Actor.*

Banks, J. A. (1954) *Prosperity and Parenthood: A Study of Family Planning among the Victorian Middle Classes.*

Barker, F. (1957) *The House That Stoll Built: The Story of the Coliseum Theatre.*

Barker, K. (1976) *Bristol at Play: Five Centuries of Live Entertainment* (Bradford on Avon).

Barrett, M., Corrigan, P., Kuhn, A. and Wolff, J. (eds) (1979) *Ideology and Cultural Production*.

Barth, G. P. (1980) *City People: The Rise of Modern City Culture in Nineteenth Century America* (New York).

Beauroy, J., Bertrand, M. and Gargan, E. T. (eds) (1977) *Popular Culture in France from the Old Regime to the Twentieth Century* (Saratoga, Cal.).

Bennett, T., Martin, G., Mercer, C. and Woollacott, J. (eds) (1981) *Culture, Ideology and Social Process*.

—— Mercer, C. and Woollacott, J. (eds) (1986) *Popular Culture and Social Relations* (Milton Keynes).

Benson, J. (1980) *British Coalminers in the Nineteenth Century: A Social History* (Dublin).

Berger, P. L., Berger, B. and Kellner, H. (1974) *The Homeless Mind: Modernisation and Consciousness*.

Best, G. (1971) *Mid-Victorian Britain, 1851–75.*

Bettany, F. G. (1926) *Stewart Headlam: A Biography.*

Bienefeld, M. A. (1972) *Working Hours in British Industry: An Economic History.*

Binfield, C. (1973) *George Williams and the YMCA: A Study in Victorian Social Attitudes.*

Bowen, R. (1970) *Cricket: A History of its Growth and Development throughout the World.*

Boyson, R. (1970) *The Ashworth Cotton Enterprise: The Rise and Fall of a Family Firm, 1818–80* (Oxford).

Bradby, D., James, L. and Sharratt, B. (eds) (1980) *Performance and Politics in Popular Drama* (Cambridge).

Bratton, J. S. (1975) *The Victorian Popular Ballad.*

—— (1980) *Wilton's Music Hall* (Cambridge).

—— (ed.) (1986) *Music Hall: Performance and Style* (Milton Keynes).

Briggs, A. (1960) *Mass Entertainment: The Origins of a Modern Industry* (Adelaide).

Bristow, E. J. (1977) *Vice and Vigilance: Purity Movements in Britain since 1700* (Dublin).

Britain, I. (1982) *Fabianism and Culture: A Study in British Socialism and the Arts* (Cambridge).

Brown, W. E. (1970) *Robert Heywood of Bolton* (Wakefield).

Burke, P. (1978) *Popular Culture in Early Modern Europe.*

Burn, W. L. (1964) *The Age of Equipoise: A Study of the Mid-Victorian Generation.*

Bushaway, B. (1982) *By Rite: Custom, Ceremony and Community in England 1700–1880.*

Carr, R. (1976) *English Foxhunting: A Social History.*

Chanan, M. (1980) *The Dream that Kicks: The Prehistory and Early Years of Cinema in Britain.*

Chapman, G. (1940) *Culture and Survival*.

Checkland, S. G. (1964) *The Rise of an Industrial Society in England, 1815–1885*.

Cheshire, D. F. (1974) *Music Hall in Britain* (Newton Abbot).

Christie, O. F. (1927) *The Transition from Aristocracy, 1832–1867*.

Clark, P. (1983) *The English Alehouse: A Social History, 1200–1830*.

Clarke, J., Critcher, C. and Johnson, R. (eds) (1979) *Working Class Culture: Studies in History and Theory*.

—— and Critcher, C. (1985) *The Devil Makes Work: Leisure in Capitalist Britain*.

Cohen, S. and Scull, A. (eds) (1983) *Social Control and The State: Historical and Comparative Essays* (Oxford).

Colls, R. (1977) *The Collier's Rant: Song and Culture in the Industrial Village*.

Couvares, F. G. (1984) *The Remaking of Pittsburgh: Class and Culture in an Industrialising City 1877–1919* (Albany, NY).

Crauford, A. L. (1933) *Sam and Sallie: A Romance of the Stage*.

Crawford, A. and Thorne, R. (1975) *Birmingham Pubs, 1880–1939*.

Crossick, G. (ed.) (1977) *The Lower Middle Class in Britain, 1870–1914*.

Cunningham, H. (1975) *The Volunteer Force: A Social and Political History, 1859–1908*.

—— (1980) *Leisure in the Industrial Revolution, c. 1780–1880*.

Darwin, B. (1935) *John Gully and His Times, 1783–1863*.

Daunton, M. J. (1983) *House and Home in the Victorian City, 1850–1914*.

Davidoff, L. (1973) *The Best Circles: Women and Society in Victorian England* (Totowa, NJ).

Deem, R. (1986) *All Work and No Play? The Sociology of Women and Leisure* (Milton Keynes).

de Grazia, S. (1964) *Of Time, Work and Leisure* (New York, Anchor paperback edn).

de Grazia, V. (1981) *The Culture of Consent: Mass Organisation of Leisure in Fascist Italy* (Cambridge).

Dent, J. J. (1932) *Hodgson Pratt, Reformer: An Outline of His Work*.

Donajgrodzki, A. P. (ed.) (1977) *Social Control in Nineteenth Century Britain*.

Dumazedier, J. (1967) *Toward a Society of Leisure* (New York).

—— (1974) *Sociology of Leisure* (Amsterdam).

Dunning, E. (ed.) (1972) *Sport: Readings from a Sociological Perspective* (Toronto).

Dunning, E. and Sheard, K. (1979) *Barbarians, Gentlemen and Players: A Sociological Study of the Development of Rugby Football* (Pittsburgh).

Dyos, H. J. and Wolff, M. (eds) (1973) *The Victorian City*, 2 vols.

Earl, J. and Stanton, J. (1982) *The Canterbury Hall and Theatre of Varieties* (Cambridge).

Ehrlich, C. (1976) *The Piano: A History*.

—— (1985) *The Music Profession in Britain since the Eighteenth Century*.

Elbourne, R. (1980) *Music and Tradition in Early Industrial Lancashire, 1780–1840*.

Farson, D. (1972) *Marie Lloyd and Music Hall.*

Formations of Pleasure (1983).

Frankenberg, R. (1966) *Communities in Britain: Social Life in Town and Country.*

Fraser, W. H. (1981) *The Coming of the Mass Market, 1850–1914.*

Frith, S. (1983) *Sound Effects: Youth, Leisure and the Politics of Rock 'n' Roll.*

Furbank, P. N. (1985) *Unholy Pleasure: The Idea of Social Class.*

Gerth, H. H. and Mills, C. W. (1964) *Character and Social Structure* (New York, Harbinger paperback edn).

Girouard, M. (1975) *Victorian Pubs.*

Goffman, E. (1972) *Encounters: Two Studies in the Sociology of Interaction* (Penguin University edn).

—— (1972) *Interaction Ritual* (Penguin University edn).

Golby, J. and Purdue, A. W. (1984) *The Civilisation of the Crowd: Popular Culture in England, 1750–1900.*

Gorer, G. (1955) *Exploring English Character.*

Gorham, M. and Dunnett, H. McG. (1950) *Inside the Pub.*

Gosden, P. H. J. H. (1961) *The Friendly Societies in England, 1815–1875* (Manchester).

Gray, R. Q. (1976) *The Labour Aristocracy in Victorian Edinburgh* (Oxford).

Green, G., Witty, J. R. and Usill, H. V. (1953) *The History of the Football Association.*

Gruneau, R. (1983) *Class, Sports and Social Development* (Amherst, Mass.).

Haley, B. (1978) *The Healthy Body and Victorian Culture* (Cambridge, Mass.).

Hamer, H. (1938) *Bolton, 1838–1938* (Bolton).

Hamilton, C. and Bayliss, L. (1926) *The Old Vic.*

Hammond, J. L. and Hammond, B. (1930) *The Age of the Chartists, 1832–1854: A Study of Discontent.*

—— (1933) *The Growth of Common Enjoyment* (Oxford).

Hargreaves, Jennifer (ed.) (1982) *Sport, Culture and Ideology.*

Hargreaves, John (1986) *Sport, Power and Culture: A Social and Historical Analysis of Popular Sports in Britain* (Cambridge).

Harker, D. (1980) *One for the Money: Politics and Popular Song.*

Harrison, B. H. (1971) *Drink and the Victorians: The Temperance Question in England, 1815–1872.*

Harrison, J. F. C. (1961) *Learning and Living, 1790–1960: A Study in the History of the English Adult Education Movement.*

—— (1973) *The Early Victorians, 1832–1851* (Panther edn).

Hebdige, D. (1979) *Subculture: The Meaning of Style.*

Hobsbawm, E. J. (1968) *Industry and Empire.*

—— (1984) *Worlds of Labour.*

Hoggart, R. (1957) *The Uses of Literacy.*

Hole, C. (1949) *English Sports and Pastimes.*

Holt, R. (1981) *Sport and Society in Modern France.*

Honri, P. (1985) *John Wilton's Music Hall: The Handsomest Room in Town.*

Houghton, W. E. (1957) *The Victorian Frame of Mind, 1830–1870* (New Haven, Conn.).

Howard, D. (1970) *London Theatres and Music Halls, 1850–1950.*

Howkins, A. (1973) *Whitsun in Nineteenth Century Oxfordshire* (Oxford).

—— and Lowerson, J. (1979) *Trends in Leisure, 1919–1939.*

Itzkowitz, D. (1977) *Peculiar Privilege: A Social History of Fox Hunting, 1753–1885.*

Inglis, K. (1963) *The Churches and the Working Classes in Victorian England.*

Jackson, B. (1968) *Working Class Community.*

James, C. L. R. (1964) *Beyond the Boundary.*

James, L. (1974) *Fiction for the Working Man.*

—— (1976) *Print and the People, 1819–1851.*

Jamieson, D. A. (1943) *Powderhall and Pedestrianism: The History of a Famous Sports Enclosure, 1870–1943* (Edinburgh).

Jones, G. Stedman (1971) *Outcast London: A Study in the Relationship Between Classes in Victorian Society* (Oxford).

—— (1983) *Languages of Class: Studies in English Working Class History 1832–1982* (Cambridge).

Jones, P. d'A. (1968) *The Christian Socialist Revival, 1877–1914: Religion, Class and Social Conscience in Late-Victorian England* (Princeton, NJ).

Johnson, L. (1979) *The Cultural Critics: From Matthew Arnold to Raymond Williams.*

Joyce, P. (1980) *Work, Society and Politics: The Culture of the Factory in Later Victorian England* (Brighton).

Kaplan, S. (ed.) (1984) *Understanding Popular Culture: Europe from the Middle Ages to the Nineteenth Century* (Berlin).

Kelly, J. R. (1983) *Leisure Identities and Interactions.*

Kidd, A. J. and Roberts, K. W. (eds) (1985) *City, Class and Culture: Studies of Social Policy and Cultural Production in Victorian Manchester* (Manchester).

Kitson Clark, G. S. R. (1962) *The Making of Victorian England.*

Laqueur, T. (1976) *Religion and Respectability: Sunday Schools and Working Class Culture* (New Haven, Conn.).

Leach, R. (1985) *The Punch and Judy Show: History, Tradition and Meaning.*

Lovesey, P. (1968) *Kings of Distance.*

—— and McNab, T. (1969) *Guide to British Track and Field Literature, 1275–1968.*

Lowerson, J. and Myerscough, J. (1977) *Time to Spare in Victorian England* (Hassocks).

MacInnes, C. M. (1967) *Sweet Saturday Night.*

McIntosh, P. C. (1963) *Sport in Society.*

—— (1968) *Physical Education in England Since 1800* (second edn).

Mack, E. C. (1938) *The Public Schools and British Opinion, 1780–1860.*

—— and Armytage, W. H. G. (1952) *Thomas Hughes.*

McKechnie, S. (1931) *Popular Entertainments Through the Ages.*

Mackenzie, J. M. (ed.) (1986) *Imperialism and Popular Culture* (Manchester).

Mackerness, E. D. (1964) *A Social History of English Music.*

Maitland, S. (1986) *Vesta Tilley.*

Malcolmson, R. W. (1973) *Popular Recreations in English Society, 1700–1850* (Cambridge).

Mander, R. and Mitchenson, J. (1965) *The British Music Hall* (second edn, 1974).

Mangan, J. A. (1981) *Athleticism in the Victorian and Edwardian Public School: The Emergence and Consolidation of the Educational Ideology* (Cambridge).

Marples, M. (1954) *A History of Football.*

Marrus, M. R. (1974) *The Rise of Leisure in Industrial Society* (St Charles, Mo.).

—— (ed.) (1974) *The Emergence of Leisure* (New York).

Martin, D. E. and Rubinstein, D. (eds) (1979) *Ideology and the Labour Movement.*

Mason, A. (1980) *Association Football and English Society, 1863–1915* (Brighton).

Mayer, D. (1969) *Harlequin in his Element: The English Pantomine, 1806–1836* (Cambridge, Mass).

Meacham, S. (1977) *A Life Apart: The English Working Class, 1890–1914.*

Meller, H. E. (ed.) (1971) *Nottingham in the 1880s: A Study in Social Change* (Nottingham).

—— (1976) *Leisure and the Changing City, 1870–1914.*

Mellor, G. J. (1970) *The Northern Music Hall: A Century of Popular Entertainment* (Newcastle upon Tyne).

Morris, P. (1960) *Aston Villa.*

—— (1965) *West Bromwich Albion: Soccer in the Black Country.*

Mortimer, R. (1958) *The Jockey Club.*

Mottram, R. H. (1936) *Portrait of an Unknown Victorian.*

Munford, W. A. (1951) *Penny Rate: Aspects of British Public Library History, 1850–1950.*

Nettel, R. (1944) *Music in the Five Towns, 1840–1914: A Study in the Social Influence of Music in an Industrial District* (Oxford).

Neuburg, V. (1977) *Popular Literature: A History and Guide.*

Newsome, D. (1961) *Godliness and Good Learning: Four Studies on a Victorian Ideal.*

Olsen, D. J. (1976) *The Growth of Victorian London.*

Open University (1981) *Popular Culture*, course U203 (Milton Keynes).

Orens, J. R. (1979) *The Mass, the Masses and the Music Hall: Stewart Headlam's Radical Anglicanism.*

Parker, S. (1983) *Leisure and Work.*

Pearsall, R. (1973) *Victorian Popular Music* (Newton Abbot).

Pearson, G. (1983) *Hooligan: A History of Respectable Fears.*

Pelling, H. (1968) *Popular Politics and Society in Late Victorian Britain.*

Perkin, H. (1969) *The Origins of Modern British Society, 1780–1880.*

Pimlott, J. A. R. (1947) *The Englishman's Holiday: A Social History* (Brighton).

—— (1968) *Recreations.*

Plumb, J. H. (1974) *The Commercialisation of Leisure in Eighteenth Century England* (Reading).

Pollard, S. (1959) *A History of Labour in Sheffield* (Liverpool).

—— (1968) *The Genesis of Modern Management.*

Poole, R. (1982) *Popular Leisure and the Music Hall in Nineteenth Century Bolton* (Lancaster).

Prochaska, F. K. (1980) *Women and Philanthropy in Nineteenth Century England* (Oxford).

Pudney, J. S. (1953) *The Thomas Cook Story.*

Raban, J. (1974) *Soft City.*

Raistrick, A. (1938) *Two Centuries of Industrial Welfare.*

Rearick, C. (1985) *Pleasures of the Belle Epoque* (New Haven, Conn.).

Reid, J. C. (1971) *Bucks and Bruisers: Pierce Egan and Regency England.*

Reynolds, J. (1983) *The Great Paternalist: Titus Salt and the Growth of Nineteenth Century Bradford.*

Roberts, K. (1981) *Leisure.*

Rojek, C. (1985) *Capitalism and Leisure Theory.*

Rosenzweig, R. (1983) *Eight Hours for What We Will: Workers and Leisure in an Industrial Society, 1870–1920* (Cambridge).

Rowell, G. (1978) *The Victorian Theatre, 1792–1914* (Cambridge).

Russell, J. F. and Elliot, J. H. (1936) *The Brass Band Movement.*

Schlicke, P. (1985) *Dickens and Popular Entertainment.*

Scott, H. (1946) *The Early Doors: Origins of Music Hall* (second edn, 1977).

Senelick, L., Cheshire, D. F. and Schneider, U. (eds) (1981) *British Music-Hall 1840–1923: A Bibliography and Guide to Sources* (Hamden, Conn.).

Shipley, S. (1971) *Club Life and Socialism in Mid-Victorian London* (Oxford).

Simey, M. B. (1951) *Charitable Effort in Liverpool in the Nineteenth Century* (Liverpool).

Simmons, G. W. (1947) *Tottenham Hotspur Football Club.*

Simon, B. (1965) *Education and the Labour Movement, 1870–1918.*

—— and Bradley, I. (eds) (1975) *The Victorian Public School* (Dublin).

Smith, M. A., Parker, S. and Smith, C. S. (eds) (1973) *Leisure and Society in Britain.*

Solloway, R. A. (1969) *Prelates and People: Ecclesiastical Social Thought in England, 1783–1852.*

Sparke, A. (1913) *Bibliographia Boltoniensis* (Manchester).

Spiller, B. (1972) *Victorian Public Houses* (Newton Abbot).

Springhall, J. (1977) *Youth, Empire and Society: British Youth Movements, 1883–1940.*

—— Fraser, B. and Hoare, M. (1983) *Sure and Steadfast: A History of the Boys' Brigade.*

Stearns, P. N. (1975) *Lives of Labour: Work in a Maturing Industrial Society.*

Storch, R. D. (ed.) (1982) *Popular Culture and Custom in Nineteenth Century England.*

Sutcliffe, C. E. and Hargreaves, F. (1928) *History of the Lancashire Football Association, 1878–1928* (Blackburn).

Swingewood, A. (1977) *The Myth of Mass Culture.*

Tannenbaum, E. R. (1976) *1900: The Generation before the Great War* (New York).

Taylor, J. (1972) *From Self-Help to Glamour: The Working Man's Club, 1860–1972* (Oxford).

Tholfsen, T. R. (1976) *Working-Class Radicalism in Mid-Victorian England.*

Thompson, E. P. (1963) *The Making of the English Working Class* (New York, Vintage paperback edn).

Tischler, S. (1981) *Footballers and Businessmen: The Origins of Professional Soccer in England* (New York).

Tomlinson, A. (ed.) (1981) *Leisure and Social Control* (Brighton).

Tomlinson, A. (ed.) (1983) *Leisure and Popular Cultural Forms* (Brighton).

Tomlinson, A. (ed.) (1983) *Explorations in Football Culture* (Brighton).

Traies, J. (1980) *Fairbooths and Fitups* (Cambridge).

Turner, R. E. (1934) *James Silk Buckingham, 1786–1855: A Social Biography.*

Tylecote, M. (1957) *Mechanics' Institutes of Lancashire and Yorkshire before 1851* (Manchester).

Vamplew, W. (1976) *The Turf: A Social and Economic History of Horse Racing.*

Vicinus, M. (ed.) (1972) *Suffer and Be Still: Women in the Victorian Age* (Bloomington, Ind.).

—— (1974) *The Industrial Muse: A Study of Nineteenth Century British Working-Class Literature.*

—— (1977) *A Widening Sphere: Changing Roles of Victorian Women.*

Vincent, D. (1981) *Bread, Knowledge and Freedom: A Study of Nineteenth Century Working-Class Autobiography.*

Waites, B., Bennett, T. and Martin, G. (eds) (1982) *Popular Culture: Past and Present.*

Walker, B. M. (ed.) (1980) *Frank Matcham: Theatre Architect* (Belfast).

Walton, J. K. (1978) *The Blackpool Landlady: A Social History* (Manchester).

—— (1983) *The English Seaside Resort: A Social History, 1750–1914* (Leicester).

—— and Walvin, J. (eds) (1983) *Leisure in Britain, 1780–1939* (Manchester).

Walvin, J. (1975) *The People's Game: A Social History of British Football.*

—— (1978) *Beside the Seaside: A Social History of the Popular Seaside Holiday.*

—— (1978) *Leisure and Society, 1830–1950.*

Watson, I. (1983) *Song and Democratic Culture in Britain: An Approach to Popular Culture in Social Movements.*

Weber, W. (1975) *Music and the Middle Class: The Social Structure of Concert Life in London, Paris and Vienna.*

Wickham, E. R. (1957) *Church and People in an Industrial City* (Lutterworth).

Wiener, M. J. (1981) *English Culture and the Decline of the Industrial Spirit, 1850–1980* (Cambridge).

Wigley, J. (1980) *The Rise and Fall of the Victorian Sunday* (Manchester).

Wilkinson, R. (1964) *The Prefects: British Leadership and the Public School Tradition* (Oxford).

Williams, R. (1961) *Culture and Society, 1780–1850.*

—— (1981) *Culture.*

Williamson, B. (1982) *Class, Culture and Community: A Biographical Study of Social Change in Mining.*

Wilmeth, D. B. (1980) *American and English Popular Entertainment: A Guide to Sources* (Detroit).

Wolff, J. (1981) *The Social Production of Art.*

Wroth, W. (1907) *Cremorne and the Later London Gardens.*

Wymer, N. (1949) *Sport in England.*

Yeo, E. and S. (eds) (1981) *Popular Culture and Class Conflict 1590–1914: Explorations in the History of Labour and Leisure* (Brighton).

Yeo, S. (1976) *Religion and Voluntary Organisations in Crisis.*

Young, G. M. (ed.) (1934) *Early Victorian England, 1830–65*, 2 vols (Oxford).

Young, M. and Willmott, P. (1973) *The Symmetrical Family: A Study of Work and Leisure in the London Region.*

Young, P. M. (1959) *The Wolves .*

—— (1961) *Bolton Wanderers.*

—— (1962) *Football in Sheffield.*

—— (1963) *Football on Merseyside.*

—— (1968) *A History of British Football.*

Essays and journal articles (NB *Most items from collections in the major subject area are not individually referenced here*)

Bailey, P. C. (1977) '"A mingled mass of perfectly legitimate pleasures": the Victorian middle class and the problem of leisure', *Victorian Studies*, xxi, 7–28.

—— (1979) '"Will the real Bill Banks please stand up?" A role analysis of mid-Victorian working-class respectability', *Journal of Social History*, xii, 336–53.

—— (1983) '*Ally Sloper's Half-Holiday*: comic art in the 1880s', *History Workshop*, 16, 4–31.

Barker, C. (1971) 'A theatre for the people', in K. Richards and P. Thomson (eds), *Essays on Nineteenth Century British Theatre* (Manchester), 1–17.

—— (1979) 'The audiences of the Britannia theatre, Hoxton', *Theatre Quarterly*, ix, 27–41.

Barker, W. J. (1979) 'The making of a working-class football culture', *Journal of Social History*, xiii, 241–51.

Berger, B. M. (1962) 'The sociology of leisure: some suggestions', *Industrial Relations*, i, 31–45.

Burns, T. (1973) 'Leisure in industrial society', in M. A. Smith, S. Parker and C. S. Smith (eds), *Leisure and Society in Britain*, 40–55.

Cannadine, D. (1978) 'The theory and practice of the English leisure classes', *Historical Journal*, 445–67.

Constantine, S. (1981) 'Amateur gardening and popular recreation in the nineteenth and twentieth centuries', *Journal of Social History*, xiv, 387–406.

Cross, G. S. (1986) 'The political economy of leisure in retrospect: Britain, France and the origins of the eight hour day', *Leisure Studies*, v, 69–90.

Crossick, G. (1976) 'The labour aristocracy and its values: a study of mid-Victorian Kentish London', *Victorian Studies*, xix, 301–28.

Cunningham, H. (1985) 'Leisure', in J. Benson (ed.), *The Working Class in England, 1875–1914*, 133–164.

Dickinson, B. (1983) 'In the audience', *Oral History Journal*, xi, 52–61.

Dingle, A. E. (1972) 'Drink and working-class living standards in Britain, 1870–1914', *Economic History Review*, xxv, 608–22.

Dunae, P. (1977) 'Penny dreadfuls: late nineteenth century boys' literature and crime', *Victorian Studies*, xxii, 133–50.

Gammon, V. (1982) 'Problems of method in the historical study of popular music', in P. Tagg and D. Horn (eds), *Popular Music Perspectives* (Exeter), 16–31.

Gaskill, S. M. (1980) 'Gardens for the working class: Victorian practical pleasure', *Victorian Studies*, xxiii, 479–501.

Gottdiener, M. (1985) 'Hegemony and mass culture: a semiotic approach', *American Journal of Sociology*, xc, 979–1001.

Gray, R. Q. (1973) 'Styles of life, the "labour aristrocracy" and class relations in later nineteenth century Edinburgh', *International Review of Social History*, xviii, 428–52.

Griffin, C., Hobson, D., MacIntosh, S. and McCabe, T. (1982) 'Women and leisure', in Jennifer Hargreaves (ed.), *Sport, Culture and Ideology*, 88–116.

Haley, B. E. (1968) 'Sports and the Victorian world', *Western Humanities Review*, xii, 115–25.

Hall, S. (1980) 'Cultural Studies and the Centre: some problematics and problems', in S. Hall, D. Hobson, A. Lowe and P. Willis (eds), *Culture, Media, Language*, 15–47.

—— (1981) 'Notes on deconstructing "the popular"', in R. Samuel (ed.), *People's History and Socialist Theory*, 227–40.

Hargreaves, J. A. (1985) ' "Playing like gentlemen while behaving like ladies": the formative years of women's sport', *British Journal of Sports History*, 40–52.

Harker, D. (1981) 'The making of the Tyneside concert hall', *Popular Music*, i, 27–56.

Harrison, B. H. (1965) 'The Sunday trading riots of 1855', *Historical Journal*, viii, 219–45.

—— (1967) 'Drink and sobriety in England, 1815–1872', *International Review of Social History*, xii, 204–76.

—— (1968) 'Two roads to social reform: Francis Place and the "Drunken Committee" of 1834', *Historical Journal*, xi, 272–300.

—— (1968) 'Religion and recreation in nineteenth century England', *Past and Present*, 38, 98–125.

—— (1973) 'Pubs', in H. J. Dyos and M. Wolff, *The Victorian City*, 2 vols, i, 161–90.

Johnson, R. (1970) 'Educational policy and social control in early Victorian England', *Past and Present*, 49, 96–119.

—— (1986) 'The story so far: and further transformations?', in D. Punter (ed.), *Introduction to Contemporary Cultural Studies*, 277–313.

Jones, G. Stedman (1974) 'Working-class culture and working-class politics in London, 1870–1900: notes on the remaking of a working class', *Journal of Social History*, vii, 460–508, reprinted in Jones, *Languages of Class* (Cambridge, 1983).

Jones, S. G. (1985) 'The leisure industry in Britain, 1918–39', *Service Industries Journal*, v, 90–106.

Kent, C. (1974) 'The Whittington Club: a bohemian experiment in middle-class social reform', *Victorian Studies*, xviii, 31–55.

—— (1986) 'Presence and absence: history, theory and the working class', *Victorian Studies*, xxix, 437–62.

Kent, J. H. S. (1973) 'The role of religion in the cultural structure of the later Victorian city', *Transactions of the Royal Historical Society*, xxiii, 153–73.

Korr, C. P. (1978) 'West Ham United and the beginning of professional football in east London, 1895–1914', *Journal of Contemporary History*, xiii, 211–32.

Lowerson, J. (1983) '"Scottish croquet": the English golf boom, 1880–1914', *History Today* (May), 25–30.

—— (1984) 'Sport and the Victorian Sunday: the beginnings of middle-class apostasy', *British Journal of Sports History*, i, 202–20.

McCrone, K. E. (1984) '"Play up and play the game!": sport at late Victorian girls' public schools', *Journal of British Studies*, xxiii, 106–34.

McGregor, O. R. (1957) 'Social research and social policy in the nineteenth century', *British Journal of Sociology*, viii, 146–57.

McKibbin, R. (1979) 'Working-class gambling in Britain, 1880–1939', *Past and Present*, 82, 147–78.

—— (1983) 'Work and hobbies in Britain, 1880–1950', in J. M. Winter (ed.), *The Working Class in Modern British History: Essays in Honour of Henry Pelling* (Cambridge), 127–46.

—— (1984) 'Why was there no Marxism in Great Britain?', *English Historical Review*, xcix, 297–331.

Malchow, H. L. (1985) 'Public gardens and social action in late Victorian London', *Victorian Studies*, xxix, 97–124.

Malcolmson, R. W. (1981) 'Leisure', in G. E. Mingay (ed.), *The Victorian Countryside*, 2 vols, i, 603–15.

Mandle, W. F. (1972) 'The professional cricketer in England in the nineteenth century', *Labour History*, xxiii, 1–16.

—— (1973) 'Games people played: cricket and football in England and Victoria in the late nineteenth century', *Historical Studies*, xv, 511–35.

Marrus, M. R. (1974) 'Social drinking in the belle époque', *Journal of Social History*, vii, 115–41.

Meacham, S. (1972) '"The sense of an impending clash": English working-class unrest before the First World War', *American Historical Review*, lxxvii, 1343–64.

Merton, R. K. (1957) 'The role-set: problems in sociological theory', *British Journal of Sociology*, viii, 112–20.

Metcalfe, A. (1982) 'Organised sport in the mining communities of south Northumberland, 1800–1889', *Victorian Studies*, xxv, 469–95.

Middleton, R. (1985) 'Articulating musical meaning/re-constructing musical history/locating the "popular"', *Popular Music*, v, 5–43.

Morris, R. J. (1970) 'Leeds and the Crystal Palace', *Victorian Studies*, xiii, 283–300.

—— (1970) 'The history of self-help', *New Society*, 3 December.

Myerscough, J. (1974) 'The recent history of the use of leisure time', in I. Appleton (ed.), *Leisure Research and Policy* (Edinburgh), 3–16.

Parry, N. C. A. (1983) 'Sociological contributions to the study of leisure', *Leisure Studies*, ii, 57–81.

Perkin, H. J. (1975–6) 'The social tone of Victorian seaside resorts in the North-West', *Northern History*, xi, 180–94.

Plumb, J. H. (1972) 'The public, literature and the arts in the eighteenth century', in P. Fritz and D. Williams (eds), *The Triumph of Culture: Eighteenth Century Perspectives* (Toronto), 27–48.

Price, R. N. (1971) 'The working men's club movement and Victorian social reform ideology', *Victorian Studies*, xv, 117–47.

Reid, D. (1976) 'The decline of Saint Monday, 1766–1876', *Past and Present*, 71, 76–101.

—— (1980) 'Popular theatre in Victorian Birmingham', in D. Bradby, L. James and B. Sharratt (eds), *Performance and Politics in Popular Drama* (Cambridge), 65–89.

Rubinstein, D. (1977) 'Cycling in the 1890s', *Victorian Studies*, xxi, 47–71.

Samuel, R. (1983) 'The middle class between the wars', *New Socialist*, January/February, March/April, May/June.

Sandiford, K. A. P. (1981) 'The Victorians at play: problems in historiographical methodology', *Journal of Social History*, xv, 271–88.

—— (1982) 'Cricket and the Victorians: an historiographical essay', *Historical Reflexions*, ix, 421–36.

—— (1983) 'Sport and Victorian England', *Canadian Journal of History*, xviii, 111–17.

Scott, P. (1970) 'Cricket and the religious world in the Victorian period', *Church Quarterly*, iii, 134–44.

Senelick, L. (1975) 'Politics as entertainment: Victorian music-hall songs', *Victorian Studies*, xix, 149–80.

Shiman, L. L. (1973) 'The Band of Hope movement: respectable recreation for working-class children', *Victorian Studies*, xviii, 49–74.

Shipley, S. (1983) 'Tom Causer of Bermondsey: a boxer hero of the 1890s', *History Workshop*, 15, 28–59.

Smith, M. A. (1983) 'Social usages of the public drinking house: changing aspects of class and leisure', *British Journal of Sociology*, xxxiv, 367–85.

Springhall, J. (1980) 'Leisure and Victorian youth: the penny theatre in London, 1830–1890', *History of Education Society Proceedings*, 101–124.

Stearns, P. N. (1980) 'The effort at continuity in working-class culture', *Journal of Modern History*, lii, 626–55.

'Sport, Labour and Society', Conference Report, Bulletin of the Society for the Study of Labour History, 50 (Spring, 1985), 4–12.

Storch, R. D. (1975) 'The plague of blue locusts: police reform and popular resistance in northern England, 1840–57', *International Review of Social History*, xx, 61–90.

Storch, R. D. (1976) 'The policeman as domestic missionary: urban discipline and popular culture in northern England, 1850–1880', *Journal of Social History*, ix, 481–509.

Summerfield, P. (1986) 'Patriotism and empire: music hall entertainment, 1870–1914', in J. M. Mackenzie (ed.), *Imperialism and Popular Culture* (Manchester), 17–48.

Taylor, I. R. (1971) 'Soccer consciousness and soccer hooliganism', in S. Cohen (ed.), *Images of Deviance*, 134–64.

Thomas, K. (1964) 'Work and leisure in pre-industrial society', *Past and Present*, 29, 50–62.

Thompson, E. P. (1967) 'Time, work-discipline, and industrial capitalism', *Past and Present*, 38, 56–97.

—— (1974) 'Patrician society, plebeian culture', *Journal of Social History*, vii, 382–405.

Thompson, F. M. L. (1981) 'Social control in Victorian Britain', *Economic History Review* (May), 189–208.

Thorne, R. (1980) 'Places of refreshment in the nineteenth century city', in A. D. King (ed.), *Buildings and Society*, 228–53.

Vamplew, W. (1979) 'The sport of kings and commoners: the commercialisation of British horse-racing in the nineteenth century', in R. Cashman and M. McKernan (eds), *Sport in History* (Hemel Hempstead), 307–25.

—— (1979) 'Ungentlemanly conduct: the control of soccer-crowd behaviour in England, 1885–1914', in T. C. Smout (ed.), *The Search for Wealth and Stability*, 139–54.

Waites, B. (1981) 'The Music hall', in The Open University, *Popular Culture, The Historical Development of Popular Culture*, 1, block 2 (Milton Keynes), 43–78.

Walton, J. K. (1981) 'The demand for working-class seaside holidays in Victorian England', *Economic History Review*, xxxiv, 249–65.

Waters, C. (1981) '"All sorts of outlandish recreations": history, sociology and the study of leisure in England, 1820–70', *Historical Papers of the Canadian Historical Association*, 8–33.

Weber, E. (1971) 'Gymnastics and sports in *fin de siècle* France: opium of the classes?', *American Historical Review*, lxxvi, 70–97.

Weber, W. (1978) 'Artisans in concert life in mid-nineteenth century London and Paris', *Journal of Contemporary History*, xiii, 253–67.

Wiener, M. J. (1978) 'Social control in nineteenth century Britain', *Journal of Social History*, xii, 314–21.

Wilson, C. (1965) 'Economy and society in late-Victorian Britain', *Economic History Review*, xviii, 183–98.

'Work and leisure in industrial society: conference report', *Past and Present*, 30 (1965), 96–103.

'Working-class culture: conference report', *Bull.SSLH*, 9 (1964), 3–8.

'The working class and leisure–class expression and/or social control: conference report', *Bull.SSLH*, 32 (1976), 5–18.

Index